Wagering on Transcendence

The Search for Meaning
in Literature

Wagering on Transcendence

The Search for Meaning in Literature

Edited by Phyllis Carey

Sheed & Ward
Kansas City

Sheed & Ward™ is a service of The National Catholic Reporter Publishing Company.

Library of Congress Cataloguing-in-Publication Data
Wagering on transcendence : the search for meaning in
    literature / Phyllis Carey, editor.
            p.   cm.
    Includes bibliographical references and index.
    ISBN: 1-55612-982-3 (alk. paper)
    1. Transcendence (Philosophy) in literature.
2. Literature—Philosophy. 3. Religion and literature.
4. Literature, Modern—History and criticism. I. Carey, Phyllis.
PN49.W24 1997
809'.93384—dc21   97-14762
                                                        CIP

Published by: Sheed & Ward
            115 E. Armour Blvd.
            P.O. Box 419492
            Kansas City, MO 64141-6492

To order, call: (800) 333-7373

www.natcath.com/sheedward

Contents

I. The Journey

II. Transcendence through Nature

III. Time and Space

IV. Transcendence and the Human Story

V. *Self and Society*

VI. *The Wager*

To the Spirit who sustained the writing and the writers, to the Spirit who keeps us wagering – alone and together.

Permissions

For permission to reprint copyright material, the contributors gratefully acknowledge the following:

Angel Books for excerpts from "Tristia," "#124," and "#307" from *Selected Poems* by Osip Mandelstam, translated by James Greene, 1991.

Christianity and Literature for permission to reprint "Face to Face: Samuel Beckett and Václav Havel" by Phyllis Carey. This essay was originally published in the autumn 1994 issue of *Christianity and Literature* (Volume 44, Number 1).

The Ecco Press for excerpts from "Hymn," Cafe," "To Raja Rao," by Czeslaw Milosz; "Encounter" and "From the Rising of the Sun" translated by Czeslaw Milosz and Lillian Vallee; "Throughout Our Lands" translated by Czeslaw Milosz and Peter Dale Scott; "The Year" translated by Czeslaw Milosz and Richard Lourie; "A Mistake" translated by Renata Gorczynski and Robert Hass; "Six Lectures in Verse" translated by Czeslaw Milosz and Leonard Nathan; "City without a Name" translated by Czeslaw Milosz, Robert Hass, Robert Pinsky and Renata Gorczynski; "A Legend," "Thankfulness," "With Her," "Old Women" and "How It Should Be In Heaven" translated by Czeslaw Milosz and Rober Hass, all from *The Collected Poems by Czeslaw Milosz.* Copyright 1988 by Czeslaw Milosz Royalties, Inc. Published by The Ecco Press.

Farrar, Straus & Giroux, Inc. for excerpts from *The Habit of Being* by Flannery O'Connor, copyright 1979 by Regina O'Connor; excerpts from *Mystery and Manners* by Flannery O'Connor, copyright 1969 by the Estate of Mary Flannery O'Connor; and excerpts from *The Violent Bear It Away* by Flannery O'Connor, copyright 1960 by Flannery O'Connor, copyright renewed 1988 by Regina O'Connor. Harold Matson Company, Inc. for non-exclusive British Commonwealth rights for excerpts from *The Violent Bear It Away,* copyright 1956 by Flannery O'Connor, copyright renewed 1984 by the Estate of Regina Cline O'Connor.

exclusive British Commonwealth rights for excerpts from *The Violent Bear It Away,* copyright 1956 by Flannery O'Connor, copyright renewed 1984 by the Estate of Regina Cline O'Connor.

Farrar, Straus & Giroux, Inc. and Faber and Faber Ltd. for excerpts from "The Peninsula" from *Selected Poems 1966-1987* by Seamus Heaney, copyright 1990 by Seamus Heaney.

Harcourt Brace & Company and Faber and Faber Ltd. for excerpts from "The Dry Salvages" in *Four Quartets,* copyright 1943 by T. S. Eliot, renewed 1971 by Esme Valerie Eliot; and excerpts from *The Family Reunion,* copyright 1939 by T.S. Eliot, renewed 1967 by Esme Valerie Eliot.

HarperCollins for excerpts from *Teaching a Stone to Talk* by Annie Dillard, copyright 1982.

Charles James Kaiser for cover design: "Grace," copyright Charles James Kaiser. Prismacolor pencil on pigmented board, 1996.

Magistra: A Journal of Women's Spirituality in History for permission to reprint "Attentive to Transcendence: The Life of Etty Hillesum" by Joan Penzenstadler, S.S.N.D. This essay was originally published in the summer 1996 issue of *Magistra, A Journal of Women's Spirituality in History* (Volume 96, 2, No.1).

The Modern Schoolman for permission to reprint "Camus: Wagering on Immanence" by James Conlon. This essay was originally published in the May 1995 issue of *The Modern Schoolman* (Volume 72).

Pantheon Books, a division of Random House, Inc.; and Uitgevery Balans, The Netherlands, for excerpts from *An Interrupted Life: The Diaries of Etty Hillesum 1941-43*, edited by J. G. Gaarlandt and translated by Arno Pomerans. English translation copyright 1983 by Jonathan Cape Ltd. Copyright 1981 by De Haan/Uniboek b.v., Bussum. (The most recent U.S. edition of this volume is by Metropolitan Books, Henri Holt and Company, 1996.)

Russell and Volkening, Inc. for excerpts from *Bread and Wine* by Ignazio Silone, translated by Eric Mosbacher.

Sheed & Ward Publishers for excerpts from *The Spiritual Canticle* (1961) by John of the Cross, translated and edited by E. Allison Peers and *The Life of Teresa of Avila* (1960) by Teresa of Avila, translated and edited by E. Allison Peers.

Preface

Once, when sitting with Walker Percy in his Covington, Louisiana home, a tape-recorder whirling, bourbon near at hand, I heard this physician and metaphysician, both, this learned and wise man who was also an exceedingly humble pilgrim, exclaim with some conviction: "The abstract mind feeds on itself, takes things apart, leaves in its wake all of us, trying to live a life, get from the here of now, today, to the there of tomorrow." I sat back and let those words settle in my head – the shrewd arrow directed at the apple of knowledge become something else: the sin of pride. Dr. Percy was being a novelist when he spoke in that way – worried sick (he was) by the inclination of many (as he would put it), in these last days of the second millennium, to take us away from the concrete particulars of a lived life (the hopes and worries and fears such a life prompts) in favor of an all-too-clever kind of conceptual analysis that gives short shrift to human experience as it befalls every person who is born, lives, and knows full well of death's certainty.

As I read the introduction to this book, and contemplated its subject matter, I kept remembering Dr. Percy, his struggle to find some larger meaning in this late-twentieth-century life, with its prominent, persuasive secular materialism so much a part of our thinking. Like many of us, he was not ready to withdraw from that world – he welcomed our efforts to explore, to understand, to figure out. Darwin and Freud and Einstein are a big part of our contemporary lives, and what they have to tell us mattered to him, matters to all of us. Yet, ironically, those individuals were themselves their own kind of seekers – anxious to learn something beyond "data." Freud called himself a "conquistador," and dreamed of a world somehow transformed morally by the ideas he had shaped. Einstein's sense of wonder, even of mystery, is well-known. Darwin was a wonderfully bold and brave observer of things present and past who knew how to tell a wonderfully convincing story – in his head he constructed a way of seeing time itself, and too, fate and chance, as they all take part in a vast drama, imperceptible at any given moment, but hugely decisive over the longer haul of things.

So with some of our novelists and poets, and too, our critics, thank God – they are still unwilling to settle for less than *meaning:* the effort, through words, to find out who we are, what matters and why. In the pages that follow, the reader is brought close to such human aspiration – the desire to have some larger notion about life's nature and purpose: a sense of destiny, really, if not destination. Still among us are poets and novelists who are trying with all their might (with every resource given the storyteller, with the images and metaphors allowed the poet) to strengthen our collective moral and spiritual imagination, that of writers, that of readers, that of our culture. We are wayfarers, they know – as Walker Percy so often put it; and so we are on a journey – there is something ahead (above, beyond) for us to consider. As such, as wayfarers, we need all the help we can find; we need compasses, guides, thoughts and suggestions – hence our artists and philosophers and theologians, all of whom join us in trying to imagine what might be, even as they try to observe and render faithfully what presently is.

To gather together these essays, which in turn are responses to stories and poems of certain writers, is to bring the reader companionship in a sense of that word Silone, for one, told us to keep in mind: with bread, as in communion – the food for which we so hunger, called inspiration. If is of no small significance, then, that this book comes to us – graces us, some will surely conclude: a devoted, even passionate effort of certain scholars to take their bearings in the largest sense of that expression, to link arms with those they have studied on behalf of the rest of us who seek out volumes like this, in the hope that together we might reflect upon what it is like, these days, to live a life, and too, wonder what, if anything, who, if anyone, might be waiting around the great corner that is death.

Robert Coles

Acknowledgments

Over the time this project has been in progress, we have incurred numerous debts of gratitude to many people. First, to Luetta Wolf, S.S.N.D., the other contributors and I owe a great deal that extends far beyond this project. For this collection, she read most of the original essays and offered invaluable suggestions for revisions. Without her initial help and enduring support and encouragement, this volume would not have materialized.

Mary Kay Mader formatted several of the essays early on, which aided greatly in revisions. Thomas Artz, a long-time friend of Mount Mary and currently co-publisher of ACTA Publications, gave encouragement and helpful advice when the manuscript was beginning to take shape. Aldy Hagen provided invaluable computer and copy-editing expertise in getting the manuscript into its final form. We thank each of them sincerely.

Kathleen Scullin, Chair of the Mount Mary English Department, and Theresa Lamy, S.S.N.D., Vice President for Academic Affairs, have provided much-needed moral support as well as funds for typing, copy-editing, and duplicating. For copyright permission fees, we are indebted to the John Francis Schuh, S.S.N.D., Chair of English Fund. For technical assistance and suggestions, we thank Mary Cain, Susan Seiler, Joseph Rozman, Mike Tucci, Jan Weinfurt, and the incomparable Mount Mary Library staff, whose individual and collective expertise contributes to a wide variety of Mount Mary projects. We are especially grateful to Charles J. Kaiser for his inspiring art and his participation in this volume. The faculty, administration, and staff of Mount Mary College have contributed in many ways with helpful suggestions and encouragement.

I wish also to extend my personal thanks to the authors of the essays, who had to rise above heavy teaching schedules, committee work, and personal obligations in order to compose essays for the volume.

To Robert Heyer and the staff at Sheed & Ward we owe a tremendous debt for their willingness to wager on a volume that did not fit neatly into any of the standard categories. It is because of their interest, enthusiasm, and willingness to work with us that we are now able to address a larger audience. In particular, we wish to thank Sarah Smiley for her extensive help in producing the finished text, Sylvia Fox for her many efforts in marketing the book, and Andy Apathy for his accessibility, wise suggestions, and editorial expertise.

Finally, to Robert Coles, who gave a memorable keynote address at the Mount Mary Symposium, "Friendship: An Ethical Concept" in April, 1991, we extend our deep gratitude for his compelling preface, which articulates clearly and eloquently what this project is all about. We welcome his companionship and that of our readers as we continue in our individual and communal searches for meaning.

Introduction

Let us weigh the gain and the loss involved by wagering that God exists. . . . if you win, you win all; if you lose, you lose nothing.

— Pascal, Pensées

A few years ago, a small group of Mount Mary faculty members met on a Friday afternoon to discuss George Steiner's *Real Presences* over a glass of wine in the faculty lounge. From the lively discussion that ensued – which was part of an ongoing dialogue at Mount Mary about meaning – the idea for this volume emerged. Steiner's book sparked a conversation about the relationship of God's existence to a variety of issues. It struck me that in our own time – as opposed to almost the entire recorded history of Western civilization – God's nonexistence has become a given. The death of God, the silence of God, the absence of God – all implicitly acknowledging the significance of God – have succumbed to the irrelevance of God. The fact that Steiner has to *argue* for the reality of transcendent experiences suggests the extent to which the secularism of our age controls our modes of discourse and our means of measuring reality.

In my own area of expertise (literary criticism), readings dominated by deconstruction, semiotics, dialogism, postcolonialism, and other forms of postmodernist theories vie for intellectual superiority and refined sophistication, limiting literature to what can be described in intellectual terms and sometimes reducing it to technical jargon that few but other specialists in the area can understand. The current disdain for the spiritual in many critical circles, however, while frequently equating transcendence with authoritarianism, hierarchy, paternalism, discrimination, and a putative logocentrism, itself seems to operate, as John Milbank observes, from "an unknowable transcendent source" that uses a secular, nonreligious indifference as its own transcendent criterion for judgment.[1]

George Steiner argues that even secular transcendence implicitly depends on God's existence: "any coherent understanding of what language is and how language performs, . . . any coherent account of the capacity of human speech to communicate meaning and feeling is, in the final analysis, underwritten by the assumption of God's presence. . . . The experience of aesthetic meaning in particular, that of literature, of the arts, of musical form, infers the necessary possibility of this 'real presence.'"[2] Steiner summarizes his point thus:

> The meaning of meaning is a transcendent postulate. To read the poem responsibly ('respondingly'), to be answerable to form, is to wager on a reinsurance of sense. It is to wager on a relationship – tragic, turbulent, incommensurable, even sardonic – between word and world, but on a relationship precisely bounded by that which reinsures it.[3]

Having spent the last several years exploring the latest literary theories, appreciating the value of their diverse perspectives but bemoaning their general disdain for transcendence as a spiritual dimension, I was convinced after our *Real Presences* discussion that a volume "wagering on transcendence" – asserting the real presence of that which goes beyond the human in literature and in life – could be a valuable contribution to individuals, to discussion groups, to college classes and ultimately, to society at large.[4] If current critical discourse in largely ignoring transcendence seems ostensibly at

---

1. See John Milbank, "Problematizing the secular: the postmodern agenda," in *Shadow of Spirit: Postmodernism and Religion,* ed. Philippa Berry and Andrew Wernick (London: Routledge, 1992), 30-44.

2. George Steiner, *Real Presences* (Chicago: The University of Chicago Press, 1989), 3.

3. Ibid., 216.

4. Recent books and articles suggest that the "ravenous hunger for authentic spiritual experience" is a growing phenomenon. See, e.g., Bill Peatman, "We are consuming religious books with fury," *National Catholic Reporter* (8 September 1995): 25.

least to be wagering on God's nonexistence, then those who have experienced the reality of the transcendent in their own life stories and in the stories of others must accept the challenge to explore the terms of their own wagering.

The response from the Mount Mary faculty to the concept for this collection was indeed amazing. Although several contributors are not literary critics, they nevertheless wanted to write about their individual dialogues with particular thinkers and writers. In the process, they communicated their own fascination with various forms and shapes of transcendence in literature. In poetry, fiction and drama, they have experienced "real presences" through some extension of reason that reaches out to the whole person, allowing for intuition, feeling, imagination, analogy, faith, and other valid ways of knowing. As Kathleen Scullin, a colleague and contributor to this collection puts it, "Literature traffics with the transcendent almost universally and certainly shamelessly. Those who *write* literature know they wrestle with angels. Should not those who *read* it recognize that reality?"

While each of the contributors focused on the question of transcendence as it impinges on meaning, the essays evolved into a kaleidoscope of perspectives, offering a variety of definitions, insights, and approaches to the topic. The final grouping of the essays, imposed after they were written, provides a loose schema for some of the points where the essays converge: transcendence through individual quests, through nature, through the re-seeing of time and space, through the shaping of lived experiences in stories, through communal experiences of suffering, violence, sin and reconciliation, through confronting the options available to humans. The wager itself emerges under differing guises in various essays: from an obvious choice to a compelling force, to a subtle prodding, to a long, painful process, to an instantaneous recognition, to a growing perspective, to an accumulation of evidence, to an agonizing hunger, to a problematic paradox, to a fundamental dimension of being human.

The title of the collection comes most immediately from Steiner, whose *Real Presences* "argues a wager on transcendence."[5]

---

5.   Steiner, 214.

More distantly, the title evokes the famed Pascalian wager. For Blaise Pascal, the options humans face regarding God's existence point clearly to a gamble on transcendence; quantitatively at the very least, the longest life on earth full of earthly pleasures cannot outweigh endless bliss. One should, therefore, bet on the existence of God, "the prospect of an infinite return on one's investment."[6]

In the Pascalian wager, the reality of God's existence seems to rest largely with human choice and may appear simply self-interested – a calculated investing in the future. Although Pascal reacted strongly against Cartesian rationalism, his wager emphasizes, ironically, making the more rational decision. Unlike Descartes' *cogito*, however, Pascal's wager recognizes a limit to human rationality: "we know something and yet not enough."[7] As Kierkegaard later excavated the abyss between human agony and belief, providing a springboard for transcendence, Pascal measured the gap humans experience between their finite limitations and their infinite potential, mapping the stakes for a wager on the infinite.

While Pascal argued from the perspective of the individual, in our own day, Václav Havel, playwright and president of the Czech Republic, who has written provocatively on the nature of hope and transcendence, uses communal and historical perspectives as a context for the individual wager. Havel points out that the diverse cultures throughout the world each evolved from some sense of the sacred, some sense that "we are not here alone nor for ourselves alone, but that we are an integral part of higher, mysterious entities. . . ."[8] For Havel, the recognition of something beyond the human is not merely in keeping with traditional beliefs but is actually essential for survival: "Transcendence [is] the only real alternative to extinction."[9] According to Havel, the degradation of the planet and the alienation of modern humans derive in large part from a modern anthropomorphism which, in attempting to

6. Leslie Armour, *"Infini Rien"*: *Pascal's Wager and the Human Paradox* (Carbondale, Ill.: Southern Illinois University Press, 1993), 70.

7. Ibid., xii.

8. Václav Havel, "A Time for Transcendence," *Utne Reader* (January, February 1995): 113.

9. Ibid.

exalt humans through scientific rationality to the place of gods, actually results in a dehumanizing that amounts to self-destruction.

As Havel stresses what is at stake for humanity as a whole in the wager on transcendence, Frederick Buechner, a contemporary Presbyterian minister and writer, asserts that the wager itself is inescapable for humans:

> If you had to bet your life, which would you bet it on? On "Yes, there is God in the highest," or, if that language is no longer viable, "there is mystery and meaning in the deepest"? Or on "No, there is whatever happens to happen, and it means whatever you choose it to mean, and that's all there is"?
>
> Of course we can bet Yes this evening and No tomorrow morning. We may know we're betting; we may not know. We may bet one way with our lips, our minds, even our hearts, and another way with our feet. But we all of us bet, and it's our lives themselves we're betting with, in the sense that the betting is what shapes our lives. And of course we can never be sure we bet right because the evidence both ways is fragmentary, fragile, ambiguous. . . . Whether we bet Yes or No is equally an act of faith.[10]

"The betting is what shapes our lives," both individually and communally. It rests on what Jan Patoccka, a Czech philosopher, described as "the experience of dissatisfaction with the given and sensory, intensified by the growing awareness that the given and the sensory is neither all there is nor definitive."[11]

This "growing awareness" of the inadequacy of "the given" forced Viktor Frankl to confront the question of meaning in the depths of human degradation. *Man's Search for Meaning,* Frankl's unforgettable account of the horrors of Nazi prison camps and his depiction of the human ability to endure life's miseries and challenges by finding transcendent meaning, inspired the subtitle for this volume: "The Search for Meaning in Literature." In many

---

10. Frederick Buechner, "Faith and Fiction," in *Spiritual Quests*, ed. William Zinsser (New York: Quality Paperback Book Club, 1988), 110.

11. Jan Patoccka, quoted in Richard Rorty, "The Seer of Prague," *The New Republic* (1 July 1991): 36.

literary works, including those of such contemporary writers as Eli Wiesel, Toni Morrison, Shusaku Endo, Maya Angelou, Iris Murdoch, Seamus Deane, Brian Friel, Seamus Heaney, Wole Soyinka, Czeslaw Milosz, Denise Levertov, and Frederick Buechner, to name only a few, the experience of "the given and the sensory" – from the brutal to the pleasurable – is shaped in various ways that enable the reader to glimpse potential realities beyond the concrete and the immediate, to reach what Seamus Heaney has termed in the title of one of his volumes, "the spirit level." In empowering their readers to see the here and now through imaginative perspectives, in arousing a dissatisfaction with "the given" as definitive, writers, both past and current, have illuminated paths for the human spirit in the enduring search for meaning.

Periodically over the years, critical studies have explored in literature the nature of the human thirst for transcendence. George Panichas' *Mansions of the Spirit: Essays in Literature and Religion* (1967) and Harry T. Mooney, Jr., and Thomas F. Staley's *The Shapeless God: Essays on Modern Fiction* (1968) come immediately to mind. In recent years, however, such collections of essays have become increasingly rare.

The present volume is intended to reawaken readers to the question of ultimate meaning in literature and to encourage others to share their encounters with the "real presences" that dwell in literature and the arts. In the essays that follow, readers are invited into a larger community of searchers that includes such thinkers and writers as Augustine of Hippo, Teresa of Avila, John of the Cross, Jean Jacques Rousseau, Miguel Unamuno, Jean Genet, T. S. Eliot, Flannery O'Connor, Czeslaw Milosz, Albert Camus, Frederick Buechner, Ignazio Silone, Etty Hillesum, Annie Dillard, Samuel Beckett, Václav Havel, Russell Hoban, Seamus Heaney, Osip Mandelstam, Joan Didion, and Italo Calvino. We have tried to discern and illuminate their struggles with the question of ultimate meaning in their own life stories and in their poetry, fiction, and drama.[12]

---

12. We did not attempt in this collection to be totally comprehensive or representative, and so the list of subjects we chose reveals gaps of various kinds – in historical periods and ethnic representation in particular. There are rich possibilities for exploring transcendent meaning in literature in every era and every cultural group; this volume represents only a few of the possible choices.

The volume opens with an overview of the search for transcendence in five autobiographies. Patricia Ann Preston, S.S.N.D., explores the reshaping of the quest from Augustine, through St. Teresa, through Jean Jacques Rousseau, through Miguel Unamuno, to Jean Genet. In the course of her study of these "lives," Preston shows how spiritual quests have undergone radical transformations in increasingly rational and subjective times.

Preston's essay is complemented by those of Joan Penzenstadler, S.S.N.D., and Mary Ellen Kohn. Penzenstadler explores the quest for transcendence in a modern woman, Etty Hillesum, whose diaries and letters comprise her own spiritual autobiography. Despite the degradation of Nazi death camps, Hillesum's increasing attentiveness to mystery enables her to enter spiritually into what Penzenstadler terms "the free, unmerited gift of God's love." Hillesum finds transcendence in becoming attuned to an inner dialogue with God, what she herself called "a deeper rhythm . . . the most important thing we have to learn in this life."[13] Her "wager," then, emerges not from cognition but from attentiveness to her own deepest rhythm and voices.

Although many of us are aware that mystics have used erotic images to describe their quest for union with God, most of us have not pondered the obverse: that the stages of our own love relationships might actually correspond to the stages of mysticism. Mary Ellen Kohn explores this thesis in her essay on John of the Cross and his use of erotic imagery in *The Spiritual Canticle.*

The essays by Preston, Penzenstadler, and Kohn focus on individual – albeit divergent – journeys for meaning through personal experience; two essays by Carolyn Sur, S.S.N.D., and Patricia Ann Obremski, S.S.N.D., shift the focus to transcendence in and via nature. Sur foregrounds the transcendent element in Annie Dillard's nature writings. Dillard, according to Sur, demonstrates how one can "lose" oneself in nature, seeing beyond an isolated element and moment "to the connectedness of all within the cosmos." Obremski explores Italo Calvino's fictions and finds

---

13. Etty Hillesum, *Letters from Westerbork,* trans. Arnold Pomerans (New York: Random, 1986), 116.

in his characters, who frequently embody a law of physics, a contemporary affirmation of the infinite potential of the universe.

Obremski's discussion of Calvino's cosmic fictions leads into the next two essays, which follow poetic explorations of the ostensible limits of time and space. Mary Hester Valentine, S.S.N.D., discusses the poetry of Czeslaw Milosz. She concludes that "in Milosz's poems we share the universal tension between our existence in time and our inability to cope with it, other than metaphysically." Catharine Malloy juxtaposes the poetry of Osip Mandelstam and Seamus Heaney. Malloy finds that despite noticeable differences, "both Mandelstam and Heaney create places with language that resist the erosion of time; both poets use place as a wager on transcendence."

From the poetry of Milosz, Mandelstam, and Heaney, the essays move to the fiction and other prose writings of Frederick Buechner, Russell Hoban, and Ignazio Silone. For all three of these authors, stories and the telling of stories are vehicles of various kinds of transcendence. For Buechner, as Heidi Sjostrom argues, the events of our lives are God's speaking to us; Buechner's fiction embodies his advice for anyone seeking the transcendent: "Listen to your life." Jane Thompson explores the storytelling process itself in Russell Hoban's *Riddley Walker*. In that futuristic science-fiction novel, Hoban, in Thompson's analysis, demonstrates how narrative not only gives shape to human experience but also "allows individuals to reach beyond themselves; to maintain relationships and communities; and ultimately to perceive the social, natural, and spiritual worlds as interdependent." The archetypal stories of human experience can, moreover, transform the individual as Paul J. McGuire, S.C.J., finds in Ignazio Silone's *Bread and Wine*. In that novel, McGuire argues, Pietro Spina, in playing a role, is inwardly transformed through his experience and through rereading the stories of his youth; he moves from fictions to reality, to actually becoming who he pretended to be.

The transformation of the individual vis-à-vis the larger community is explored further in three essays by Ann Angel, Kathleen Scullin, and Mary Beth Duffey. Ann Angel uses the journalism of Joan Didion to raise questions about the relationship between actions and values, between moral ambiguity and societal decay.

Kathleen Scullin examines the role of violence vis-à-vis transcendence in Flannery O'Connor's *The Violent Bear It Away*. In Scullin's analysis, O'Connor sees the struggle toward self-consciousness as an inherently spiritual struggle: violence toward self and toward others often results when humans oppose God's grace with self-will, when humans refuse transcendence. Mary Beth Duffey also explores the effects of violence on the individual and the community in T. S. Eliot's *The Family Reunion*. Duffey demonstrates how Eliot fuses Greek and Christian archetypal themes of coming home and reconciliation to show that individual transformation and transcendence are inextricably linked to community.

The final two essays in the collection focus on the wager itself: "Let us weigh the gain and the loss involved by wagering that God exists. . . . if you win, you win all; if you lose, you lose nothing." James Conlon argues that Albert Camus in his *The Stranger* and *The Plague* actually offers a counterargument to Pascal's wager: It is more reasonable to wager on the certainty of earthly joys than on the uncertainty of eternity; nonbelief actually intensifies human efforts toward alleviating suffering in this world. By taking the role of a "devil's advocate" or, more accurately, of the human attuned to the joys and sufferings of this world, Conlon confronts us with the fundamental issues at stake in the wager. Finally, in her analysis of two plays that Samuel Beckett and Václav Havel dedicated to each other, Phyllis Carey uses the philosophy of Emmanuel Lévinas to argue that Pascal's wager on transcendence is in essence the only alternative if one is to be truly human. Carey uses Beckett's and Havel's drama to demonstrate that human identity itself depends on a response to the *other,* and that it is through that response that humans become open to the totally *other,* the transcendent source of all being.

Each essay in the volume concludes with an "Author's Note," which suggests why the author of the essay was attracted to the particular writer(s) discussed, which questions about transcendence are implicit in the essay, and further points for reflection. The "Notes" are intended as open invitations to readers for contemplation and discussion.

The collection as a whole attests to our wider communal attempt at Mount Mary to ponder the meaning of human existence in our Search for Meaning classes, in the Literature of the Religious Imagination course and in many other forums, both formal and informal. In our efforts, we join a long history of human searchers, aware that the ultimate answers elude us despite the most sophisticated techniques of contemporary scholarship. As Leslie Armour points out in assessing our latest theories:

> Postmodern thought promises to free us from science, bourgeois rationality, and traditional religion alike, but it does not seem to give us a way of facing up to the infinite . . . anyone who thinks that we are not simply mechanisms in a complex physical and economic system still has to bet. For if we are not fully programmed, we have to choose, and no final certainties seem to be forthcoming.[14]

If Armour is right, wagering itself is an expression of transcendence over our increasingly mechanized and computerized existences. It expresses the desire that all human endeavor may not simply be for this world or for nought. Czeslaw Milosz, for one, saw clearly what is at stake, and his words seem appropriate as a final gloss on the human desire that both motivated this collection and that underlies our many forms of wagering on transcendence:

> And what if Pascal had not been saved
> and if those narrow hands in which we laid a cross
> are all he is, entire, like a lifeless swallow
> in the dust, under the buzz of the poisonous-blue flies?
>
> And if they all, kneeling with poised palms,
> millions, billions of them, ended together with their
>   illusion?
> I shall never agree. I will give them the crown.
> The human mind is splendid; lips powerful,
> and the summons so great it must open Paradise.[15]

---

14. Armour, 84.

15. Czeslaw Milosz, "Throughout Our Lands," *The Collected Poems 1931-1987* (New York: Ecco Press, 1988), 150-51.

Works Cited

Armour, Leslie. *"Infini Rien": Pascal's Wager and the Human Paradox.* Carbondale, Ill.: Southern Illinois University Press, 1993.

Buechner, Frederick. "Faith and Fiction." In *Spiritual Quests.* Edited by William Zinsser, 105-29. New York: Quality Paperback Book Club, 1988.

Havel, Václav. "A Time for Transcendence." *Utne Reader* (January February, 1995): 111-13.

Hillesum, Etty. *Letters from Westerbork.* Translated by Arnold Pomerans. New York: Random, 1986.

Millbank, John. "Problematizing the secular: the postmodern agenda." In *Shadow of Spirit: Postmodernism and Religion.* Edited by Philippa Berry and Andrew Wernick, 30-44. London: Routledge, 1992.

Milosz, Czeslaw. "Throughout Our Lands." In *The Collected Poems 1931-1987.* New York: Ecco Press, 1988. 150-51.

Mooney, Harry J. and Thomas F. Staley. *The Shapeless God: Essays on Modern Fiction.* Pittsburgh: University of Pittsburgh Press, 1968.

Panichas, George, ed. *Mansions of the Spirit: Essays in Literature and Religion.* New York: Hawthorn Books, 1967.

Pascal, Blaise. *Pensées: Notes on Religion and Other Subjects.* Edited by Louis LaFuma. Translated by John Warrington. London: J. M. Dent & Sons, 1960.

Peatman, Bill. "We are consuming religious books with fury." *National Catholic Reporter* (8 September 1995): 25.

Rorty, Richard. "The Seer of Prague." *The New Republic* (1 July 1991): 35-40.

Steiner, George. *Real Presences.* Chicago: The University of Chicago Press, 1989.

I.

The Journey

Chapter One

The Search for Transcendence as Manifested Through Autobiography

Patricia Ann Preston, S.S.N.D.

The word "autobiography" conjures up many questions in the mind of the prospective reader. Will it be a documentary recording of facts, an interpretation of events, a psychoanalysis of a "self," a novelized version of the author's tragedies and dreams? It is possible to approach autobiographies from many different perspectives. A recent reading of autobiographies by famous figures of Western civilization, however, has led me to a reflection on the human person's search for transcendence throughout history. Although I read the autobiographies with questions about the difference between reality and fiction, about the social environment surrounding the autobiographer, about the motives of the author in writing his or her story, about the style, philosophy, theology and aesthetics of the work, the one common thread that kept attracting my attention was the quest that each writer conveyed. Whether saint or sinner, artist or literary great, philosopher or criminal, each narrator presented in one way or another a personal search for meaning and ultimately spoke to me, the reader, about that person's search for the transcendent.

In stating their reasons for writing their stories, the autobiographers rarely identify this search as a motivating force or even a factor, but as the various writers sought to present their lives as they viewed them, or as they wanted others to view them, the sensitive reader discerns the universality of the human quest for the transcendent. One characteristic of all these autobiographers is that they were restless people.[1] They were constantly questioning the traditional world they lived in and seeking to push the limits of their understanding, their emotions, their places in the world surrounding them to something beyond their apparent human limits.

The first autobiography I remember reading was the *Confessions* of St. Augustine. As a young woman of sixteen, already devoured by intellectual and theological questions, I was touched very personally by Augustine's story of his quest for truth and for God. As the book has prompted readers of all times, from St. Teresa of Avila to the present, to ask questions, to affirm their right and duty to continue their personal search, so it did to me, an adolescent in the mid-twentieth century.

At the end of the twentieth century I found that Augustine could still speak to me. He aroused in me that same affirmation of the human person's need to pursue truth, to search for the transcendent, to find something beyond the limits of one's self. I was reminded again of the fundamental principle, so often repeated by great moral teachers, that the search for God, for fulfillment, for freedom starts in the inner self. Reflecting his own search for God, Augustine asks,

> How, then, do I look for you, O Lord? For when I look for you, who are my God, I am looking for a life of blessed happiness. . . . How, then, am I to search for this blessed life? For I do not possess it until I can rightly say, "This is all that I want. Happiness is here." . . . Surely happiness is what everyone wants, so much so that there can be none who do not want it. But if they desire it so much, where did they learn what it was? If they have learnt to love it, where did they see it?[2]

---

1. Almost all the autobiographies were written by people who were from what would now be called middle-class families and were raised as Christians. The one exception, Jean Genet, spent his first years with a French bourgeois family and obviously, from his writings, obtained a fair amount of education. Genet closely guarded the total story of his youth.

2. Saint Augustine of Hippo, *Confessions*, trans. R. S. Pine-Coffin (London: Penguin Books, 1961), Book X, 226; hereafter, cited parenthetically in the text as Augustine.

Augustine explores his inner self, particularly memory, to find true happiness. He confesses the various stages of his search:

> These were the stages of my pitiful fall into the depths of hell, as I struggled and strained for lack of the truth. My God, you had mercy on me even before I had confessed to you; but I now confess that all this was because I tried to find you, not through the understanding of the mind, by which you meant us to be superior to the beasts, but through the senses of the flesh. (Augustine III, 62)

In Book VI, Augustine had recognized, "I was looking for you outside myself and I did not find the God of my own heart" (Augustine VI, 111). He went looking for the God of reason, and he began to discover that what was needed was to find "the God of my own heart."

Augustine had started his *Confessions* with the observation: "you [God] made us for yourself and our hearts find no peace until they rest in you" (Augustine I, 21). He proceeded to narrate the story of his personal search for God, along with other details of his life, and reached a climax when he exclaimed:

> I have learnt to love you late, Beauty at once so ancient and so new! I have learnt to love you late! You were within me, and I was in the world outside myself. I searched for you outside myself and, disfigured as I was, I fell upon the lovely things of your creation. You were with me, but I was not with you. . . . You called me; you cried aloud to me; . . . your radiance enveloped me; you put my blindness to flight. . . . I tasted you, and now I hunger and thirst for you. You touched me, and I am inflamed with love of your peace. (Augustine X, 231-32)

Augustine, influenced by his early fascination with Aristotle, Plato, Manichaeism and later his interest in the works of Plotinus, stresses the discontinuity between the "inner" realm and the "outer" realm, between the "natural" and the "supernatural." As Robert Meagher describes it, "Augustine . . . has in mind types of life actually available to individual human beings when he explains 'One kind of life is earthly, another is heavenly; there is a life of beasts, another of human beings, and another of angels' (*In Joann. cv.*, 18.7)."[3]

The saint's search for the transcendent leads him "within" himself, but when he seems to come in contact with the "divine," he experiences that the encounter is not of this life: "And sometimes you allow me to experience a feeling quite unlike my normal state, an inward sense of delight which, if it were to reach perfection in me, would be something not encountered in this life, though what it is I cannot tell" (Augustine X, 249).

Peter Brown emphasizes that Augustine is a continuing seeker. He points out that religious autobiographies of the early Christian times had been the stories of successful conversions. However, as Brown says, "The amazing Book Two of the *Confessions* is not the affirmation of a cured man: it is the self-portrait of a convalescent."[4] In Section 30 of Book X, Augustine writes: "By your [God's] grace it [my soul] will no longer commit in sleep these shameful, unclean acts inspired by sensual images, which lead to the pollution of the body: it will not so much as consent to them" (Augustine X, 234). Later he adds, "Day after day without ceasing these temptations [of the bodily senses] put us to the test, O Lord. . . . Give me the grace to do as you command, and command me to do what you will!" (Augustine X, 245). The saint laments, "The pleasures I find in the world, which should be cause for tears, are at strife with its sorrows, in which I should rejoice, and I cannot tell to which the victory will fall" (Augustine X, 232). Augustine in his middle age is still striving mightily to reach those limits where the human touches the divine. He does not see himself as a work accomplished.

Santa Teresa of Avila, in her *Life*, also shows that she is a seeker of happiness and truth. However, her search for the transcendent is not through reason. Explaining the stages of prayer leading to mystical union with God, Teresa says, "This is a prayer

3. Qtd. in Robert E. Meagher, *An Introduction to Augustine* (New York: New York University Press, 1978), 99-100. In a footnote to this section Meagher points out that "Augustine would have been familiar with this conception of human beings as occupying a middle position among essences in the Plotinian formation: 'Human being lies mid-way [*en meso*] between gods and beasts and inclines towards both. Some human beings become like gods and others become like beasts. Most, however, remain in the middle' (*Enneads* [n.3, 100])."

4. Peter Brown, *Augustine of Hippo* (Berkeley: University of California Press, 1967), 177.

[the Prayer of Quiet] that comprises a great deal and achieves more than any amount of meditation on the part of the understanding. . . . Let it [the will] make certain acts of love . . . concerning what it will do for Him to Whom it owes so much, without allowing the understanding to make any noise. . . ."[5] She seeks through love, an abundance of love. In fact, when Teresa draws closest to the transcendent, "the understanding becomes silent."

The historian Gerda Lerner points out that "the thinkers of Classical Antiquity and the fathers of the Church had iterated man's rationality, his ability to reason logically and without the subjectivity of emotions, to a divine gift."[6] However, she notes that there was another ancient tradition which allowed for a different "mode of cognition and enlightenment. Mysticism . . . asserted that transcendent knowledge came not as a product of rational thought, but as a result of a way of life, of individual inspiration and sudden revelatory insight."[7]

In Chapter IX of the *Vida*, Teresa tells of her first reading of Augustine's *Confessions*. "When I started to read the *Confessions*, I seemed to see myself in them and I began to commend myself often to that glorious Saint. When I got as far as his conversion and read how he heard that voice in the garden, it seemed exactly as if the Lord were speaking in that way to me, or so my heart felt" (Teresa IX, 117).

In Chapters XXIII and XXIV of her *Life* Teresa tells of her own conversion. This conversion has to be seen against the backdrop of twenty years of life as a faithful, but not too particular, nun. As she says, "Until now the life I was describing was my own; but the life I have been living since I began to expound these matters concerning prayer is the life which God has been living in me" (Teresa XXIII, 219). Teresa's fear of herself and her weakness leads her to seek the advice of spiritual persons. The first holy men she

---

5. Saint Teresa of Avila, *The Life of Teresa of Jesus,* ed. and trans. E. Allison Peers (Garden City, N.Y.: Doubleday, 1960), Chap. XV, 157; hereafter cited parenthetically in the text as Teresa.

6. Gerda Lerner, *The Creation of Feminist Consciousness: From the Middle Ages to 1870* (New York: Oxford University Press, 1989), 65.

7. Ibid., 66.

consults tell her that her spiritual favors might really be the work of an evil spirit. Teresa nevertheless rejects their decisions and seeks out other holy men. Fortunately, she found some who reassured her and helped her on her way to seek ever closer union with God. However, ultimately she relies on the Lord Himself as her spiritual director:

> My confessor then asked me who told me it was Jesus Christ. "He often tells me so Himself," I replied. . . . The Lord is pleased that this knowledge should be so deeply engraven upon the understanding that one can no more doubt it than one can doubt the evidence of one's eyes – indeed, the latter is easier, for we sometimes suspect that we have imagined what we see, whereas here, though that suspicion may arise for a moment, there remains such complete certainty that the doubt has no force. (Teresa XXVII, 250)

When a confessor suspects that her visions are imagined and commands her to hold up a cross and snap her fingers at the vision to chase the devil away, thus causing Teresa much distress, she again relies on the Lord: "He told me not to worry about it and said I was quite right to obey, but He would see that my confessor learned the truth. When they made me stop my prayer He seemed to me to have become angry, and He told me to tell them that this was tyranny" (Teresa XXIX, 270).

Teresa's spiritual consciousness became so fine-tuned that she professed, "Any offence, however slight, which I might commit against God I would feel in my soul so deeply that if I had anything I did not need I could not become recollected again until it had been taken away" (Teresa XXIV, 229).

The modern reader of Teresa sometimes finds these assertions of the need for asceticism to be sick, or twisted. However, for most of the mystics and saints, asceticism was merely a way to free the body, in a *gloriosa passio* which springs from an ardent love of God, and for many, a blessed opportunity to share in the *passio* of Jesus which manifested, made incarnate, God's love for human beings.[8] Thus, when Teresa talks about sufferings and asceticism,

---

8. Erich Auerbach, *Literary Language and Its Public in Late Latin Antiquity and in*

she does so in the sense of the *gloriosa passio*. The true reason for asceticism and seeking suffering is to share in the glory of the love of God, not just in the future, but as Santa Teresa teaches, even here on earth through one's experience of the transcendent through prayer. An analogy of this asceticism can be seen in the demanding stress that the modern athlete or fitness advocate exerts on his or her body when seeking a coveted athletic prize or the goal of perfect physical health.

Of course, in our modern post-Freudian society, every bodily act, as well as almost all human aspirations, is linked automatically to the human sexual drive – either through exaltation, sublimation, or repression. Thus modern readers rather often give a sexual coloration to Teresa's early life, her relationship with her confessors, and her frequent mention of her sinfulness in the *Life*. There is no doubt in my mind that Teresa did experience physical sexual attraction toward some men in her life – she was very human and filled with tender emotions. However, to interpret all her references to "sin" or human *afición* only in terms of sexual drives is to misread the Teresa of the late Middle Ages in Spain. All women, and religious women in particular, were so hedged in and bound by meticulous rules of honor and safeguards to protect their virginity that any small transgression of one of the elaborate rules would be considered a serious sin by Teresa.

Moreover, as the spiritual person draws more closely to the *numen* of the Godhead, any action or thought that does not lead one directly toward God is considered a sin, in an ever more fine recognition of the human person's propensity to turn away from God. This manifests itself in some as an aberration called scrupulosity, which actually keeps one from God. But the spiritually positive process can be likened to the good hostess' inspection of her crystal for a dinner party, taking each piece closer to real light in order to find and remove the specks of dust or water deposits that mar the perfect clarity of the crystal. Thus, Teresa's references to her wretchedness and sinfulness, which many readers find excessive in the *Life*, have to be seen in the context of her approach

---

the Middle Ages, trans. Ralph Manheim (New York: Pantheon Books, 1965), 67-69.

to the *numen*, the perfect light of God, through her ever-increasing mystical union with God. Teresa says, "Not only does the soul perceive the cobwebs which disfigure it and its own great faults, but so bright is the sunlight that it sees every little speck of dust, however small" (Teresa XX, 201).

In her *Life* Santa Teresa describes her never-ending inward drive to unite herself with the transcendent. She makes it very clear that the human person cannot do this alone, but only with the assistance of the Divine, but she also stresses the importance of the individual's constant quest and response to any divine initiative. "It is quite clear what [Divine] union is – two different things becoming one. O my Lord, how good Thou art! . . . Let all things praise Thee, my God, Who hast so loved us that we can truly say that Thou hast communication with souls even in this exile: even if they are good, this is great bounty and magnanimity" (Teresa XVIII, 174).

"Those with whom the soul has to do keep thinking it has reached its summit, but soon afterwards they find it higher still, for God is always giving it new favors" (Teresa XXI, 207). "I have also been thinking of the comparison which follows. Assuming that what is given to the most advanced soul is the same as what is given to beginners, it is like food shared by many people; those who eat very little of it experience the pleasant taste only for a short time; those who eat more derive some sustenance from it; while those who eat a great deal derive life and strength!" (Teresa XXII, 217).

Throughout the *Life* and in some of her later writings, especially the *Interior Castle*, Santa Teresa shows that she is pushing her quest for the transcendent, for union with God, to the utmost boundaries of human limitations. Her famous raptures, ecstasies, and other physical manifestations of divine union are human evidence of this testing of the limitations of the human, physical world. Toward the end of the *Life*, she describes one of her greatest raptures:

> . . . my spirit became so completely transported that it seemed to have departed almost wholly from the body; or, at least, there was no way of telling that it was in the body. . . . I cannot possibly explain how this happened,

but, without seeing anything, I seemed to see myself in the presence of the Godhead. . . . I think it is the sublimest vision which the Lord has granted me grace to see. . . . It is a great flame, which seems to burn up and annihilate all life's desires. (Teresa XXXVIII, 367-68)

Santa Teresa's search has led her into the experience of transcendence through the fires of mysticism. Her asceticism has helped to free her from the finite.

Several centuries later, Jean-Jacques Rousseau takes up the Augustinian tradition by a declaration of his interior being, even entitling his autobiography *"Confessions,"* as had Augustine. However, "the source of unity and wholeness which Augustine found only in God is now to be discovered in the self. . . . Rousseau is the starting point of a transformation in modern culture towards a deeper inwardness and a radical autonomy."[9] Where Augustine needed to understand himself and his quest for God, and Santa Teresa needed to reassure herself that her quest for and experience of God were valid, Rousseau, at the dawn of the Age of Enlightenment, through his autobiography needs to understand himself and also to have others understand him. The assurance that Augustine and Teresa had (in spite of their confessions of uncertainty and false starts or falls) that they were on the right path to the transcendent, to God, to pure truth, happiness and beauty has begun to erode. While Rousseau does not deny God, he nevertheless defines the end of man's striving for perfection, which Augustine and Teresa identified as God, as man's ultimate freedom and self-dependence. Rousseau seeks to find the motives for his good actions within himself, not in the impulses to good placed in the human person by God.

Interestingly, the word "transcendent" as defined in the *Oxford English Dictionary* is given first as, "surpassing or excelling others of its kind; going beyond ordinary limits; . . ." A later definition is the theological meaning "of the Deity: In His being, exalted above and distinct from the universe. . . . Distinguished from 'Immanent.'"[10] In Rousseau's autobiography the shift in the

---

9. Charles Taylor, *Sources of the Self* (Cambridge, Mass.: Harvard University Press, 1989), 362-63.

search for meaning, for self, is entering a new era. The original Greek word from which the modern "transcend" evolves, σκαυδαλου *(scandalon),* means "to climb, to mount." At the time of Augustine, this Greek word, from which the Latin *transcendo* derives, changes from the meaning of "to climb over, to step over, to pass over," and comes to mean "to ascend."[11] It seems that from the time of Rousseau onward, many autobiographers of Western civilization saw their need for surpassing the boundaries and limitations found in their human "self" through returning to that original Greek/Latin meaning of *transcendo,* to climb over, to step over, heading toward the primary modern English meaning of "to surpass or go beyond the physical limits of the human." Rousseau clearly sets himself as the best of humankind, as a transcendent being in himself.

Even though Rousseau does not deny the existence of God, he sees humans as capable of producing works equal to the works of God. Sightseeing at the Pont du Gard (a Roman aqueduct), Rousseau exclaims,

> This once the object surpassed my expectations. . . . The aspect of this simple and noble work struck me so much the more, as it is in the middle of a desert, whose silence and solitude render the object more striking, and our admiration more lively; . . . We ask ourselves what power transported these enormous stones so far from any quarry, or united the hands of so many thousand people in a place where there is not a single one? I went up the three stories of this superb edifice, which respect almost prevented me from treading on. The sound of my steps under these immense vaults made me imagine I heard the magnanimous voices of those who built them. . . . While feeling my own littleness, I experienced something that elevated my soul; I said to myself with a sigh, Why am not I a Roman! I remained there several hours in a ravishing contemplation.[12]

---

10. *Oxford English Dictionary,* 2nd ed., s.v. "transcendence."

11. Ibid.

12. Jean-Jacques Rousseau, *The Confessions of Jean-Jacques Rousseau,* anonymous translation revised and completed by A. S. B. Glover (New York: Heritage

This is terminology that was formerly used mainly to talk of the wonders of God's creation.

Nowhere is Rousseau's new sense of the self and of the self's search for that which is over, above and beyond him more evident than in the opening lines of the *Confessions:*

> I am undertaking a work which has no example, and whose execution will have no imitator. I mean to lay open to my fellow-mortals a man just as nature wrought him; and this man is myself.
>
> I alone. I know my heart, and am acquainted with mankind. I am not made like anyone I have seen; I dare believe I am not made like anyone existing. If I am not better, at least I am quite different. Whether Nature has done well or ill in breaking the mould she cast me in, can be determined only after having read me.
>
> Let the trumpet of the day of judgement sound when it will, I shall appear with this book in my hand before the Sovereign Judge, and cry with a loud voice. This is my work, these were my thoughts, and thus was I . . . Eternal being! assemble around me the numberless throng of my fellow-mortals; let them listen to my Confessions. . . . Let each of them, in his turn, lay open his heart with the same sincerity . . . and then say, if he dare, *I was better than that man.* (Rousseau 3-4)

Rousseau, like Alexander Pope, believes that the proper study of mankind is man. He is unique; Nature (not God) "broke the mold" when he was made. He professed this uniqueness proudly throughout his *Confessions.* As Ernst Cassirer notes, "And yet, no matter how strongly he remained aware of this uniqueness, Rousseau was animated by the strongest urge for communication and mutual understanding."[13] Although Rousseau apparently addresses his *Confessions* to God and mankind in the third paragraph of Book I, this God is noticeable only here. "Within the body of the book there is scarcely a single invocation or apostrophe to God. We note the diffuse presence of the reader, . . . a putative witness. . . . He

---

Press, 1955), 230; hereafter cited parenthetically in the text as Rousseau.

13. Ernst Cassirer, *The Question of Jean-Jacques Rousseau,* trans. and ed. Peter Gay (Bloomington: Indiana University Press, 1963), 128.

strives to convince him [the reader, the interlocutor] of the absolute truth of his narrative, as of the abiding innocence of his intentions."[14]

In his autobiography Rousseau shows that he truly believed that later in life – at the point of writing his *Confessions* – he really understood himself. In Book IV he exclaims, "Ah! how little I knew of it [myself]! Mine [my life] had been a hundred times more charming, had I been less a fool, and known better how to enjoy it" (Rousseau 120). Now that he supposedly understands himself, he knows how he should respond to life.

Rousseau's personal experience of growing lucidity is reflected in his autobiography. In Rousseau's system of belief, humans originally possessed happiness and joy. There was no "fallen nature," no "original sin." However, in that original state of happiness, the human was also "originally a brute deprived of 'light,' his reason still asleep."[15] The present, in contrast to the dark past, is a time of lucid reflection and enlarged consciousness. "In Rousseau's work the private emotions and conscience inherit some of the functions assigned to God in traditional theological discourse."[16]

Rousseau describes his early childhood, particularly his life at Bossey, as a time of Paradise. "The manner I lived in at Bossey was so agreeable, that nothing but its continuance was necessary absolutely to fix my character. Tender, affectionate, peaceable sentiments were its basis. . . . I raised myself by transports to sublime emotions. . ." (Rousseau 11). His Paradise ended not because he had sinned, but because he had suffered injustice from others: "We were there, as the first man is represented in the terrestrial paradise, but having ceased to enjoy it" (Rousseau 17-18). This pattern of blaming others, of paranoia, was to mark his examination of his entire life. He tries to "unravel the immense chaos of sentiments" in his life by doubly painting the state of his

---

14. Jean Starobinski, "The Style of Autobiography," trans. Seymour Chatman, in *Autobiography: Essays Theoretical and Critical*, ed. James Olney, (Princeton: Princeton University Press, 1980), 80.

15. Starobinski, 83.

16. Ibid., 81.

soul, "namely at the moment when the event happened to me and the moment when I wrote it."[17]

At the beginning of the second half of his *Confessions,* Rousseau makes very clear that "the real object of my confessions is to communicate an exact knowledge of what I interiorly am and have been in every situation of my life. I have promised the history of my mind" (Rousseau 250). For him, his "virtuous sentiments" are the central part of his life. "I may omit facts, transpose events and fall into some errors of dates; but I cannot be deceived in what I have felt, nor in that which from sentiment I have done; and to relate this is the chief end of my present work" (Rousseau 250).

The second part of Rousseau's *Confessions* shows his increasing paranoia, but in Book XII he unequivocally states the same assertion that he had made at the beginning of the *Confessions:*

> But notwithstanding what they may think or say, I will still
> continue faithfully to state what J. J. Rousseau was, did
> and thought; without explaining or justifying the singular-
> ity of his sentiments and ideas, or endeavouring to dis-
> cover whether or not others have thought as he did.
> (Rousseau 623-24)

Rousseau finds his validity, his transcendence, in his own sentiments and ideas. His search for transcendence as revealed in his *Confessions* is principally to have his transcendent self accepted by others. Santa Teresa had used her experience of union with God to assert her certainty about the truth of what she was experiencing and reporting. Rousseau ends his *Confessions* with the validation of his words based on his own words and works:

> I have written the truth: if any person has heard of things
> contrary to those I have just stated, were they a thousand
> times proved, he has heard calumny and falsehood . . .
> and if he refuses thoroughly to examine and compare them
> with me whilst I am alive, he is not a friend either to justice
> or truth. For my part, I openly and without the least fear,
> declare, that whoever, even without having read my
> works, shall have examined with his own eyes my dispo-
> sition, character, manners, inclinations, pleasures, and

---

17. Rousseau, quoted in Starobinski, 81-82, n. 12.

habits, and pronounce me a dishonest man, is himself one who deserves a gibbet. (Rousseau 635)

Georges Gusdorf, discussing the conditions and limits of autobiography, points out that "confession of the past realizes itself as a work in the present: it effects a true creation of self by the self. Under guise of presenting myself as I was, I exercise a sort of right to recover possession of my existence now and later."[18] He continues, "Every autobiography is a work of art and at the same time a work of enlightenment. . . . What is in question is a sort of revaluation of individual destiny."[19] Augustine ostensibly wrote his *Confessions* to praise God; Santa Teresa wrote to satisfy the demands of her confessors in order to validate her experiences. Upon leaving the "Age of Belief," Rousseau, the eighteenth-century autobiographer, appears to need to assure his transcendence, his destiny, through his own existence and works.

A century later, at the end of his lucid life, Friedrich Nietzsche felt compelled to write the story of his life. His autobiography, *Ecce Homo*, is subtitled *How One Becomes What One Is*. Nietzsche's question is "what," not "who"; one's existence is a construction, an artifact or object. The title of his work is also significant: *Ecce Homo,* "Behold the Man," a phrase known to all his readers as the words of Pontius Pilate about Christ. In Walter Kaufmann's introduction to *Ecce Homo*, he notes that Nietzsche calls himself "the Man" in the sense of Dionysius, as contrasted with Jesus, the Crucified. "In the later works of Nietzsche, 'Dionysius' is no longer the spirit of unrestrained passion, but the symbol of life with all its suffering and terror."[20] Thus Nietzsche proclaims himself "the Man" in a total affirmation of life, of himself, willing to live amidst suffering, as opposed to the crucified Jesus of resigned suffering. As Charles Taylor has pointed out:

---

18. Georges Gusdorf, "Conditions and Limits of Autobiography," trans. James Olney, in *Autobiography: Essays, Theoretical and Critical*, ed. James Olney, 44.

19. Ibid., 45.

20. Walter Kaufmann, "Editor's Introduction," in Friedrich Nietzsche, *On the Genealogy of Morals / Ecce Homo*, trans. and ed. Walter Kaufmann (New York: Random House, 1969), 209.

What we have in this new issue of affirming the goodness of things is the development of a human analogue to God's seeing things as good: a seeing which also helps effect what it sees. This can mean, of course, that the self-attribution of this power is a resolutely atheist doctrine, the arrogation to man of powers formerly confined to God.[21]

In a prefatory note to the book, Nietzsche tells why he is writing his autobiography: "On this perfect day . . . the eye of the sun just fell upon my life: I looked back, I looked forward, and never saw so many and such good things at once. . . . *How could I fail to be grateful to my whole life? –* and so I tell my life to myself."[22]

We have now come a full swing toward the individual: Augustine addressed God; Teresa wrote at the command of her confessor; Rousseau addressed his fellow mortals and alluded to his day before the Sovereign Judge; Nietzsche addresses only himself. He alone is sufficient for the discovery of the good. The titles of his chapters show clearly that he is supposedly addressing himself: "Why I Am So Wise," "Why I Am So Clever," "Why I Write Such Good Books," "Why I Am a Destiny." Like Rousseau, Nietzsche proclaims himself unique. He begins his "Preface" with the words *"Hear me! For I am such and such a person. Above all, do not mistake me for someone else"* (Nietzsche 217).

Nietzsche affirms that the way to find meaning in life is to live life. One understands only what one experiences. Selfishness is good. The search for "philosophy" "means living voluntarily among ice and high mountains – seeking out everything strange and questionable in existence, everything so far placed under a ban by morality" (Nietzsche 218). "How much truth does a spirit endure?" he asks himself (Nietzsche 218). The early philosophers had found the search for truth through the order of reason. In the eighteenth century, many leading thinkers turned to the providential design of nature to find the constitutive good.[23] Now Nietzsche

---

21. Taylor, 449.

22. Friedrich Nietzsche, *On the Genealogy of Morals / Ecce Homo,* trans. and ed. Walter Kaufmann (New York: Random House, 1969), 221; hereafter cited parenthetically in the text as Nietzsche.

states that the search for meaning in life is to be found only in turning in on oneself, in to selfishness. "And thus I touch on the masterpiece of the art of self-preservation – of *selfishness*" (Nietzsche 253). Nietzsche rejects reason, or even consciousness, in his search for meaning:

> The whole surface of consciousness . . . must be kept clear of all great imperatives. . . . Meanwhile the organizing "idea" that is destined to rule keeps growing deep down . . . one by one, it trains all *subservient* capacities before giving any hint of the dominant task, "goal," "aim," or "meaning."
>
> . . . For the task of a *revaluation of all values* more capacities may have been needed than have ever dwelt together in a single individual . . . the long, secret work and artistry of my instinct. Its *higher protection* manifested itself to such a high degree that I never even suspected what was growing in me – and one day all my capacities, suddenly ripe, *leaped forth* in their ultimate perfection. (Nietzsche 254-55)

Thus the Dionysian ruling force, passion, leaped forth in Nietzsche in contrast to the birth of Athena, reason, from the head of Zeus. All of Nietzsche's "search" takes place within himself, in his own feelings, apart from his consciousness. As Yves Le Gal puts it, "Nietzsche sends us back . . . to a different criterion from that of truth, that of *force*, of life as rising or declining energy."[24]

Nietzsche is positioned "with one foot beyond life" (Nietzsche 217) and he talks about his "instinctive sureness in practice" (Nietzsche 226). He seems to find his transcendence in solitude, in a return to himself (Nietzsche 233-34). Zarathustra overcomes his nausea, finds his redemption, in solitude, cleanliness, purity. Nietzsche sees himself as utmost perfection. He claims "by my mere existence I outrage everything that has bad blood in its veins" (Nietzsche 258). "My formula for greatness in a human being is

---

23. See Taylor, 361.

24. Yves Le Gal, "*Unzeitgemass*: Out of Season," in *Nietzsche and Christianity*, ed. Claude Geffré and Jean-Pierre Jossua, English Language ed. Marcus Lefébure (New York: Seabury Press, 1981), 9.

amor fati [love of fate] that one wants nothing to be different, not forward, not backward, not in all eternity" (Nietzsche 258).

As Kaufmann asserts:

> To be sure, in *Ecce Homo* Nietzsche attempts what might be called a deliberate self-mythologization; some of his statements obviously make no claim to literal correctness; and poetic license is in places extended beyond all boundaries of reason and good taste. The mythological mask, however, that Nietzsche seeks to create for himself is not that of a prophet who establishes a new religion; it is the antithesis of Zarathustra.[25]

However, Nietzsche also recognized that his words had power. In the opening lines of the chapter "Why I Am a Destiny," he declares, "I know my fate. One day my name will be associated with the meaning of something tremendous. . . . I am no man, I am dynamite" (Nietzsche 326). Nietzsche identifies with Dionysus, the God of passion, and sees that his role is to bring back the Dionysian emphasis on the excess of life (Nietzsche 274). Thus, he finds transcendence in a complete exaltation of human life, but human life according to his own definition of "the will to power as no man ever possessed it" (Nietzsche 275). Kaufmann explains this "will to power" as

> a striving that cannot be accurately described either as a will to affect others or as a will to "realize" oneself; it is essentially a striving to transcend and perfect oneself. Nietzsche's opposition to the conception of a will to live or of a desire for self-preservation is due to this insistence that nothing that is alive is sufficient unto itself.[26]

Speaking of inspiration, Nietzsche asserts that God does not invade him, carry him into rapture as Santa Teresa had explained, but rather that "Everything happens involuntarily in the highest degree but as in a gale of a feeling of freedom, of absoluteness, of power, of divinity" (Nietzsche 300-301). It comes not from outside, but from within oneself.

---

25. Walter Kaufmann, *Nietzsche: Philosopher, Psychologist, Antichrist,* 3d ed. (New York: Vintage Books, 1968), 117.

26. Ibid., 248.

This sense of divinity, however, does not come without suffering. In speaking of the creation of the piece he considered his masterwork, *Zarathustra,* Nietzsche recalls, "One pays dearly for immortality: one has to die several times while still alive" (Nietzsche 303). However, in the work, his "concept of the 'Dionysian' . . . became a *supreme deed"* (Nietzsche 304), the total affirmation of negation:

> The psychological problem in the type of Zarathustra is how he that says No and *does* No to an unheard-of degree, to everything to which one has so far said Yes, can nevertheless be the opposite of a No-saying spirit; how the spirit who bears the heaviest fate, . . . can nevertheless be the lightest and most transcendent . . . how he that has the hardest, most terrible insight into reality, that has thought the "most abysmal idea" nevertheless does not consider it an objection to existence, not even to its eternal recurrence — but rather one reason more for being himself the eternal Yes to all things, "the tremendous, unbounded saying Yes and Amen." (Nietzsche 306)

Nietzche's revaluation of all values, which he described in the chapter "Why I Am a Destiny," arises from his internal certitude about his own divinity: "that is my formula for an act of supreme self-examination on the part of humanity, become flesh and genius in me. It is my fate that I have to be the first *decent* human being. . . ." (Nietzsche 326).

For Nietzsche, transcendence is found in the "will to power," the self-sufficiency and certainty of the eternal recurrence because of the "overman's," Nietzsche's, purity, cleanliness, solitude. Taylor remarks, "The profoundly Christian resonance which remains paradoxically in Nietzsche in spite of his virulent opposition to Christianity lies in his aspiration to affirm the whole of reality, to see it as good, to say 'yes' to it all."[27]

In his quest for transcendence, Nietzsche moved inwardly toward a conviction of his own divinity in the will to power; Jean-Paul Sartre and Miguel de Unamuno, in some ways Nietzsche's successors, founded their search for the transcendent in "the Word,"

---

27. Taylor, 452.

in language. Jean-Paul Sartre even named his autobiography *The Words*. In it he talks mainly about his young years. Whereas other children found the transcendent in God or in nature, Sartre declares, "I never tilled the soil or hunted for nests. I did not gather herbs or throw stones at birds. But books were my birds and my nests, my household pets, my barn and my countryside."[28] *The Words* was written late in Sartre's life, and so he cannot help but insert a bit of his adult search for meaning at the end. He sees that he took his pen for a sword during much of his life, as the "priest" of doubt. He states, "Dogmatic though I was, I doubted everything except that I was the elect of doubt" (Sartre 252).

He finds his transcendence in his words: "I write and will keep writing books; they're needed; all the same, they do serve some purpose. Culture doesn't save anything or anyone, it doesn't justify. But it's a product of man: he projects himself into it, he recognizes himself in it; that critical mirror alone offers him his image" (Sartre 254).

Sartre ends his autobiography with his profession of his mission in life:

> . . . my sole concern has been to save myself . . . by work and faith. As a result my pure choice did not raise me above anyone. Without equipment, without tools, I set all of me to work in order to save all of me. If I relegate impossible Salvation to the proproom, what remains? A whole man, composed of all men and as good as all of them and no better than any. (Sartre 255)

In the existentialists we find the final exaltation of man as man, the destruction of both religion and the bourgeois life as *raison d'etre*. Life is the process of becoming, and one transcends one's becoming only by leaving behind one's words. Miguel de Unamuno shows this clearly, not in his autobiography, but in one of his novels, *Niebla*, when a character (who is thinking of committing suicide in the novel) comes to don Miguel, the author, to talk about his fate. The author and character, Augusto, debate about Augusto's intention to commit suicide, and the character tells

---

28. Jean-Paul Sartre, *The Words*, trans. Bernard Frechtman (New York: George Braziller, 1964), 49; hereafter cited parenthetically in the text as Sartre.

don Miguel that he is assured of continuance, of transcending this mortal life, even if the author kills him. He will live beyond don Miguel because he lives in the book. Augusto finally dies, but it is an ambiguous end – the reader does not know if don Miguel, the author, killed him or if he killed himself.[29]

In his quasi-autobiography, *How To Make a Novel*, Unamuno states that "all novels, all works of fiction, all poems, when they are alive, are autobiographical. Every fictional being, every poetic character that an author creates becomes a part of the author himself."[30] He explains that to write his autobiography he has to create a character, whom he names U. Jugo de la Raza – all parts of his name. He identifies himself with Jugo de la Raza, but then states, "But poor Jugo de la Raza could not live without the book, without that book; his life, his intimate existence, his reality, his true reality was already definitively and irrevocably one with the character of the novel" (Unamuno 137). Unamuno's mirror is a fluid mirror, one in which the person, the work of fiction/reality is always becoming.

He opens his autobiography with the words "Here I am before these white pages – white like the black future: terrible whiteness! – seeking to hold back the time that passes, to fix the fleeting today, to eternalize me or immortalize me finally, since eternity and immortality are not one and the same thing. Here I am before these white pages, my future, trying to pour out my life, to snatch myself from death in each instant" (Unamuno 122). Thus Unamuno also finds his transcendence in his words, his novels, his life, which are all the same for him.

Like Nietzsche, Unamuno believes that he is creating himself. He uses the title "How One Makes a Novel" to describe his life. He is both a seeker and a creator of his self, his future. "All creatures are their creator" (Unamuno 129). In the Prologue that he wrote to the Spanish edition of his book in 1927,[31] Unamuno states:

---

29. Miguel de Unamuno, *Niebla / Abel Sanchez* (Mexico: Editorial Porrúa, S.A., 1992), 106.

30. Miguel de Unamuno, *San Manuel Bueno, Mártir / Como se hace una novela* (Madrid: Alianza Editorial, 1966), 128. Translation from the original Spanish by Patricia Ann Preston; hereafter cited parenthetically in the text as Unamuno.

31. Originally the work had been published in the *Mercure de France* in 1926 in

I do not want to again go through that intimate, most tragic experience [writing the work while in Paris]. . . . That would revive in me, to torture me with the delicious torture – Santa Teresa spoke of the "delicious pain" – of the hopeless production, of the production that seeks to save us . . . all the hours that I devoted to *The Tragic Sentiment of Life*. My whole life weighed on me, that which was and is my death. Not only my sixty years of individual, physical life weighed on me, but more, much more than them; centuries of a silent tradition weighed on me, centuries gathered together in the most hidden corner of my soul; ineffable unconscious memories of the beyond-the-cradle weighed on me. Because our hopeless hope of a personal life of beyond-the-tomb is nourished and thrives in this vague remembrance of our roots in the eternity of history. (Unamuno 86)

Unamuno remained all of his life agonizing over the question of life after death, never able to affirm it, but never able to escape it.

Just when it seems that the autobiographers have come full circle in their search for transcendence to find it in their own product, language, the twentieth century confronts us with new twists to the old search.

Jean Genet, of doubtful origins, but raised for a number of years in a French bourgeois, religious family, turns his search for the transcendent in the absolutely opposite direction, in the degradation of evil. In his search he says,

I kept no place in my heart where the feeling of my innocence might take shelter. I owned to being the coward, traitor, thief and fag they saw in me . . . within myself, with a little patience, I discovered, through reflection, adequate reasons for being named by these names. And it staggered me to know that I was composed of impurities. . . . The contempt in which I was held changed to hate: I had succeeded.[32]

a translation to the French by Jean Cassou while Unamuno was in exile in Paris.

32. Jean Genet, *The Thief's Journal*, trans. Bernard Frechtman (France: Grove Weidenfeld Press, 1964), 176; hereafter cited parenthetically in the text as Genet.

For Genet, the transcendent goal is paradoxical: "Saintliness means turning pain to good account. It means forcing the devil to be God. It means obtaining the recognition of evil. . . . It remains to specify whether the fulfillment of my legend consists of the boldest possible criminal existence" (Genet 205). He finds his moment of transcendence in total despair, irremediable destruction:

> I would give all the wealth of this world – indeed it must be given – to experience the desperate – and secret – state which no one knows I know. Hitler, alone, in the cellar of his palace, during the last minutes of the defeat of Germany, surely experienced that moment of pure light – fragile and solid lucidity – the awareness of this fall. (Genet 208)

He claims, "the greater my guilt, . . . the greater will be my freedom" (Genet 84). But at the same time Genet states that,

> Though saintliness is my goal, I cannot tell what it is. My point of departure is the word itself, which indicates the state closest to moral perfection. Of which I know nothing, save that without it my life would be vain. Unable to give a definition of saintliness – no more than I can of beauty – I want at every moment to create it, . . . though it is unknown to me. . . . I am being led to it by a constant groping. No method exists. . . . Starting from the elementary principles of morality and religion, the saint arrives at his goal if he sheds them. Like beauty – and poetry, with which I merge it – saintliness is individual. Its expression is original. However, it seems to me that its sole basis is renunciation. I therefore also associate it with freedom. But I wish to be a saint chiefly because the word indicates the loftiest human attitude, and I shall do everything to succeed. I shall use my pride and sacrifice it therein. (Genet 208-209)

Thus, Genet searched for saintliness, for freedom, through degradation. Both Genet and Santa Teresa expressed in their autobiographies their quest for the outmost limits of humanity. Santa Teresa strives for unity with God through pursuit of the utmost perfection. Genet's quest for saintliness is through pursuit of the utmost debasement. Sartre called Genet "Saint Genet," and these two saints in their narrations of their lives seem to express the very edges of the yin-yang circle of the two complementary forces that make up the phenomena of life, the search for the utmost light and the utmost darkness.

Through the centuries, the quest for transcendence has changed. The journey to perfection and union with God has been rejected. Rousseau's quest that others accept his conception of himself has not been fulfilled. Nietzsche's pursuit of the will to power has been misunderstood and perverted by other interpreters, and the existentialists' belief in their transcendence through their words is called into question in our electronic age: There is no permanent word – books are disintegrating; much communication is done electronically, and texts can be lost forever due to one power outage. St. Teresa and St. Genet have explored the outer limits of human life, both seeking sanctity: the one through utmost striving for the good, the divine, the other in pursuit of the deepest limits of degradation. But the search continues. The definitions of perfection and degradation continue to change. The pull of the yin-yang of life continues.

All of the autobiographers mentioned in this essay spoke of love – whether love of the good, of the self or of evil. I believe that somehow, as the search continues, human beings will begin to find a closer relationship again between love and transcendence, however those experiences and terms are defined.

Author's Note:

At sixteen, I read St. Augustine's and Benvenuto Cellini's autobiographies and decided (though it was years before I read Pascal's elegant words) that I would continue to practice a belief in God until some definitive alternative satisfied me. At the dawn of my senior years, I revisited or read for the first time many great European autobiographies. I had expected to find echoes of myself in Augustine, Teresa, and Unamuno, but was amazed that other autobiographers revealed a similar quest.

If I can understand the meaning even of Genet's beautifully-written search for degradation, then is my personal search also universal? Does each person stumble into widely varied paths within one's individual quest? Is our own quest intertwined with the variety and complexity of the searches of those with whom we interact throughout our lives?

P.A.P.

Works Cited

Auerbach, Erich. *Literary Language and Its Public in Late Latin Antiquity and in the Middle Ages.* Translated by Ralph Manheim. New York: Pantheon Books, 1965.

Augustine of Hippo, Saint. *Confessions.* Translated by R. S. Pine-Coffin. London: Penguin Books, 1961.

Brown, Peter. *Augustine of Hippo.* Berkeley, Calif.: University of California Press, 1967.

Cassirer, Ernst. *The Question of Jean-Jacques Rousseau.* Translated and edited by Peter Gay. Bloomington: Indiana University Press, 1963.

Genet, Jean. *The Thief's Journal.* Translated by Bernard Frechtman. France: Grove Weidenfeld, 1964.

Gusdorf, Georges. "Conditions and Limits of Autobiography." Translated by James Olney. In *Autobiography: Essays, Theoretical and Critical.* Edited by James Olney, 28-48. Princeton: Princeton University Press, 1980.

Kaufmann, Walter. *Nietzsche: Philosopher, Psychologist, Antichrist,* 3d. ed. New York: Vintage Books, 1968.

LeGal, Yves. "Unzeitgemass: Out of Season." In *Nietzsche and Christianity.* Edited by Claude Geffré and Jean-Pierre Jossua. English language editor Marcus Lefébure, 3-10. New York: Seabury Press, 1981.

Lerner, Gerda. *The Creation of Feminist Consciousness: From the Middle Ages to 1870.* New York: Oxford University Press, 1989.

Meagher, Robert E. *An Introduction to Augustine.* New York: New York University Press, 1978.

Nietzsche, Friedrich. *On the Geneology of Morals. Ecce Homo.* Translated and edited by Walter Kaufmann. New York: Random House, 1969.

Rousseau, Jean-Jacques. *The Confessions of Jean-Jacques Rousseau*. Anonymous translation revised and completed by A. S. B. Glover. New York: Heritage Press, 1955.

Sartre, Jean-Paul. *The Words*. Translated by Bernard Frechtman. New York: George Braziller, 1964.

Starobinski, Jean. "The Stages of Autobiography." Translated by Seymour Chatham. In *Autobiography: Essays Theoretical and Critical*. Edited by James Olney, 73-83. Princeton: Princeton University Press, 1980.

Taylor, Charles. *Sources of the Self*. Cambridge, Mass.: Harvard University Press, 1989.

Teresa of Avila, Saint. *The Life of Teresa of Jesus*. Translated and edited by E. Allison Peers. Garden City, N.Y.: Doubleday, 1960.

Unamuno, Miguel de. *Niebla/Abel Sanchez*. Mexico: Editorial Porrúa, S. A., 1992.

_____. *San Manuel Bueno, Mártir. Como se hace una novela*. Madrid: Alianza Editorial, 1966.

Chapter Two

Attentive to Transcendence: The Life of Etty Hillesum

Joan Penzenstadler, S.S.N.D.

Truly, my life is one long hearkening unto my self and unto others, unto God. And if I say that I hearken, it is really God who hearkens inside me. The most essential and deepest in me hearkening unto the most essential and deepest in the other. God to God.

– Hillesum, *An Interrupted Life*

Is there a Mystery which beckons beyond our present reality, a something (or someone) that is greater than the self, more than the human, more than anything creation can contain? What would make us suspect that there is such a reality? Are there any clues in human experience which would warrant such a belief? If there truly is a self-transcending rhythm, or, as T. S. Eliot puts it, a "music heard so deeply/That it is not heard at all"[1] is there any way to become attuned to it so that we could live in greater harmony with what is deepest within us?

Indeed, notes of the transcendental melody echo throughout the centuries and resound in people who dared to place themselves at the disposal of a life-giving rhythm greater than themselves. Etty Hillesum, a young Jewish woman living in Amsterdam in the early

This essay was originally published in the Summer of 1996 issue of *Magistra, A Journal of Women's Spirituality in History* (Volume 96, No. 1). It is reprinted here by permission.

1. T. S. Eliot, "The Dry Salvages," in *Four Quartets. Complete Poems and Plays* (New York: Harcourt, Brace and World, 1952), 136.

1940s, is one of these mediators of the transcendent in our world. Her commitment to discover that which was deepest in her, and to face the sometimes frightening discords which seemed to obscure the melody, was motivated by a desire which reached far beyond her own self. Struggling through setbacks, obstacles, and diversions, she came to a realization that what was deepest within her was intimately linked with transcendent reality. Thus, she interpreted the source of her being truly "at home" as being intimately connected with God: "There is a really deep well inside me. And in it dwells God. Sometimes I am there too. But more often stones and grit block the well, and God is buried beneath. Then He must be dug out again."[2] From her life in Amsterdam, to the labor camp, to Auschwitz, she underwent a dramatic transformation in what it meant to live and love with authenticity.

The Etty Hillesum who began her diaries at age twenty-seven in 1941 was a woman torn by conflicting forces. Through her written reflections, we first meet an intelligent, passionate woman imprisoned by erotic drives, self-consciousness, and waves of depression. The restrictions on Dutch Jews and forebodings of concentration camps in Poland played a minor role in her life at this time because of the war she continually experienced raging within her. She described her own state: "I long for something and don't know what it is. Inside I am totally at a loss, restless, driven, and my head feels close to bursting again" (18-19). Yet, it was precisely at this desperate point in her life that she began the discipline of what she called "working on herself" as she declared, "my awareness is growing apace and everything that was locked up in my head until now in the shape of precisely worked-out formulae is about to flow into my heart. But my exaggerated self-consciousness will have to go first – I still enjoy this in-between state too much" (9). Despite any embarrassment or pain or feeling of destitution, her desire to discover the truth beckoned her "to live fully, outwardly and inwardly, not to ignore external reality for the sake of the inner life, or the reverse. . ." (24). It was the decisions which flowed from this resolve to be attentive that

---

2. Etty Hillesum, *An Interrupted Life: The Diaries of Etty Hillesum 1941-1943*, ed. J. G. Gaarlandt, trans. Arnold Pomerans (New York: Washington Square Press, 1985), 44; hereafter cited parenthetically in the text.

constituted her life. She shifted from a narcissistic self-consciousness to a reflection on self that was passionately centered in her desire to live an authentic human life.

This kind of attentiveness was not an exercise reserved for times of tranquility. Rather, it was an activity that permeated all the patterns of her life and came to grips with successes as well as breakdowns. It was spurred by a desire for what was of value rather than for what merely satisfied at the moment. She regarded forebodings and intuition as part of the data from which to draw, but practiced "mental hygiene" in organizing the data, lest she drown in imagination and emotions. When she thought she was about to collapse under the weight of her own sufferings and the pogroms taking place around her, she did not dismiss her feelings but squarely encountered them. In the ensuing struggle, she discovered that many of her desperate questions gave way to a deep sense of the order and meaning in life. By facing the conflict in and about her, she was able to say:

> I feel like a small battlefield, in which the problems or some of the problems of our time are being fought out. All one can hope to do is to keep oneself humbly available, to allow oneself to be a battlefield. After all, the problems must be accommodated, have somewhere to struggle and come to rest and we, poor little humans, must put our inner space at their service and not run away. (30)

Hillesum did *not* run away as she continually searched for clarity and the truly human life in opposition to the inhumanity that closed in upon her and upon all she loved during the war years in Europe. In the process, she developed a religious sensibility that sprang, not from dogmas or ritual, theology or tradition, but from a "reposing in herself" through which she came to know herself and to know that the sufferings of the Jewish people could be filled with meaning. In the beginning of her writings, the word "God" is used almost as an exclamation, but as she progressed in awareness, "God" became the most sacred of words and kneeling the most intimate of gestures.

Her spirituality, however, remained unconventional as she discovered her religious rhythm without any affiliation with synagogue or church. Although she was not a practicing Jew, Hillesum clarified her understanding through the Hebrew and the Christian Scriptures, which stimulated her further reflection. The loving attentiveness with which she hearkened to the Scriptures parallels a contemporary of hers who was also unconventional, Simone Weil. Both women were drawn into a relationship with God that was profoundly mystical without any apparent knowledge of the mystical tradition. In fact, Weil writes,

> I had never read any mystical works because I had never felt any call to read them. . . . God in his mercy had prevented me from reading the mystics, so that it should be evident to me that I had not invented this absolutely unexpected contact.[3]

For both women, the contact with God was as unexpected as it was real. Both continued to work on themselves in order to become more keenly attuned to the working of God.

Hillesum's understanding of "working on herself" had nothing to do with escaping from this world but everything to do with a perception of creation as good and a developing sense of her unity with all of humanity. As Gestapo regulations began to stifle her world, she wrote:

> I don't feel in anybody's clutches; I feel safe in God's arms, to put it rhetorically, and no matter whether I am sitting at this beloved old desk now, or in a bare room in the Jewish district or perhaps in a labor camp under SS guards in a month's time – I shall always feel safe in God's arms. They may well succeed in breaking me physically, but no more than that. I may face cruelty and deprivation the likes of which I cannot imagine in even my wildest fantasies. Yet all this is as nothing to the immeasurable

---

3. Simone Weil, *Waiting for God,* trans. Emma Craufurd (New York: G. P. Putnam's Sons, 1951), 69. On this same page, Weil states,

    In my arguments about the insolubility of the problem of God I had never foreseen the possibility of that, of a real contact, person to person, here below, between a human being and God. . . . Moreover, in this sudden possession of me by Christ, neither my senses nor my imagination had any part, I only felt in the midst of my suffering the presence of a love, like that which one can read in the smile on a beloved face. (69)

expanse of my faith in God and my inner receptiveness. (184-85)

Are such outbursts the Pollyanna-like retort of someone not yet attuned to the monstrous challenge which confronted the Jewish community? Marie Syrkin, author of *The State of the Jews*, ponders a similar question when writing a critique of Hillesum's diaries: "Willful bravado or a consistent philosophy? It will become the latter. . . . If in one mood she sounds irritatingly like Pippa Passes, 'God's in his heaven, all's right with the world,' in another she has the insight to pray, 'Oh, God, give me the strength to bear the suffering you have imposed on me and not just the suffering I have chosen for myself.'"[4]

The transcending melody to which Hillesum was becoming attuned permeated and transformed her desires and feelings and even her questions and insights. In her earliest entries, for example, we see a woman struggling to give clarity to things in her own words and coming to grips with her sensuous life: "I yearned physically for all I thought was beautiful, wanted to own it" (13). She squarely faced this painful longing and admitted that for her it was a "mental masturbation" that sapped her creative energy. By reflecting on the myriad desires that crowded her life, she began to distinguish between petty feelings and more noble ones, although she admitted that she still lacked "a basic tune," the proper rhythm for her life. Even in these beginnings, she already realized that the harmonious pattern for her life was not to be found some place outside of herself. She was intent on probing her motivations and becoming a receptive, questioning listener in times of emotional chaos in order to take responsibility for the shape of her own life.

The kinds of questions she asked herself reflect the depth of her pondering, especially in regard to her relationships. Intimate with Han Wegerif with whom she lived, Hillesum was also the lover of Julius Spier, a therapist/lecturer with whom she worked and who became her spiritual mentor. Early in her diaries she wondered:

---

4. Marie Syrkin, "Do Not Go Gently," *The New Republic* (March 1984): 34-35.

I am really faithful to him [Spier] inwardly. And I am faithful to Han as well. I am faithful to everyone. I walk down the street next to a man. . . . Yet just twelve hours ago I lay in the arms of another man and loved him then and love him now. Is that sordid? Is it decadent? To me it feels perfectly all right. Perhaps because the physical thing is not so essential to me, no longer so essential. The love I now feel is different, wider. Or am I fooling myself? Am I too vague? Even in my relationships? (73)

In the past, she had attempted to dismiss such upsetting questions with a reasoning process which never seemed to reconcile mind and heart. With her intellect she worked out solutions, but her erotic drives still seemed to rule, and her fears did not subside. She now realized that the philosophical base which she had inherited from her father had become a shield preventing her from plumbing the depths she suspected within her. Sadly, she reflected on her father's resigned philosophy which she summarized: "Oh, well, which of us knows anything, all is chaos within and without." It was this capitulation to chaos which Hillesum realized was threatening her life, too, and which she resolved to "make . . . [her] life's task to shake off instead of reverting to it time and again" (70).

The concentration of her inner forces curbed her sometimes out-of-control, erotic curiosity, bringing an inner peace and helping her realize that what had often immobilized her was a vague sort of fear, a fear that she now began to dissipate by living more fully in the present. She wrestled with fear several times throughout her diaries – from the fear of losing another's love if all expectations were not met, to fear of the total extermination of the Jews. No matter what motivated her fear, she concluded, "[D]on't we live an entire life each one of our days, and does it really matter if we live a few days more or less? . . . It is a question of living life from minute to minute and taking suffering into the bargain" (159).

Paying attention to the fear or hatred or benevolence within her, Etty became aware that she had a choice about the role those feelings would play in her life. Her appreciation for the importance of being attentive to and taking responsibility for her own self had far-reaching ramifications, for she firmly believed that nothing could be changed in this world unless one first changed one's self. She was deeply aware of the relation between self-constitution and the constitution of society. As her struggle to look upon the Nazis as human beings made in the image of God became more acute, she did not dwell on their dehumanizing atrocities but reflected on her own capacities for evil. In regard to hatred, she wrote: "I see no alternative, each of us must turn inward and destroy in himself all that he thinks he ought to destroy in others. And remember that every atom of hate we add to this world makes it still more inhospitable" (222). In a more positive light, she just as strongly believed in the importance of leading an authentic and faithful life so that those who succeeded her would have a legacy on which to build.

Toward the end of her diaries and with the certainty of her return to the concentration camp where she had already spent several months,[5] Hillesum again reflected on what she had discovered about fear:

> I think what weakens people most is fear of wasting their strength. If after a long and arduous process, day in day out, you manage to come to grips with your inner sources, with God, in short, and if only you make certain that your path to God is unblocked – which you can do by 'working on yourself' – then you can keep renewing yourself at these inner sources and need never again be afraid of wasting your strength. (228)

Becoming attentive to fear in a way that detached her from its awful control, Hillesum discovered a freedom of operation and a strength of which she did not even know she was capable.

In searching for the roots of her feelings, she was reflectively conscious of the afflictions within her own body. At twenty-seven, she was often depressed, pent-up inside herself, and subject to

---

5. In the introduction to *An Interrupted Life*, J. G. Gaarlandt explains: "From August 1942 until September 1943 Etty remained in Westerbork camp [where she voluntarily decided to go with the trapped Jews], working in the local hospital, but thanks to a special permit from the Jewish Council she was able to travel to Amsterdam a dozen times. . . . Etty's health was often very bad and on one occasion she was hospitalized in Amsterdam during one of her leaves" (xv-xvi).

headaches and illness, but she was determined not to allow physical maladjustments to determine who she was becoming: "It can't be just this stupid cold in my head that makes everything look so black. But what is the truth of the matter? . . . I feel negative about everything, keep carping and complaining. And all this must be the direct result of a blocked nose! After all, it's not really me, this dislike of my fellow men" (42-43). She concluded that when she felt physically wretched, she needed to rest from thinking things through because her thought process was disparagingly slanted. On the other hand, she continued to suspect that her melancholy and headaches had a deeper root than the physical, although she admitted that her desire to know the root was still too clouded by self-interest.

After her bouts with physical illness, the rhythm of her reflective questioning resumed: Would I rather have Spier's love all to myself? Am I being much too physical? Much too selfish? These ponderings eventually led to a more refined question: "Do I demand absolute love from others because I'm unable to give it myself?" (50). She discovered that she dwelt so much on sensuality because her concept of love was as yet too romanticized, too self-centered and not grounded in the ordinariness of everyday life. Becoming aware of this pattern within her, she also began to realize that "one should accept things as they are and not try to lift them to impossible heights; only if you let them be will they reveal their true worth" (51).

Hillesum struggled to free herself from demanding unconditional love from those who could not give it. She was aware of the lack of freedom that such desire had already brought into her life. What seemed to see her through the pain of these struggles was her overriding yearning to know the truth about herself and her world and the underlying conviction that the truth was ultimately good. As she reflected, with a more detached desire to know in the foreground, she realized the contingency of all human relationships and longed for a harmony between her feelings and her beliefs and ideas. Already she was becoming aware of a "fruitful loneliness" inside her – the paradox of emptying herself in order to become full, of experiencing the solitude that gives rise to profound Presence. It was an awareness reminiscent of the paradox in the writing of St. John of the Cross:

> O living flame of love
> That tenderly wounds my soul
> In its deepest center! . . .
> O sweet cautery,
> O delightful wound! . . .
> In killing you changed death to Life.[6]

Only one attuned to her deepest center would know how utter emptiness can also be fruitful, how death can be life at the same time. She was realizing how her life, hollowed clean of blockages, could be filled by something greater than herself.

At times, amidst her struggles, she experienced a tremendous peace through which she forgot about herself and her yearning after this or that particular thing. A feeling of being at one with all existence enveloped her. She deeply affirmed the goodness of creation and was attuned to the rhythm that pulsed through all of life. Hillesum described this moment of acute awareness: "It is in these moments – and I am so grateful for them – that all personal ambition drops away from me, that my thirst for knowledge and understanding comes to rest, and that a small piece of eternity descends on me with a sweeping wingbeat" (75).

Through her contemplation of the goodness of life and the infinite riches and possibilities she carried within her, something she had only an inkling of before became a conviction: "Life" must be her motivating force, not another person. She was concerned about women drawing their strength and sense of identity from others, particularly from men. This painful journey to trust herself and be obedient to the source of life (which she later named "God") calling from within her was intimately connected to her questioning of the "proper" longings of a woman. She wondered to what extent her search to love and be loved by one man was a woman's handicap. Was this desire to be totally enveloped by one man an ancient tradition from which she needed to liberate herself, or was it so much a part of her essence that she would be doing violence

---

6. *The Collected Works of St. John of the Cross*, trans. Kieran Kavanaugh and Otilio Rodriguez (Washington, D.C.: Institute of Carmelite Studies, 1979), 578-79.

to herself if she gave up this quest and bestowed love on all of humankind instead? Could a woman move from exclusivity to an expansive, all-encompassing kind of love? Could this love be sustained by a passion as intense as sexual love? She even wondered if that was why there were so few women scientists and artists: "A woman always looks for the one man on whom she can bestow all her wisdom, warmth, love and creative powers. She longs for a man, not for mankind" (33).

She tested these questions out through her own experience, and later, after she learned to draw on the deepest source of her life, she again addressed this topic. When she was forced to see a doctor because of her weakened condition after the stresses of camp life, the doctor suggested that she take time to enjoy life's physical pleasures. She was leading "too cerebral a life" and didn't "let herself go enough." He even charged that Hillesum no longer lived in "the real world." She illumined the doctor's words and implications with her own insights as she wrote:

> The real world! All over the real world men and women are being kept apart. . . . That is the real world. And you have to come to terms with that. And not just stoke your desires. . . . Why not turn the love that cannot be bestowed on another, or on the other sex, into a force that benefits the whole community and that might still be love? And if we attempt the transformation, are we not standing on the solid ground of the real world of reality? A reality as tangible as a bed with a man or a woman in it. (218)

Her convictions developed dramatically from the time she started writing her reflections to this proclamation of the validity of an intense love that is all-inclusive. She began her diaries with, "I should think to be counted among the better lovers, and love does indeed suit me to perfection, and yet it remains a mere trifle, set apart from what is truly essential, and deep inside me something is still locked away" (1). By September 1942, the "something locked away" had been revealed, and she could respond to the doctor's innuendoes with courage and spiritual insight. Hillesum was indeed serious about self-reflection, but that in itself could not bring about the radical transformation that happened within her. Change occurred in synchronization with her relationship with

God. Hillesum admitted that sometimes she did think with an ecstatic intensity, but she also knew how to refresh herself by drawing on a source that resided deep within her.

The more she came to an understanding of who she was, the more her desire to know God increased. The horizon of Hillesum's attentiveness began to shift as God took a central place in her consciousness. With the shift, her frank, erotic drives were at first interwoven with her search for an authentic spiritual life. However, this interweaving led to further questions that she needed to resolve: "Has S. [Spier] unleashed things deep down inside me that yet can't come out but carry on their subterranean existence with Han? I can hardly believe that. Or is it perversity? A matter of convenience? To pass from the arms of one man into those of the other? What sort of life am I leading?" (128).

Even later, in June 1942, when her understanding of intimacy far transcended the physical, her desires could still take on a strongly selfish cast. Etty caught herself longing for Spier to love only her, but she no longer became discouraged by these setbacks. Instead, she understood that such desires emerged because of the extensive strain and fatigue she was undergoing. She simply acknowledged them and said, "But I have come quite a long way and shall have to persevere. And suffer relapses on the way" (148). The manner of her attentiveness, though more acute than ever, was now more accepting than desperate, more loving than fearful.

In the process of purifying her own feelings, she learned the difference between self-centered feelings and more universal sentiments. For example, as German regulations against the Jews became more stringent in Amsterdam, Hillesum noted the need to distinguish between genuine moral indignation and petty personal hatred. She saw the latter as usually meaning little more than using fleeting incidents to fan the fires of a personal hurt. Moral indignation, on the other hand, was one of the "big emotions" which sprang from outrage at the injustice of an entire people being stripped of their human dignity. She noted a further distinction. She could be defenseless before German persecutors yet never totally acquiesce to their demands. She knew that no matter how vulgar the soldiers became, she had sovereignty over her own attitude.

Grounded in the conviction that life was fundamentally good, beyond anything humans could do to pervert it, and that her life, therefore, had meaning, Hillesum was able to reconcile the paradox of dying in a concentration camp and yet finding life beautiful. Contemplating writers and poets and the wonders of nature from her little room in South Amsterdam, she learned to love life. Later, living in the barracks bursting with frightened, persecuted people, she found the confirmation of her love for life. She was under no illusion as to what awaited her and empathized with those Jews already sent to Poland:

> I am in Poland every day, on the battlefields, if that's what one calls them. I often see visions of poisonous green smoke; I am with the hungry, with the ill-treated and the dying, every day, but I am also with the jasmine and with the piece of sky beyond my window; there is room for everything in a single life. For belief in God and for a miserable end. (159)

She keenly felt her responsibility and need to be part of the community and did not wish to be exempt from the fate of the Jewish people. Her belief was that she could do justice to life only if she did not abandon those in danger. She expressed her desire: "I want to be at every front, I don't ever want to be what they call 'safe.' I want to be there, I want to fraternize with all my so-called enemies, I want to understand what is happening and share my knowledge with as many as I can possibly reach. . ." (234). As survivors of the camp to which Hillesum was sent have attested, she did become "the thinking heart of the barracks" and remained a source of joy and hope to the last.

Hillesum's understanding of love steadily developed from the first entries in her diary to the time she decided to join her people in Westerbork Camp. She learned a great deal about self-giving love from Julius Spier, yet even with him, her loving was initiated by an exterior factor: the one she perceived as beautiful and good. As commendable as it was to be drawn by a goodness which activated her love, she was eventually able to transcend the kind of loving that originated in the object of love. She began to act out of a creative freedom which preceded any estimation of the value of the beloved.[7] She chose camp life without Spier and liberated her highest spontaneity to love purely for the sake of loving. Through suffering she learned that she needed to share her love with the whole of creation. She was attentive to the activity through which her love was being purified, and articulated what she had learned, even before Westerbork, about suffering and love: "Through suffering I have learned that we must share our love with the whole of creation. Only thus can we gain admittance to it" (154). The harmony for which Hillesum longed became more defined in her loving. It was not so much a harmony that she herself composed as it was one to which she attuned herself.

Another aspect of Etty's life which was intertwined with her loving and which developed just as dramatically was the quality of her prayer. On June 8, 1941, her search for "a basic tune" took a significant turn. She decided to meditate half an hour each morning before work in order to become more attentive to her "inner voice." Thirty minutes of physical exercise were already part of her daily routine, so by combining this regimen with spiritual exercise she hoped to be able to reconcile body and spirit. She took into account the discipline required in order to let go of the myriad distractions that so easily cluttered silence. The goal of her meditation was to open up her innermost being, "with none of that treacherous undergrowth to impede the view. So that something of 'God' can enter . . . and something of 'Love' too" (27). She was passionate about encountering reality with a clarity which anxieties and cares and petty desires had too readily obscured.

Six months after beginning to listen to the silence within her, Etty declared that something new was occurring in her life, although as yet it was so subtle that she could not discern whether it was something crucial or merely a passing mood. A prayer spilled out of her in which she vowed to live life to the full, no matter where it might lead, as long as God continued to direct her. She sometimes imagined a life of quiet contemplation, but knew her calling was really to seek God "amongst people, out in the world." Appreciating the importance of remaining open to questions if she truly wished to live a full life, she made a further

---

7. An article by Beatrice Bruteau develops an understanding about this kind of transcendent love. See "Trinitarian Personhood," *Cistercian Studies* 22 (Fall 1987): 199-212.

commitment: "I shall allow myself to become thoroughly perplexed by whatever comes my way and apparently diverts me, yes, I shall allow myself to be perplexed time and again perhaps, in order to arrive at greater certainty. Until I am no longer perplexed and a state of balance has been achieved, but with all paths still open to me" (65).

A few days after her prayer of commitment and openness to the workings of God, she found herself on her knees in the middle of a large room. She who had considered herself "the woman who could not kneel," and then "a kneeler in training," now experienced "something stronger than herself" forcing her to the ground (76). She acknowledged her embarrassment, since she considered this gesture as intimate as any act of love that could not be put into words. After that first incident, she more and more regularly dropped to her knees, and, as she put it: "I listen in to myself, allow myself to be led, not by anything on the outside, but by what wells up from within" (81).

For the first time in her life, Hillesum became attentive to her praying self. She did not experience God through any particular religious tradition, but she did have a strong sense of the reality of God and of the possibility of her operating with that transcendent reality as her source. From that moment to the end of her life, she attended to all matters from a different horizon.

The attentiveness Etty developed came through prayer and fasting, but rather than abstaining from food she caught onto the discipline of fasting from anxiety, a discipline which freed her heart to be attentive to deeper movements. This kind of asceticism alerted her to and freed her from radical evil by giving her a taste for the radically good.[8] It took effort to acquire such an attentiveness, but it was the effort of receptivity, of being attuned to the mystery greater than herself, of giving herself over to loving contemplation. Developing a contemplative spirit, Etty became alert to the things within her own self that fostered distraction and a flight from silence and, thus, she was able to perceive the roots

---

8. Regarding the connection between the journey to holiness and fasting from anxiety, John Garvey quotes Meister Eckart: "It is often more fitting to keep yourself from anxiety than to abstain entirely from food." See "Asceticism and the Evil One," *Commonweal* (May 1987): 312.

of destruction in the world as well as the source of truth and goodness.

Even in her most fruitful and creative acts, Hillesum was attentive to the self-destructive forces which all too easily could be unleashed if left unguarded. It was in moments such as these that her urge to kneel down and keep watch over her heart came as a strong mandate, lest her energies be wildly dissipated. A desire to kneel also pulsed through her body in moments of deep gratitude. It was a gesture, whether acted out on the rough coconut matting of her bathroom floor or in the recesses of her heart, that became part of the fundamental melody of who she was.[9]

In one of her prayers she talked about her inability to safely hide herself in her room and shut out all that was happening around her. She attempted to look things "straight in the face," even the most heinous crimes, and be attentive to the human being left scarred and battered because of others' senseless deeds. She continued her prayer: "I try to face up to Your world, God, not to escape from reality into beautiful dreams – though I believe that beautiful dreams can exist beside the most horrible reality – and continue to praise your creation, God, despite everything" (141).

Prayer for Hillesum resulted in the conviction that there was something deep within her that would never desert her again. At home in contemplation, she could sit for hours and bear everything and grow stronger. Prayer brought her a sense of wholeness and helped her to integrate within her own being the contradictions so blatant in her world: the derision spewed out by a German soldier and the welcoming cup of coffee shared with friends; the blisters caused by walking for miles after all public transportation was banned and the white blossoms of jasmine which bloomed behind her house.

---

9. Because of the way Hillesum became absorbed with the presence of God – that deepest and richest part in which she reposed – some have called her a mystic. Perhaps she did have mystical tendencies, but not in the sense that some, inaccurately, have understood mysticism: a flight from the world and a life dedicated to solitary contemplation of another realm. Hillesum was clear about her convictions regarding the mystical life: "Mysticism must rest on crystal-clear honesty, can only come after things have been stripped down to their naked reality" (149).

Through prayer, her love became more and more expansive. In July 1942, she wrote how her whole being had become a prayer for Spier, but she immediately questioned why her prayer would be only for him. Why not also for the sixteen-year-old girls who were being sent to the labor camp? A few entries later, she was able to say: "All the strength and love and faith in God which one possesses, and which have grown so miraculously in me of late, must be there for everyone who chances to cross one's path and who needs it" (175). Her love grew apace with her awareness, and her awareness was enriched because of love, embracing more and more of God's creation.

Etty's loving attentiveness to the depths within her and within others became the all-encompassing work of her spirit. She discovered a word in German which came closest to describing this work: *hineinhorchen,* which means "hearken unto." She understood that "hearkening unto" does not mean listening to what is said so much as being attentive to what is meant. In this mode of listening, she learned to identify the source out of which something flowed. Hillesum described her life as "one long hearkening unto my self and unto others, unto God. And if I say that I hearken, it is really God who hearkens inside me. The most essential and the deepest in me hearkening unto the most essential and deepest in the other. God to God" (214).

Most of us have not developed the art of hearkening to the music deep within ourselves that T. S. Eliot describes:

> there is only the unattended
> Moment, the moment in and out of time,
> The distraction fit, lost in a shaft of sunlight,
> The wild thyme unseen, or the winter lightning
> Or the waterfall, or music heard so deeply
> That it is not heard at all, but you are the music
> While the music lasts.[10]

Etty, on the contrary, mastered the discipline of poised listening that is required in order to *hineinhorchen.* Her moments were not unattended. She heard the music and identified it with her deepest self. The intimacy between the music and the self were in such

---

10. Eliot, 136.

profound harmony within Etty that her attentiveness carried a quality of presence which reconciled and instilled hope. It was grounded in a loving heart. By responding to the initiative of God in her life as wholeheartedly as she did, she allowed her spirit to take responsibility over her body, and the vast silence in her, which embraced all that life offers, continued to grow.

Amazingly, Hillesum's attentiveness to transcendence developed even more profoundly when she found herself in Westerbork, a Nazi work camp in the Netherlands.[11] Westerbork, the last stop before Auschwitz, was a camp built for 1,500 that teemed with 30,000 to 40,000 frightened, broken men, women and children by the time Etty arrived. The values for which she had struggled and on which she had come to base her life were most deeply confirmed behind the barbed wire of the camp. There was hardly any room to breathe much less to write, yet she was able to scribble down a few words as she cramped herself in a wheelbarrow, and a few more in the workshop or behind the infirmary. The result was a host of letters, written between August 1942, and September 1943, and smuggled to her friends. In them, we catch glimpses of how she continued to be with herself as she was present to the other.

In a detailed letter dated 18 December 1942, Hillesum wrote of her concern that people all around her in the barracks did not want to think about or feel or remember what was happening to them. If the only thing that mattered was that the Jews save their bodies, she said, that would never suffice. What mattered was *not* how many lives were preserved no matter what the cost, but *how* people chose to preserve them. She sometimes thought that

---

11. On July 15, 1942, Hillesum began working as a typist for the Jewish Council in Amsterdam. The Germans instigated the formation of the Council to help them organize the massive number of Jews living in the country, but they promoted the illusion that those working in the Council could save their comrades from the worst and even defer their own deportation. In this same month, the first big "round-up" took place in Amsterdam, and Hillesum voluntarily decided to go with the imprisoned Jews to Westerbork, a transit camp in the east of the Netherlands. At this point, she strongly felt her personal destiny bound to the destiny of the Jewish people and believed she could do justice to life only by using her strength to instill some strength and hope into the lives of others.

every new situation, good or bad, can enrich us with new insights. But if we abandon the hard facts that we are forced to face, if we give them no shelter in our heads and hearts, do not allow them to settle and change into impulses through which we can grow and from which we can draw meaning – then we are not a viable generation.[12]

Hillesum had learned to house unsettling events, to live with them, and to allow life-giving insights to emerge from them.

While moving from one barracks to another, she observed that it was not the environment that was solely responsible for creating who the inmates became. The barren spaces of the camp could be filled only with what people carried within them. For Hillesum, Westerbork became "home," because she let go of any nostalgia that may have held her back from living totally in the present. Her memories and her loved ones were always with her, but in the present moment. She wrote to Maria Tuinzing: "I can live here as well as I do just *because* I remember everything from 'before' (it's not really a 'before' for me), and I go on living" (*Letters* 53).

Etty noted that people were dissipating their energies by allowing details to wear them down. This distracted them from what really mattered in life and, thus, they soon looked on life as meaningless. They needed to attune themselves to the few "big things" that made life meaningful and quietly abandon the rest. Hillesum was convinced that "you can find those big things anywhere, you have to keep rediscovering them in yourself so that you can be renewed. And in spite of everything you always end up with the same conviction: life is good after all. . ." (*Letters* 63). Continuously drawing on the source within her, she renewed her energies and perceived the world from the horizon of love. Someone enclosed the quotation "And yet God is love" in a letter to her, and she agreed that it was truer now than ever.

Accommodating the paradox of God's love in the midst of Nazi atrocities became Etty's trademark. The most gruesome nights occurred when the trains were loaded with a thousand Jews bound

---

12. *Letters from Westerbork*, trans. Arnold Pomerans (New York: Random, 1986), 31; hereafter cited parenthetically in the text as *Letters*.

for Poland. On those nights, the screaming children, harassed mothers, confused elderly, and last-minute suicides converged into one long nightmare. Hillesum was present to it all, offering her care and courage wherever possible. She sometimes collapsed with fatigue and became "infinitely sad"; nevertheless, she felt her spirit growing stronger. Even after the most miserable day, she found herself walking with a spring in her step along the barbed wire; a feeling that life was glorious soared straight from her heart. Her disciplined heart remained free to contemplate both the horrors and the joys of life.

Hillesum's understanding of life was deepened and purified because of her attentiveness to the source of her love. She responded, not to a previously existing situation or value, but in an act of "creative freedom" which stripped away labels of "enemy" or "friend." She simply loved the other because the other was. She remarked that people at Westerbork did not give others much occasion to love them; therefore, many felt their love for humanity drying up for lack of nourishment. But she kept discovering that "there is no causal connection between people's behavior and the love you feel for them. . . . The fellow man himself has hardly anything to do with it." She admitted that "it's a little bit bare of love here, and I myself feel so inexpressibly rich; I cannot explain it" (*Letters* 107).[13]

The harmony that permeated her being met perhaps its greatest challenge on September 7, 1943. Etty, with her father, mother, and brother, was suddenly scheduled for the next train to Auschwitz. She continued her writing even in the stifling freight car and tossed a postcard out the window which farmers found

---

13. What Hillesum seemed to be attentive to but could not explain was the quality of loving which Beatrice Bruteau highlights in her article on "Trinitarian Personhood." She refers to St. Augustine's observation that "the saint is one who seeks God not for any reason." When we love purely for the sake of loving, then we become "impartial as God is impartial, who makes the sun rise on the evil and on the good, and sends the rain on the just and on the unjust" (Matt. 5:43-48). We are overwhelmingly enriched, because our refreshment, as well as our capacity to freely give of ourselves, comes from the very Source of love. When we try to base our loving on motivation from the environment, the responses of others, or even on our human nature, we usually experience strain and fatigue.

and mailed a week later. In it she said, "We left the camp singing. . . ." Red Cross records show that Etty Hillesum died on November 30, 1943. Three weeks before her departure for Auschwitz, she summed up her life in a magnificent prayer which she sent to one of her friends in Holland:

> You have made me so rich, oh God, please let me share out Your beauty with open hands. My life has become an uninterrupted dialogue with You, oh God, one great dialogue. Sometimes when I stand in some corner of the camp, my feet planted on Your earth, my eyes raised toward Your heaven, tears sometimes run down my face, tears of deep emotion and gratitude. At night, too, when I lie in my bed and rest in You, oh God, tears of gratitude run down my face, and that is my prayer. I have been terribly tired for several days, but that too will pass. Things come and go in a deeper rhythm, and people must be taught to listen; it is the most important thing we have to learn in this life. . . . (*Letters* 116)

It is true that the ultimate test of her spiritual insight did not come before Auschwitz. The labor camp which she considered "hell" was only a mild hint of the exhibitions of savagery which awaited her in the death camp, and we have no way of knowing if the focus of her life shifted during her three months in Auschwitz before her death. However, throughout her diaries and letters we glimpse the way in which her ponderings, her understandings, her affirmations and her decisions led her in a dynamism toward self-transcendence. Some of the last news we know of Hillesum is her response to the horror of being suddenly selected for the transport to Poland. One of her friends, Jopie Vleeschouwer, described Hillesum's reaction to this turn of events: "For her it was a slap in the face, which did in fact literally strike her down. Within the hour, however, she had recovered and adapted herself to the new situation with admirable speed. . . . I think she really quite preferred to share the experiences they have prepared for us all" (*Life* 274).

Hillesum's last two-and-a-half-years of life were an incarnation of what it means to listen to the deeper rhythm of life, that is, to attune oneself to the self-transcending dynamism at the core of human being. Her attentiveness was grounded in her belief in the goodness of life and manifested a profound concentration and a cooperation with the free, unmerited gift of God's love. This love radically attuned her to the experiences of life, called forth questions about these experiences, evoked insights, freed her to let go of what was not in tune with reality, and affirmed what was true and good.

Etty had hoped to become an artist of sorts someday, but as the likelihood grew more dim, she conceded that there was an artistry involved in the making of one's life. The composition of Etty Hillesum's life ranks among the masterpieces. Although most of us will probably not live out our lives in a milieu such as Hillesum's, which laid bare the moral fiber of human persons in the most explicit and ruthless ways, we do have the same dynamic rhythm operative within us and calling us to self-transcendence. The invitation is present, beckoning us to participate in the life that it promises.

Author's Note:

When I first read Etty Hillesum's diaries, I was attracted to the dramatic change that took place in her when she began a form of contemplation on a daily basis. What could possibly account for such a transformation from a life imprisoned in anxious struggle to one of serenity and profound joy? What could have given her release and a sense of freedom, even as the Nazi regime was tightening its grip on the people of Holland?

Today, people of varying ages seem to be suffering from a loss of meaning, a confusion and disenchantment. We experience support systems disintegrating, dependable lifestyles crumbling, and we wonder if anything, if anyone, is trustworthy. How can the human spirit withstand such existential powerlessness, such lack of control over external circumstances? And how do we distinguish between submission that relinquishes control in defeat and surrender that opens to freedom? Can we risk entering darkness with a posture of receptivity?

J.P.

Works Cited

Bruteau, Beatrice. "Trinitarian Personhood." *Cistercian Studies* 22 (fall 1987): 199-212.

Eliot, T. S. "The Dry Salvages." In *Four Quartets. Complete Poems and Plays*, 130-37. New York: Harcourt, Brace and World, 1952.

Garvey, John. "Asceticism and the Evil One," *Commonweal* (May 1987): 311-12.

Hillesum, Etty. *An Interrupted Life: The Diaries of Etty Hillesum 1941-1943*. Edited by J. G. Gaarlandt. Translated by Arnold Pomerans. New York: Washington Square Press, 1985.

_____. *Letters from Westerbork*. Introduction by Jan Gaarlandt. Translated by Arnold Pomerans. New York: Random, 1986.

Saint John of the Cross. *The Collected Works of St. John of the Cross*. Translated by Kieran Kavanaugh and Otilio Rodriguez. Washington, D. C.: Institute of Carmelite Studies, 1979.

Syrkin, Marie. "Do Not Go Gently." *New Republic* (March 1984): 33-36.

Weil, Simone. *Waiting for God*. Translated by Emma Craufurd. New York: G. P. Putnam's Sons, 1951.

Chapter Three

The Metaphor of the Erotic Union in St. John of the Cross

Mary Ellen Kohn

Although human relationships in twentieth-century Western society are quite complex and vary greatly among different couples, there are some things that they all seem to have in common. Most romantic relationships take a certain amount of time to develop, and they usually pass through different stages on their way to completeness. Basically, these stages can be seen as three: In the first, we make room in our lives for a new partner as we try to get over past relationships; in the second, the partners fall in love and are enlightened by each other; and in the third and final stage, the relationship has fully developed into a permanent union.

These three stages of modern-day personal relationships can be equated with the three paths in the mystical union. A mystic, in his or her quest for a complete union with God, travels on the paths known as the purgative way, in which the soul is purged of sins and impurities; the illuminative way, in which the mystic acquires a vision of God as He is in our world; and the unitive way, in which there is the perfect union between God and the human soul of the mystic.

One such mystic was the Spaniard Juan de Yepes (1542-91), better known by his religious name, Saint John of the Cross. He was a member of the order of the Carmelites, a confessor for the nuns of this order, and a reformer for the order. Because of this last activity, St. John was tortured and imprisoned by the non-reforming members. It was while imprisoned in Toledo in 1578 (inspired by the solitude of incarceration and its possibilities for meditation) that he wrote the poem considered to be his masterpiece, *The Spiritual Canticle (Songs between the Soul and the Spouse)*.

At face value, *The Spiritual Canticle* can be seen simply as a beautiful pastoral poem or as an amorous dialogue between two lovers. Yet, the story of these two lovers is not the depiction of the usual couple one finds in pastoral literature, but rather that of a saint and his God, with whom he seeks the perfect spiritual union, a mystical marriage that few of us could ever hope to attain.

The expression of this mystical experience takes the form of a divine dialogue between two lovers who recreate their supernatural love in an animated conversation. Scholars such as Cristóbal García also consider *The Spiritual Canticle* to be a poem pertaining to the eclogue or pastoral genre, the cultivation of which attained unequaled success during the Renaissance.[1] The pastoral eclogue was the preferred poetic form for the expression of love by Renaissance writers, such as St. John of the Cross. The use of this genre is seen in St. John's choice of pastoral nature as an adequate locale for his amorous journey toward a symbolic nuptial consummation and in his allegorical use of animals as symbols of God's creation. The eclogue style is seen additionally in the amorous complaints to the Beloved because of the pain caused to St. John's soul by the wounds of love.[2] The exercise of love between the soul of the poet and his God is conceived as a continuous and uninterrupted sanctifying progression, and relates a living, extremely personal experience, the very semblance of the spirit of a saint.

St. John's style in *The Spiritual Canticle*, then, is not a literary one, but rather one expressing a personal experience. Because St. John of the Cross was not considered primarily a poet by profession, scholars have found few direct literary influences in his work. This does not mean, however, that the poet did not discover

---

1. See Cristóbal Cuevas García, *Cántico Espiritual. Poesías,* by St. John of the Cross (Bilbao: Editorial Alhambra, 1979), 40. In writing *The Spiritual Canticle,* St. John was most influenced by the biblical *Song of Songs* in content and by the pastoral poetry of the Spanish Renaissance lyric poet, Garcilaso de la Vega, in style.

2. See Eulogio Pacho, *Vértice de la poesía y de la mística: El "Cántico espiritual" de San Juan de La Cruz* (Burgos: Editorial Monte Caramelo, 1983), 83.

themes, symbols, allegories, and expressions proceeding from well-documented readings. In the *Canticle*, the stylistic presence of the Bible is reflected in the language, psalm-like structures, paired groupings, ideological parallelisms, exclamations, permutations, etc. Accordingly, scholars agree that the *Song of Songs* is the principal source of *The Spiritual Canticle*. However, the *Canticle* is more intimate, dynamic, symbolic, and essential in the search for the human aspect (seen in the emphasis on the amorous relationship between the lovers), and less ceremonial, plastic, sensual, and exuberant in the theme of nature (which is emphasized more in the *Song of Songs*). Some see other influences, such as those from the Greco-Latin classics.[3] All in all, however, these influences affect only external aspects and rhetorical resources; the former Juan de Yepes apparently did not receive a solid and systematic humanistic preparation from reading these classics as did, for example, the Spanish ascetic writer Fray Luis de León.

Being inspired is surely not enough for a poet; one must also be able to express through the written word one's thoughts, feelings, and experiences. St. John of the Cross was troubled by the difficulty of putting into words the uncontainable impulse that he carried within himself, but as Eulogio Pacho tells us, St. John admits that to his natural abilities as a poet is added the grace of God, an inspiration which helps him translate his supernatural experiences.[4] This divine inspiration is more powerful than any earthly poetic muse could ever be for a poet faced with the task of describing the indescribable. As a result, in spite of the emotional tone of his work, the doctrine set forth in the *Canticle* shines with precision and expository clarity.

Since the *Canticle* is an outgrowth of a personal experience, St. John turned to the power of verse to put his feelings into words. The result is similar to the type of love poetry one reads today in which the poet expresses his or her feelings for a lover.

---

3. Among the critics who comment on the similarities and differences between *The Spiritual Canticle* and the *Song of Songs* and the classical influences on St. John of the Cross are Cristóbal Cuevas García, 66; and Eulogio Pacho, 87.

4. Pacho, 76.

It is characteristic of a lover, when he or she cannot communicate directly with the partner because of absence, to make contact by whatever means possible, even by making use of intercessors and intermediaries, as is seen in the second stanza of the *Canticle*, in which the Bride supplicates the shepherds to give her message to her Beloved:

Shepherds, ye that go
Yonder, through the sheepcotes, to the hill,
If perchance ye see him that I most love,
Tell ye him that
I languish, suffer and die.[5]

The marvelous world of beauty described in the poem is not a simple string of lovely images borrowed from the pastoral tradition, for St. John had no such direct model. Instead, his inspiration grew out of his mystical state and personal experience, resulting in an account of spiritual life which later scholars have seen as ranging from the first steps of mental prayer to the highest contemplation of which the soul is capable.

As was stated earlier, however, the poem reads more as a dialogue between lovers than as an account of spiritual life. Examining the correspondence between the three mystic paths and the three basic stages of a relationship, we can see how the poem's structure leads to the ultimate goal of the fully developed relationship, a complete union with the Loved One.[6] The first eleven stanzas describe the purgative way, the period of overcoming past

---

5. St. John of the Cross, *The Spiritual Canticle*, ed. and trans. E. Allison Peers (Garden City, N.Y.: Image Books, 1961), stanza II, vv. 6-10; hereafter cited parenthetically in the text. It should be noted that both stanza numbers and verse numbers are given as cross-references so that readers may look up quotations in the original text in the manner they prefer. This means, for example, that this particular reference is for verses 6-10 of the poem as a whole and not of stanza II.

6. In this paper I have alternated between the use of the masculine and feminine pronouns and possessive adjectives when referring to the Soul, the Bride, and the Soul/Bride. This is because when referring to the Bride, it seems logical to use the feminine pronouns, but when referring to the Soul alone or the combined form Soul/Bride, the use of the pronoun shows whether the emphasis is on the literal appearance of this personage in the poem (feminine pronouns) or its symbolic reference to St. John, the poet and man (masculine pronouns).

sins (or past relationships). The tenth stanza, for example, illustrates this rejection of the past in preparation for the new "Beloved":

> Quench thou my griefs,
> Since none suffices to remove them,
> And let mine eyes behold thee,
> Since thou art their light and for thee alone I wish to have
> them.

Stanzas XII-XXVI comprise the body of the poem, corresponding to the illuminative way, the vision of God in this world (the enlightened vision of the lover, or "falling in love"). An example of this vision in the poem is seen in stanza XIX, which describes the sole importance of loving, above any other activity, a condition recognized by any one who has ever been in love:

> My soul has employed itself
> And all my possessions in his service:
> Now I guard no flock nor have I now other office,
> For now my exercise is in loving alone.

The conclusion, stanzas XXVII-XXXIX, relates the unitive way or the culmination of the soul's journey to his union with God (the final and permanent union of two lovers). In stanza XXXIII of the poem, this union is described symbolically as that of two doves, who represent the Bride and the Beloved:

> The little white dove
> Has returned to the ark with the bough,
> And now the turtle-dove
> Has found the mate of her desire on the green banks.

In this way, the poem's structure parallels the development of a relationship between two lovers: from absence or separation to union. This parallel is more clearly seen through a detailed analysis of the poem and its structure.

The poem's point of departure is the absence of the "Beloved," representing God, and the search by the "Bride," or soul, representing St. John himself, for the Loved One. Here, His presence is realized through vision; the saint is longing for the vision of God. However, St. John of the Cross follows the theological opinion that nobody "sees" God in this life. Instead, the three mystic paths must be followed in order to attain this vision of and union with God. The first path is a normal development for a religious man like St. John of the Cross, and the last one is considered unattainable in this life. Thus, it is primarily the middle path, the illuminative way, that is described in *The Spiritual Canticle*, although the third path is also mentioned later in the poem. This structure parallels secular love poetry, which emphasizes courtship and falling in love (the middle path) with a mention of the ultimate goal, a union (the final path).

This second path, then, is described in the form of a passionate dialogue between lovers, as if the painful ascension were the soul's race in pursuit of the Loved One, finally reaching Him and embracing Him in a mutual, united love. St. John explains in the prose commentary on this poem that the path described in the poem corresponds to the one ordinarily followed by souls in order to arrive at the perfection of love. What St. John does not explain, however, is the manner in which his description of the second path of mysticism corresponds to the "falling in love" stage of secular relationships. This correspondence is seen in the lovers' blindness to others and in their enjoyment of the world and of each other until they become transformed into one united being instead of two separate ones. Throughout the entire poem, while on his journey toward union with his Beloved, a certain transformation occurs in the saint-poet, and this transformation is a veritable divinization.[7] The soul of St. John becomes purified, his spirit saturated with divine resonances.[8] Therefore, *The Spiritual Canticle* is more than the story of an unforgettable moment full of love; it describes the process toward a meeting conceived as consummation.[9]

The introduction to the poem (stanzas I-IV) functions as a preview to the mystical experience. The Bride is searching for the Beloved and even questions the creatures to discover His location. Here, St. John refers to many things in nature (mountains, riverbanks, flowers, beasts, frontiers, woods, thickets, meadow) to give

---

7. See Alain Cugno, *Saint Jean de la Croix* (n.p.: Librairie Artheme Fayard, 1979), 150.

8. See Pacho, 48.

9. See Cuevas García, 42.

the sensation of the speed with which the Bride rushes past earthly things (in mystical terms, purging herself of sin) in her urgency to find her Beloved. The poet/Bride feels the same anguish that modern lovers do when they find no interest in anything until they are in the presence of their partners. This same state of anxiety (the vision of the soul wounded by love and by the absence of the Beloved) is reflected in the first four stanzas of the *Canticle* and continues through stanza XI, which concludes the purgative way as described in the poem.

The second part of the poem (stanzas XXII-XXVI) provides the mystical "core" of the poem. The Lovers meet, and the voice of the Soul, before the Beloved, grows in delight and describes all the beauty in the world. Surprisingly, the stylistic technique that best assists St. John of the Cross in writing a precise and clear poem is symbolism. Perhaps the strongest symbols in the poem are those of the wounded stag and the dove, representing the Beloved and the Bride (who, in turn, represent God and the poet St. John of the Cross), respectively:

> Withdraw them, Beloved, for I fly away.
> Return thou, dove,
> For the wounded hart appears on the hill
> At the air of thy flight, and takes refreshment.
> (stanza XII, vv. 57-60)

In his prose commentary on the poem, St. John reports that it is characteristic of the stag to climb to high places and, when wounded, to race in search of refreshment and cool water, but that if he hears the cry of his mate and senses that she is wounded, he immediately runs to her to embrace and comfort her. Likewise, St. John postulates that God (here represented by the wounded stag) comforts us when we are wounded, so throughout *The Spiritual Canticle* he tells God that he is wounded with love for Him and is seeking comfort through a union with his Beloved.

Stanzas XIII and XIV of the *Canticle* condense all of the beauties of the physical world. Now that the Bride is reunited with her Beloved, she can appreciate the wonders of nature. The Bride's thrill and excitement with all that she sees, both in the world and in her lover, cause the nature imagery of the poem to symbolize the greatness and perfection of the divine Loved One:

My Beloved, the mountains,
The solitary, wooded valleys,
The strange islands, the sonorous rivers,
The whisper of the amorous breezes,

The tranquil night,
At the time of the rising of the dawn,
The silent music, the sounding solitude,
The supper that recreates and enkindles love.
(stanzas XIII-XIV, vv. 61-68)

These two stanzas contain several references to nature (mountain, wooded valleys, rivers, islands, breezes, night and dawn), which further underscore the transcendence of the earth's limitations in the journey toward oneness with God, since the Bride has gone beyond nature, out of the earthly realm, and into that of mysticism. Stanza XV describes, through the Bride's own voice in a dialogue with her Lover, the Bride's new life (still in this world) since meeting the Beloved:

Our flowery bed,
Encompassed with dens of lions,
Hung with purple and builded in peace,
Crowned with a thousand shields of gold.
(stanza XV, vv. 69-72)

The Soul has ended his journey, his quest to unite with his Beloved, God. This is the climax of the poem. From the peak of the spiritual height, the Soul describes his itinerary thus far; from the Beloved's first glance to Union with Him. The poem's conclusion, stanzas XXVII-XXXIX, corresponds to mysticism's unitive way, the permanent union between two lovers, but immediately before arriving at this point, the divine Husband describes how these two "lovers" came to be one:

The Bride has entered
Into the pleasant garden of her desire,
And at her pleasure rests,
Her neck reclining on the gentle arms of the Beloved.
(stanza XXVII, vv. 127-30)

Then the Soul/Bride speaks, expressing her thoughts on the intimacy and privacy needed in their "marriage":

> O nymphs of Judaea,
> While mid the flowers and rosetrees the ambar sends forth
>   perfume,
> Dwell in the outskirts
> And desire not to touch our thresholds.
> Hide thyself, dearest one,
> And look with thy face upon the mountains,
> And desire not to speak,
> But look upon her companions who travel mid strange
>   islands.
> (stanzas XXXI-XXXII, vv. 143-50)

In the unitive way, the soul is constantly guided by God and the desires for glory. In *The Spiritual Canticle*, this need for guidance is seen in the form of a monologue in which the Soul/Bride, never satisfied, advances new protests and requests. In a speech to the Beloved, the Soul reveals his desires to better know the increasing greatness that he discovers within Him:

> There wouldst thou show me
> That which my soul desired,
> And there at once, my life, wouldst thou give me
> That which thou gavest me the other day.

> The breathing of the air,
> The song of the sweet philomel,
> The grove and its beauty in the serene night,
> With a flame that consumes and gives no pain.
> (stanzas XXXVII-XXXVIII, vv. 167-74)

The Soul/Bride now changes tone, from the supplicating insinuation of the desirous times of the past and the agitated description of her wanderings and anxieties to a placid serenity. The Soul/Bride now feels tranquil because of finally being able to enjoy the Beloved since all exterior movement has ceased. All impediments have disappeared; there is no reason for suspicion. But the poet also feels tranquil because of the perfect union with the Beloved: what was once lacking in the physical world is no longer lacking above, in the spiritual world.

The Spiritual Canticle offers one central symbol, the erotic union, from which comes the cohesive strength of the work. All of creation is converted, for St. John, into an immense string of divine symbols and allegories, as a Platonic reflection of the universe of ideas preexisting in the mind of God.

We average readers are not mystical saints like St. John of the Cross and, therefore, we have difficulty understanding the mystical experience. But the stages of development that our own interpersonal relationships have gone through can be seen as corresponding to the paths of mysticism. With this correspondence in mind during a careful reading of St. John of the Cross' *The Spiritual Canticle*, we can better understand what this saint-poet's experience with God was like. This understanding, then, although unlikely to make mystics out of each one of us, can assist us in our search for meaning and in our attempts to make God a part of our lives.

Author's Note:

At one point in my life, I experienced the dissolution of a romantic relationship with a young man who said that true love should have a "mystical" quality to it. I didn't understand that statement then, but my later reading of St. John of the Cross' Spiritual Canticle *helped. Just as one can never truly "know" God, in the mystical sense, without following all three paths (purgative, illuminative, and unitive), one cannot truly love another person without following a series of paths. But how many of us are too impatient to "purge" ourselves of past loves? How many of us want to arrive at the unitive path immediately through a physical relationship or attempting a permanent union?*

How can we develop the patience and discipline to follow the stages of union? Is it the earth and its "things" that prevent us from loving God? Can a realization of earthly limits help us envision how perfect a spiritual union with God can be?

M.E.K.

Works Cited

Cuevas García, Cristóbal, ed. *Cántico Espiritual. Poesías* by St. John of the Cross. Bilbao: Editorial Alhambra, 1979.

Cugno, Alain. *Saint Jean de la Croix.* N.p.: Librairie Artheme
Fayard, 1979.

Pacho, Eulogio. *Vértice de la poesía y de la mística: El "Cántico
espiritual" de San Juan de La Cruz.* Burgos: Editorial Monte
Caramelo, 1983.

St. John of the Cross. *The Spiritual Canticle.* Edited and translated
by E. Allison Peers. Garden City, N.Y.: Image Books, 1961.

II.

Transcendence
Through Nature

Chapter Four

Religious Experience and Transcendence in Annie Dillard's Eco-Spirituality

Carolyn Sur, S.S.N.D.

Transcendence often seems to be equated with a denial of the flesh, of the concrete, of nature. This essay, on the contrary, explores how oneness with nature can set the stage for a religious experience, a kind of transcendence. In a nature experience, the observer rises above the "now movement" and sees beyond one isolated component of creation to the connectedness of all within the cosmos. To attain this "overview," one must lose touch, for a while, with one's own humanity, or one must transcend what is merely human in order to enter into the world of something "other." That *other* may be a creature lesser or greater than the human personality in the broad scope of creation. In Annie Dillard's imagery, one may *descend* into the world of inorganic matter – rocks and moonbeams, or into the world of organic matter – animals, musk-rats, and weasels. One may also *ascend* into the world of the divinity. Either transcendence may happen in a flash, in a glimpse, or in some brief, acute moment. Seldom are life's transcendent experiences enduring, for to endure is to cross over from life to death, the ultimate transcendence.

Humanity's restlessness seems to document that *homo sapiens* has been programmed to yearn for what is beyond, for the "not yet." When transcendence involves the Higher Power, it is called a religious or mystical experience. When nature is the medium of such a religious experience, transcendence to a lower form of life often, paradoxically, leads to a higher form of life. "Eco-spiritual-

63

ity," the school of spirituality that deliberately emphasizes nature in one's ascent to the higher life, is so named because it is through union with that which comprises the ecosystem that one can better know God.

Annie Dillard, (1945-), who won the Pulitzer Prize for general nonfiction in 1974 and who has been described as a kind of "contemporary mystic,"[1] comes home to herself and discovers the connectedness of lower life to human life in her keen observations of nature. In order to transcend her humanness, she stalks a muskrat, she watches the moon "stalk" the earth, she observes a friend as he meditates upon a stone, and she stares down a weasel. By examining Dillard's experiences in nature, one can discover how creation leads to the Creator. Being in rhythm with nature's energies puts one in sync with God's energy, which transcended the Godhead in creation.

In Dillard's experience of stalking the muskrat, she seems to see the animal as an extension of herself. Dillard observes the muskrat not by seeing it with the eyes of a scientist, which is a left-brain analysis of the details and the surroundings; rather, she sees the muskrat with a kind of "inner eye." Dillard knows by intuition, not by analysis. She knows the muskrat, not by situating it in the logistics of time and space, not by listing observable, empirical statistics about the muskrat – its size, age or color. True knowing the muskrat is "not knowing" these nonessential facts. True knowing, for Dillard, is the *reflection* upon the experience of knowing; true seeing is the *reflection* upon the experience of seeing. This kind of knowing and seeing becomes more explicit in Dillard's nature experiences.

Dillard makes this distinction clear when she describes a specific activity in nature, the paradox of "not stalking" in order *to* stalk. This she calls the *Via negativa,* using a phrase from Meister Eckhart's thirteenth-century spirituality:

> In summer, I stalk. Summer leaves obscure, heat dazzles,
> and creatures hide from the red-eyed sun, and me. I have
> to seek things out. The creatures I seek have several

---

1. Susan M. Felch, "Annie Dillard: Modern Physics in a Contemporary Mystic," *Mosaic: A Journal for the Interdisciplinary Study of Literature* 22 (spring 1989).

senses and free will; it becomes apparent that they do not wish to be seen. I can stalk them in either of two ways. The first is not what you think of as true stalking, but it is the *Via negativa,* and as fruitful as actual pursuit. When I stalk this way I take my stand on a bridge and wait, emptied. I put myself in the way of the creature's passage, like spring Eskimos at a seal's breathing hole. Something might come; something might go. I am Newton under the apple tree, Buddha under the bo.[2]

Eckhart called his method of finding God the spirituality of subtraction. Dillard follows her description of stalking passively by describing a second way of stalking, the active approach or the *Via positiva:* "Stalking the other way, I forge my own passage seeking the creature. I wander the banks; what I find, I follow, doggedly, like Eskimos haunting the caribou herds. I am Wilson squinting after the traces of electrons in a cloud chamber; I am Jacob at Peniel wrestling with the angel" (*PTC* 184).

The contrast of the *Via negativa* and the *Via positiva* is a constant dynamic in the thorough pursuit of any subject. True knowing demands a methodical pursuit of a subject – the *Via positiva*. Only then will one have the mastery of it to pursue it passively, effortlessly – the *Via negativa*. All who master anything – a musical instrument, a sport, or a professional status – are engaged in this cyclic contrast of disciplined pursuit versus relaxed mastery. Those who pursue God will follow similar paths, eventually letting go of a learned methodology.

Meister Eckhart, thirteenth-century German mystic, whose spiritual writings are characterized by *Via negativa* and paradox, once said of this cyclic dynamic: "The eye with which I see God is the same eye with which God sees me."[3] First God envisions and creates; then I know and respond. Eckhart seemed to know that the Divine manifests itself in the integrated human person, connected to and aware of all that is life, not confined within some

---

2. Annie Dillard, *Pilgrim at Tinker Creek* (New York: Harper's Magazine Press, 1974), 184; hereafter cited parenthetically in the text as *PTC.*

3. Meister Eckhart, *Meditations with Meister Eckhart: A Centering Book by Matthew Fox* (Sante Fe: Bear & Company, 1983), 21.

separate aspect of the life force which philosophers and theologians for many centuries termed "the soul."

Correspondingly, for Annie Dillard, "stalking," while not explicitly defined, seems to be the search for the ultimate unifying principle which unites her, the subject, to all of life. Theologians call *the* ultimate unifying principle God.[4] Philosophers and scholars speak of the pursuit of Truth. Annie comes closest to this ultimate Truth when she transcends self and becomes keenly aware of another, of the animal in its natural habitat.

In stalking the muskrat, Annie catches the animal off guard. She does not simply *observe* the animal; she lets go of – "transcends" – her human boundaries and *becomes* some aspect of the animal. She transcends herself from the limitations of *homo sapiens,* just briefly, to enter into the hide of the muskrat. This is possible when she is "in sync" with the animal, a phenomenon more common to the animal world. On the spiritual path, God catches us off guard as well in order that we might move in sync with divinity.

Most of us have never stalked a muskrat for the sake of watching it in nature, but we may be familiar with watching a cat stalk a bird for its lunch. The cat, in stalking a bird, transcends its own movements of "cat-ness." It freezes "stock-still," focused for depth of perception, then moves in the cadence, the rhythm, and the energy patterns of the bird. It is completely intent on the hunt, not to be distracted by other instincts, by human presence, by mating or even by its passion for milk. Dillard stalks a muskrat and later stares down a weasel, not for food but because of her awareness, her desire to experience a connectedness with all of life. This process suggests "detachment," a central theme for

---

4. The German theologian Karl Rahner, for example, holds that to remain *true* to oneself, one must return again and again to the transcendental experience of our orientation towards the absolute mystery. See Karl Rahner, *Foundations of Christian Faith,* trans. William V. Dych (New York: Crossroads, 1992), 43, 53. Rahner holds that the transcendental experience, which is mystery, is mediated by an encounter with concrete reality in the world of events, in the world of *things* and *persons.* Therefore, the reflecting individual sees the experience as transcending, as infinitely "bigger than" his or her encounter with the event. The event is *in* the world but not limited *to* the world. Mystery "constantly reveals itself and at the same time conceals itself" (42). Infinity is both revealed by and concealed by finitude.

Meister Eckhart, the term used here to mean a shift from a kind of possessing the object for a utilitarian purpose, for example, catching the fish to eat, or capturing a scene for photography, or trapping a muskrat for its pelt. This utilitarianism is in contrast to a careless detachment – from using the object to feeling a oneness with the object. In the theological realm, God, in "stalking humanity," becomes one with humanity in Christ, and transcends "Godness."

In Eastern modes of religious thought, one's *awareness* of the connectedness of all that has lived and is living enhances an *actual* connectedness with all living things. The West compartmentalizes and detaches; the East generalizes and connects. Connectedness of one to a single other is the starting point of connectedness to the whole. In so connecting all to all, one achieves union with the unifying principle of life itself – God. In "stalking," Annie Dillard lets go of the mundane *now* of concrete life for something of the purity of living. Stalking and meditating, however, are not skills acquired in a short time. They require all the discipline of an Olympic athlete. In meditation, humanity takes the initiative and stalks God by prescribed methods. In contemplation, God takes the initiative and invites humanity in. There is no methodology in contemplation. It is pure gift, invitation.

Annie describes the tedious process of detachment, of stalking, in the following scene:

> Learning to stalk muskrats took me several years. . . . One hot summer evening three years ago, I was standing more or less *in* a bush. I was stock-still, looking deep into Tinker Creek from a spot on the bank opposite the house, watching a group of bluegills stare and hang motionless near the bottom of a deep, sunlit pool. I was focused for depth. I had long since lost myself, lost the creek, the day, lost everything but still amber depth. All at once I couldn't see. And then I could: a young muskrat had appeared on top of the water, floating on its back. Its forelegs were folded languorously across its chest; the sun shone on its upturned belly. Its youthfulness and rodent grin, coupled with its ridiculous method of locomotion, which consisted of a lazy wag of the tail assisted by an occasional dabble of a webbed hind foot, made it an

enchanting picture of decadence, dissipation, and summer sloth. I forgot all about the fish. (*PTC* 190-91)

Stalking the muskrat gives Annie a glimpse of mystery. It mesmerizes her and captures her from the concerns of everyday life – the mate, her human needs and instincts, the distracting presence of another person. Through the rhythm of the swimming muskrat, the ritual of wagging and dabbling, Dillard enters into the muskrat's mindlessness, which is akin to the mindlessness of a nun or a monk serious about the exercise of meditation. For the Zen monk, the common expression applies, "those who say, do not know; those who know, do not say." In Dillard's stalking the muskrat, one could say that she enters into an imaginary water ballet with the muskrat. Dillard, too, swims with its motions just as the cat springs with the bird, not just symbolically but in the reality of the kinetic memory. In watching the muskrat, Annie may recall the experience of her own swimming or subconsciously may remember how in her embryonic life she floated with *her* belly up and *her* forearms folded languorously across her chest within the womb. The kinetic memory recalls the stage when she was not bound by terrestrial gravity but dangled from the umbilical cord in a universe of amniotic fluid. The muskrat invites Annie to transcend one space still connected to another by the cord of life. In human death, severing the cord of life connects one to the world of spirituality.

In order to transcend from one world to another, one must allow oneself to become uncomfortable in known territory to become comfortable in unknown territory. Such unknown territory in spirituality is in the realm of mysticism, of union with the Higher Power, a realm of mystery and paradox. Dillard's "stalking" suggests a mystic stance when she takes note of opposites, of paradox, when she speaks of a forgetting in order to remember. She observes a "mindlessness" in the animals at Hollins Pond and Tinker Creek which she desires to imitate. In her mind, one learns how to live by setting aside what some term a left-brained analysis of the "how to," and by allowing the mind to muse absentmindedly. In her words, "I would like to learn, or remember, how to live. I come to Hollins Pond not so much to learn how to live as, frankly, to forget about it. . . . I might learn something of mindlessness, something of the purity of living in the physical senses and the dignity of living without bias or motive."[5] Contemporary mystics such as Dillard are at home in paradox, in *forgetting* how to live on one level in order to *learn* how to live on a higher level. Mystery not only hints at paradox; it is at home only in paradox. As a late medieval text, *The Cloud of Unknowing* describes it, paradox is the ability to "not see" in order "to see" – to *not see* the distracting, nonessentials in life, in order to *see* the essentials, the real truth.[6] In today's culture, one is deluged with information. What is needed is meaning, truth.

The mystic is one who yearns for the ultimate Truth. The real truth, the experience which is most *human*, is to face the ultimate question of God. This leads to transcendence of worldly, earthly concerns. The transcendent experience opens the human to a glimpse of infinity because he/she first truly and thoroughly experiences something *other* in the finite realm. This experience is not merely an intellectual knowing but often is a knowing with a kind of "inner eye." A mystical, transcendent experience presumes some level of conscious interaction by the individual, with some one or some thing outside of one's self, followed by a reflection period. Only a human being can know and reflect upon his/her connectedness to all things.[7]

---

5. *Teaching a Stone to Talk* (New York: Harper & Row, 1982), 15; hereafter cited parenthetically in the text as *TST*.

6. Karl Rahner warns that one will miss the experience of transcendence in life if one concentrates only upon the nonessentials. One can "devote himself to his concrete world, his work, his activity in the categorical realm of time and space. [People can] live at a distance from themselves in that concrete part of their lives and of the world around them which can be manipulated and controlled . . . recognizing and accepting the fact that everything is encompassed by an ultimate question. This question is perhaps left as a question. One believes that it can be postponed in silence and in a perhaps sensible skepticism. But when one explains that it cannot be answered, he is admitting that in the final analysis such a question cannot be evaded." See Rahner, 32-33.

7. Rahner explains that knowledge of oneself as subject helps one to know first oneself, then another as object, but beyond the limits of finite objects is the contrast, the infinite horizon. According to Rahner, infinity precedes all else. He holds that the human person is born with the instinct to know the infinite (God). Here we add, a human is born to know, to relate, to connect, as a cat is born with the instinct to stalk. Therefore, a truly human experience is a

In stalking, Dillard "remembers" her muskratness, her otherness, as does the cat in stalking the bird. The cat "remembers" its own birdness in an earlier biological phylum. Dillard's turning from "doing" in life to truly "being" in life connects her to the existence of all forms of life. This awareness is a glimpse of what the artist Frederick Franck calls "being in touch with the inner workings of life"; of "life that knows it is living"; of "a moment speaking as time and eternity"; of "seeing into the nature of things, inside and outside of myself."[8] The Eastern philosophers call this Zen. The Western theologians call it transcendence. Karl Rahner describes it as the human experience which connects one with the Transcendent. Others, like the Spanish mystic John of the Cross, who calls the Transcendent the "ah-I-don't know-what," cannot find words adequate for the experience. They know it in the *feeling* of being truly alive, in the following of one's "bliss," in Joseph Campbell's terms. In the "not naming" and "not seeing" one truly sees and one truly exists because one reflects upon being. Reflection is a unique human experience that Teilhard de Chardin equates to evolution's taxing down the runway, then suddenly becoming airborne. Reflection upon being leads to reflection upon the source of all being, the Ultimate Being.[9]

Without explicitly defining it in theological terms, Dillard senses that she is connected to the Transcendent Immanent in the various forms and stages of creation. In the single-mindedness required to enter into the hide of the muskrat, that is, in stalking the muskrat, she knows that she and the muskrat are not just *on*

---

transcendental experience out of selfness into otherness. According to Rahner, "the object of such a transcendental experience does not appear in its own reality when man [or woman] is dealing with something individual and definable in an objective way, but when in such a process he [or she] is *being* subject and not dealing with a 'subject' in an objective way." See Rahner, 31.

8. Frederick Franck, "Introduction," *The Zen of Seeing* (New York: Vintage, 1973), 9.

9. This kind of seeing into the nature of all things is similar to the Native American Indian emphasis on the connection of blood that unites beings with all of nature. Eco-Spirituality combines this reverence for nature with spirituality. "Eco-feminism," another term in current use, credits the efforts to save the earth from the dual threats of nuclear annihilation and ecocide to women in the feminist movement. The rape of the earth and violence to women are reflections of the dominant culture's devaluation of the natural.

the earth or *in* the water. They are both part *of* the earth and *of* the water. She takes on metaphorically not only the identity of Watson and Crick, squinting at the electrons in the cloud chamber; but also she *is* the electron in the cloud chamber, along with all the raw elements of the cosmic soup. Literally, part of what was in the laboratory of the universe fifteen billion years ago is now part of Annie Dillard. As life emerged from the sea to the land, evolutionists teach, life generated a continuous thread. The human alive is both *from* and *of* those primordial waters. Each person is a microcosm of the life of the universe. We, in turn, contain microcosms within us, smaller universes. It is quantum physics,[10] process theology, or DNA, depending upon one's discipline.

Stalking the muskrat triggers the subconscious of higher life to memories of more elementary connections. Annie Dillard is part of all that constitutes what scientists call the Big Bang theory, part of all which constitutes what believers call the Divine Plan, part of all that constitutes what Chief Seattle calls the Web of Life, imaged by Susan Jeffers as the web of a spider. Dillard is connected to what twentieth-century physicists term the "fundamental particles – electrons, protons, neutrons, mesons, muons, pions, taus, thetas, sigmas, pis, and so on." While "the search for the ultimate unifying particle, the quark, continues to engage the efforts of the best theoretical physicists,"[11] stalking the muskrat puts Dillard in touch with the ultimate unifying particle the theologians credit to God. Though she does not explicitly formulate it, Dillard seems to have a profound and real sense that she is connected to the muskrat and the weasel in the mysterious way that the quark unifies sub-atomic

---

10. Since the initial writing of this essay, I have continued to explore texts which connect quantum physics and theology. Among them are the following: Kevin O'Shea, *Person in Cosmos: Metaphors of Meaning from Physics, Philosophy, and Theology* (Bristol, IN: Wyndham Hall Press, lf. 1995); Robert John Russell *et al., Physics, Philosophy, and Theology: A Common Quest for Understanding* (Vatican City State: Vatican Observatory, 1995); lf. John Polkinghorne, *The Faith of a Physicist* (Princeton: Princeton University Press, 1994); David S. Toolan, "At Home in the Cosmos: The Poetics of Matter = Energy," *America* (24 February 1996):8-14; George Coyne, S.J., *The New Physics and a New Theology* (Notre Dame: The University of Notre Dame Press, 1996).

11. Carolyn Merchant, *The Death of Nature: Women, Ecology and the Scientific Revolution* (San Francisco: HarperCollins, 1990), 291.

particles. Cytologists might explain this by saying that the electron, the DNA molecule, the muskrat, and the weasel are *of* the same stuff of life which constitutes Dillard herself.

Annie Dillard shows her awareness of the connection between souls and the evolution from soil to soul in *Tickets for a Prayer Wheel*. In this text she writes: "Out of the soil the plants are taking substance, edges, like a tomato moving on its stake, ten pounds of tomatoes, and the ground blowing them up like balloons. We walk on the soil here on the continents among the plants, and eat."[12] Evolutionists with faith explain that life budded out of the earth in an unbroken flow to become sophisticated muskrats, most clever weasels, Olympic stalkers, humans who reflect upon all that is, created by One who transcends all that is.[13]

Each unit of life – the quark, the electron, DNA, the bo tree, the apple, the muskrat – is, in some way, an entity beyond itself. To use computer terminology, transcendence is programmed into all of life. When Dillard reflects upon any one microcosm in the chain of life, she transcends not only the creek or the day; she transcends herself and connects with the Ultimate Transcendence, which connects all, yet goes beyond all. In paralleling the ability of each element of life to transcend itself, *homo sapiens* imitates the generative powers of God's fecundity.

The unifying principle of life creates life which goes beyond itself. It causes amoebas to bud pseudopods, which eco-spirituality might call "amoeba-ing"; the unifying principle directs trees to flower into apples – "apple-ing"; the unifying principle instructs a cat how to stalk a bird – "cat-ing." The unifying principle programs

---

12. Annie Dillard, *Tickets for a Prayer Wheel* (Columbia, Mo.: University of Missouri Press, 1974), 19; hereafter cited parenthetically in the text as *TPW*.

13. See Annie Dillard, *Tickets for a Prayer Wheel*, 19. The evolution of life was the topic of the late Carl Sagan's book and the television series *Cosmos*. Sagan led some of the early scientific writing on subatomic particles, suggesting, for example, that protons and neutrons were in fact made of still more elementary particles called quarks. Stephen Hawkings asserts that the components of creation continued to transcend their lower level of life which evolved through the Cenozoic Era to the black hole which, according to Hawkings "burp[s] subatomic particles to another universe." If Hawkings is correct, even the universe we know may transcend itself. See Sharon Begley and Jennifer Foote, "Why Past is Past," *Newsweek* (28 December 1992): 51-53.

humans to reflect as an instinctive activity leading ultimately to reflection upon the Infinite.[14] In Rahner's terms, "Man is and remains a transcendent being, that is, he is that existent to whom the silent and uncontrollable infinity of reality is always present as mystery. This makes man totally open to this mystery and precisely in this way he becomes conscious of himself as person and as subject."[15]

Annie Dillard finds transcendence in her openness to nature; at the same time, she discovers a consciousness of herself as person and as subject. This process is exemplified in her encounter with a weasel:

> I have been reading about weasels because I saw one last week. I startled a weasel who startled me, and we exchanged a long glance. . . .
>
> The weasel was stunned into stillness as he was emerging from beneath an enormous shaggy wild rose bush four feet away. I was stunned into stillness twisted backward on the tree trunk. Our eyes locked, and someone threw away the key.
>
> Our look was as if two lovers, or deadly enemies, met unexpectedly on an overgrown path when each had been thinking of something else: a clearing blow to the gut. It was a bright blow to the brain, or a sudden beating of brains, with all the charge and intimate grate of rubbed balloons. It emptied our lungs. It felled the forest, moved the fields, and drained the pond; the world dismantled and tumbled into that black hole of eyes. If you and I looked at each other that way, our skulls would split and drop to our shoulders. But we don't. We keep our skulls. So.
>
> . . . He disappeared. This was only last week, and already I don't remember what shattered the enchantment. I think I blinked, I think I retrieved my brain from the weasel's brain, and tried to memorize what I was seeing, and the

---

14. See Michael Dowd, "The Big Picture – The Larger Context for All Human Activities," *Proceedings from the John Neumann Institute: A Call to Life – Care for Each Other, Care for Earth* (Milwaukee: Sacred Heart School of Theology, 1993), 2.

15. Rahner, 35.

weasel felt the yank of separation, the careening splash-down into real life and the urgent current of instinct. He vanished under the wild rose. I waited motionless, my mind suddenly full of data and my spirit with pleadings, but he didn't return.

Please do not tell me about "approach-avoidance conflicts." I tell you I've been in that weasel's brain for sixty seconds, and he was in mine. (*TST* 12-14)

How does one get in and get out of the brain of a weasel? What is it that causes the weasel in Annie's encounter to "shatter the enchantment?" Stephen Hawking says that "whenever a memory is made, in either a brain or a computer, the smidgen of energy required to light up a neuron or move an electron, is released as heat. Heat-roiling, chaotic heat – increases entropy. Reflecting, then because it releases heat, increases disorder, too."[16] In the disorder of Annie's rational thinking and blinking, in the disorder of changing the brain's activity from "mindlessness" to analysis, a slight charge of heat was sufficient to disturb the weasel. It is generally on the left side of the brain that analysis or abstract reflection takes place. It is the right side of the brain that a mystic engages to reflect in kataphatic images during meditation. An effortless meandering through the right side of her brain among ancient, archetypal images helps Dillard to recall that she, too, may once have had the habits of a weasel; this energy keeps her in sync with the weasel, and puts the weasel's image in her mind.

Such intimacy with the subject is so intense that in modern shamanic societies, animals are frequently referred to as relatives: "daughter chick," "sister weasel," "father muskrat." With this kind of familial affinity, Dillard would like to live as the weasel lives:

The weasel lives as he should. And I suspect that for me the way is like the weasel's: open to time and death painlessly, noticing everything, remembering nothing, choosing the given with a fierce and pointed will. . . . We could live under the wild rose wild as weasels, mute and

---

16. Stephen Hawking, quoted in Begley and Foote, 53. See also Marcia Baringa, "Visual System Provides Clues to how the Brain Perceives," *Science* (14 March 1997): 1583-85.

> uncomprehending. I could very calmly go wild. I could
> live two days in the den, curled, leaning on mouse fur,
> sniffing bird bones, blinking, licking, breathing musk, my
> hair tangled in the roots of grasses. Down is a good place
> to go where the mind is single. (*TST* 15)

Who has not had the embarrassing experience of staring at another from across the room, only to have the person glance over in recognition? Suddenly, the connection is made, and the other person feels the focused energy. The person turns our way; the eyes catch one another, even if only momentarily. The first person is likely to turn away with a "yank of separation," embarrassed to be discovered staring. Annie Dillard predicts that if two people looked at each other the way she and the weasel looked at each other, their "skulls would split and drop to [their] shoulders" (*TPW* 14). If two people really believed that God dwelled within each other, if they stared at the Ultimate Transcendent in one another – that refined remnant of the Transcendent's artistry in *homo sapiens* – they could not endure. It is less awesome to go to lower nature for transcendence. Annie Dillard goes to Hollins Pond and to Tinker Creek.

The glimpse at the Ultimate Transcendent, whom many name by the generic term *God*, is not restricted to an interaction with plant or animal life. In her book by the same name, Annie Dillard speaks of "teaching a stone to talk." In this process, she stares at a stone until it speaks to the "unspoiled core" of the self, until the stone is recognized as a microcosm of the self, until the voice within speaks because one has focused upon the stone in *Via negativa*. Annie introduces the main character in this dialogue in veiled language as "Larry," perhaps identified as the "Gary" whose name is found in the dedication of the text. She describes the rituals between "Larry" and the stone as follows:

> It is – for I have seen it – a palm-sized oval beach cobble
> whose dark gray is cut by a band of white which runs
> around and, presumably, through it; such stones we call
> "wishing stones," for reasons obscure but not, I think,
> unimaginable.
>
> He [Larry] keeps it on a shelf. Usually the stone lies
> protected by a square of untanned leather, like a canary

asleep under its cloth. Larry removes the cover for the stone's lessons, or more accurately, I should say, for the ritual or rituals which they perform together several times a day.

No one knows what goes on at these sessions. . . . I assume that like any other meaningful effort, the ritual involves sacrifice, the suppression of self-consciousness, and a certain precise tilt of the will, so that the will becomes transparent and hollow, a channel for the work. I wish him well. It is a noble work, and beats, from any angle, selling shoes. (*TST* 68)

In the ritual of talking to a stone, the will, which must become transparent and hollow, parallels the *Via negativa* of stalking. When one watches in an empty, "stalking" mode of the *Via negativa,* the path often leads to reflection and to a transcendence into a higher realm of life, to communion with God through prayer.

When Dillard empties the self for the sake of the other, she connects with the Author of Life. She can address both Lord and lover in the same breath, though the lover may be guised as human: "Lord, lover, listen: I remember kissing on the stair/dancing in the kitchen. . ." (*TPW* 17). The loves of Annie's life seem to blur together – men and muskrats, with the One who transcends life. Love Itself and her present human loves become hues of each other in the cycle of *Via negativa* to *Via positiva,* from death to life and from life back to death, or, in the vocabulary of the mystics, life with the Other and death to the self:

Come take a walk, you said. / And if I reached out / my hand could feel your shoulders move, / thin, under your shirt. . . . You tell me your dream and I'll tell you mine. I dreamed I woke in a garden. Everywhere trees were growing: everywhere flowers were growing, / and otters played in the stream, and grew. / Fruit hung down. / An egg at my feet / cracked, opened up, / and you stepped out, / perfect, intricate lover. (*TPW* 19, 21, 23)

Stalking and loving and praying can bring about *Glassenheit,* a term the Germans use to describe a kind of ultimate self-possession or calmness. To find *Glassenheit,* one must take a walk into that unknown darkness, into transcendent space, into the creative tension of growth, a place Meister Eckhart calls the ground of one's being. In creative tension, one level of creation dies; another emerges. One organism dies; a new entity lives. The egg cracks.

A chick within an egg must experience the uncomfortableness of restrained space to find the energy to break through, to transcend its "egg-ness." To hatch, it must uncoil its neck, tucked comfortably and compactly under its wing, strain outward, protrude its still delicate beak, and strike repeatedly at one spot, a kind of focusing on one zone. It pecks in blind darkness against a firm wall of calcium, a boundary.[17] The strength that the chick acquires in the struggle for transcendence of its boundary of calcium is absolutely necessary for life. A concerned farmer cannot bore a hole in the egg to make it easier for the chick to emerge. At best the experienced farmer adds only a few drops of warm water to soften the calcium layer. In the chick's own time, it will emerge to a higher life outside the egg. There, with the instinct given by the One who transcends life, it will hide from weasels, eat corn, crow and grow a comb, or it will lay and hatch another generation of eggs. Similarly, each human being pecks away at the boundaries of life to transcend them to new growth.

Life is a balance of waiting, of calmness, of *Glassenheit,* and the death throes of cracking through the shell, the boundary of new life. The chick cannot return to the egg once the shell is broken. Often new life comes from violent struggle. Annie Dillard notes, for example, that the female praying mantis devours up to seven males in the process of generating new life. The mating may endure for several hours. All the while, the male is methodically losing his life for the species: first, the female eats his head, then the thorax, then the tail. With the focus like that of the *Via positiva,* he sustains his tight embrace. "'And, all the time, that masculine stump, holding on firmly, goes on with the business! I have seen

---

17. Rahner, writing about the spiritual experience, substitutes the term "limit point" or "horizon" for boundary. Theologian Gerald O'Collins, in an attempt to explain Rahner's analysis of transcendental experience notes, "In every particular experience of someone or something we concurrently experience not only ourselves but also our openness to an unlimited horizon of being." See Gerald O'Collins, S.J., *Fundamental Theology* (New York: Paulist Press, 1981), 48.

it with my own eyes,'" says Annie in *Pilgrim at Tinker Creek,* "'and have not yet recovered from my astonishment'" (*PTC* 58).

In premodern scientific language, male stalks female for perpetuation of the species; female suffocates male for protection of the offspring. Made in God's image, we should not be surprised that God also stalks humanity as Francis Thompson suggests in his poem "The Hound of Heaven." In theological language, God reproduces Trinitarian likeness in *homo sapiens,* male and female both fashioned in God's image and likeness. The lover and the beloved beget love itself in a third entity, the child. Duality transcends unity. Three-ness transcends two-ness. The cycle of *Via positiva* – life and *Via negativa* – death combine for new meaning.

The rhythm of waiting and watching, of focus and letting be, of the *Via positiva* and the *Via negativa* that one finds in nature's pattern of living and dying is reflected also in human activities where body and mind have attained the creative tension of equilibrium. Biologists chart a peak performance of an individual with all sine waves of the Biorhythm – mental, physical, emotional – intersecting at the same critical point. Athletes name the perfect performance in which all body systems are in automatic sync with surrounding energies, "zoning." An athlete's Olympic performance happens when zoning takes place, when judgment is not rational but when body responses have reached an instinctual level. A champion ski jumper transcends human boundaries to connect with the wind's forces at takeoff in imitation of his/her ancestors in flight; the speed swimmer appears to transcend two-leggedness, in sync with amphibole roots and the surrounding water's wake; the professional basketball player bounds over nine other obstructing, moving bodies to "dunk" a rubber sphere that ascends as an extension of the human hand. Runners have a "high" when they allow body and spirit to function on automatic. Analogously, mystics communicate with the Transcendent when they lose themselves in God.

As the essence of an Olympic event is the oneness of sport, player, and the forces of nature, so the essence of Annie Dillard's eco-spirituality nature spirituality is the ability to become one with an object. The muskrat, the weasel are extensions of Annie in the universe. Human transcends subhuman when it can stalk, focus, zone in upon that which is other than its own life. Through such an exercise, one learns to transcend the natural to the supernatural. When Annie stalks a muskrat or stares down a weasel, one could say that she becomes part of them; she "zones in" upon the sheer pleasure of being alive and disengaged from the mundaneness of life.

One cannot program the athlete's perfect game, but a system of skills and diet help provide better conditions for an automatic performance. One cannot program stalking a muskrat or staring down a weasel or kissing on the stairs, as both initiator and receiver, subject and object, must be engaged in the dynamic for the event to happen. Openness and fidelity to the discipline of watching and waiting and loving, however, can at least set the stage.

Fortunately, one need not redo human nature to arrive at union with the Ultimate Transcendent. If the theologians are correct, the human is already *programmed* with this knowledge.[18] Union with the Transcendent happens in those situations in life in which the human being is most conscious, most human – in laughter, in tears, in celebration, in mourning, in the transcendent moment of a sunrise or sunset, in the scholar's discovery of a nugget of truth. Fidelity to the discipline of prayer and meditation provides the conditions for a mindless escape into a wordless dialogue with the Transcendent. This is genuine contemplation.

Modern mystics and writers, such as William James, name this connection with the Ultimate Reality a "religious experience" in which one transcends the dimensions of time, the senses, and even the human body. Artist Frederick Franck might call Dillard's "purity of living," her "unspoiled core," as "the Zen of seeing." In Franck's words, "at times it [the unspoiled core] responds to Nature, to beauty, to Life, suddenly aware again of being in the presence of a Mystery that baffles understanding and which only has to be glimpsed to renew our spirit and to make us feel that life is a supreme gift."[19] Annie Dillard, an ordinary mystic and an extraor-

---

18. See Kevin Culligan, "Are We Wired for God?" *America* (22 March 1997): 23-24.
19. Franck, x-xi.

dinary writer, finds that life's ultimate gift comes in transcendent experiences in nature.

Author's Note:

Modern humans are bombarded by our ever-expanding technology; we are over-stimulated – too much information, too many people, too fast, too loud, too often. The human heart, however, was made to rest in God; nothing in modern technology can simulate this restful God-experience. Nothing synthetic refreshes like nature.

Can nature's rhythms help us to find meaning in life, help us to transcend the mundane pace of urban life? If humans were created to connect with that which came before them on the evolutionary tree, not to dominate or exploit lower life, is God then discovered, not by controlling, but by letting go? Are the peaceful rhythms of animals and moonbeams and even stones, which quantum physics assures us really do "talk," in sync with the human heart? Can we let go of the mechanical in our lives and tune into the rhythms that modulate the music of the universe?

C.S.

Works Cited

Barinaga, Maria. "Visual System Provides Clues to How the Brain Perceives." *Science* (14 March 1997): 1583-85.

Begley, Sharon and Jennifer Foote, "Why Past is Past." *Newsweek,* 28 December 1992.

Culligan, Kevin. "Are We Wired for God?" *America* (22 March 1997): 23-24.

Dillard, Annie. *Pilgrim at Tinker Creek.* New York: Harper's Magazine Press, 1974.

_____. *Tickets for a Prayer Wheel.* Columbia, Mo.: University of Missouri Press, 1974.

_____. *Teaching a Stone to Talk.* New York: Harper & Row, 1982.

Dowd, Michael. "The Big Picture – The Larger Context for All Human Activities." In *Proceedings from the John Neumann*

Institute: A Call to Life – Care for Each Other, Care for Earth. Milwaukee: Sacred Heart School of Theology, 1993.

Eckhart, Meister. *Meditations with Meister Eckhart: A Centering Book by Matthew Fox.* Santa Fe: Bear & Company, 1983.

Felch, Susan. "Annie Dillard: Modern Physics in a Contemporary Mystic." *Mosaic: A Journal for the Interdisciplinary Study of Literature* 22 (spring 1989): 1-14.

Franck, Frederick. Introduction to *The Zen of Seeing.* New York: Vintage Books, 1973.

Merchant, Carolyn. *The Death of Nature: Women, Ecology, and the Scientific Revolution.* San Francisco: HarperCollins, 1990.

O'Collins, Gerald, S.J. *Fundamental Theology.* New York: Paulist Press, 1981.

Rahner, Karl. *Foundations of Christian Faith: An Introduction to the Idea of Christianity.* Translated by William V. Dych. New York: Crossroad, 1992.

Chapter Five

Italo Calvino: A Limit at Infinity

Patricia Ann Obremski, S.S.N.D.

Italo Calvino: myth-maker for the twenty-first century, poet laureate of quantumed space, guru to the disciples of wonder. Like an Escher illustration, Italo Calvino experiments with the invisible boundary between space and time.[1] His novel perspectives suspend ordinary viewpoints, daring the reader to enter spacetime as it processes its own destiny, spiraling toward infinity.

"The first things I wrote were realistic . . . [but] the critics said that I tended to transform reality into a fable-like vision."[2] So, out of an inexhaustible reality, out of a self-professed non-scientist's perception of possibilities and pathways, came the imagery and movement of *Cosmicomics* and *t-zero,* works which Calvino considered "among my best books."[3]

In these two works can be found more than the transcendence of ideas – that movement along interconnecting pathways that exist in models of thought. The books themselves cross classification, sometimes found under allegory, fairy tales, the philosophical novel, magical realism, or science fiction. "Calvino, in other words, calls into question established norms of thinking in a way that imparts the idea of the world's transformability."[4] "He has created a genre which weaves the variegated threads of prevailing classi-

---

1. See cover for Italo Calvino, *Cosmicomics,* trans. W. Weaver (Harcourt Brace Jovanovich, 1968); hereafter cited in text as *C.*
2. Italo Calvino, quoted in A. Stille, "An Interview with Italo Calvino," *Saturday Review* (March/April 1985): 39.
3. Ibid.
4. F. Cromphout, "From Estrangement to Commitment: Italo Calvino's *Cosmicomics* and *t-zero,*" *Science Fiction Studies* 16 (July 1989): 183.

fications of literature; . . . he is writing fiction which relativizes existing norms."[5]

There is something for everyone in a surface reading of Calvino's stories – humor, awe, jealousy, longing, malice, adventure, sex. All of these themes, and more, occur without the benefit of location, era, words, even bodies or concrete reality as we know it. The universe, after all, is only evolving the order which will enable it to quantize and direct and support thought. Yet, the reader willingly superimposes present-day experiences on the void of space. To know this is true, one must read Calvino, must experience that the story teller, whether Qfwfq or Calvino, is still the "I."

"A Sign in Space" (*C* 31-39) begins with Qfwfq, who is all eyes and all voice, narrating one of Calvino's "legends and myths of the world of science."[6] Q is riding the rim of the Galaxy and is moved to express himself by means of a sign, a simple something in space with which he could identify, something he could recognize as his own when he passed it again in some 200 million years – give or take a few. This sign is to be something utterly personal and the first one ever made. It would have to be invisible, of course, because there are no lines or curves or dots existing as yet, and no eyes to see them if there were any. It would be just a "something" to change that point in space because "a sign only has to serve as a sign" (*C* 31). Like a word, a name, Q's sign is to be an expression of his essence, a part of himself, an affirmation of Q as Qfwfq.

But who is Qfwfq? He (Q assumes a masculine persona in subsequent stories) personifies a principle of the universe, a quantum potential in operation. Q is quantized because he is given spacetime boundaries, that is, he is discrete; Q is potential because he "embodies" all the possibilities that could begin existence. Even Q's name is a palindrome based on the first law of thermodynamics, which relates internal energy (U) to the energy stored as heat (q) and to the active energy or work exchange (w) occurring constantly in a dynamic system. Since U (Qfwfq's father is Uff) is a function (f) of state which depends on existence alone and not on how that state is reached, (q) and (w) are also functions and depend on each

---

5. Ibid., 162.
6. See Stille, 39.

other. Consequently, Qfwfq's name is a quasi-cyclic device stating, in either direction, that heat (potential) is a function of work (kinetic) which is a function of heat within the state of the universe (U).

Like Bohm's holomovement, the universe begins to unfold itself before Q's consciousness, to actualize what had been enfolded before the great Cosmic Event. "Each region of space and time somehow contains the total order of (that) universe . . . (carrying) information on all parts of reality . . . an unbroken, undivided whole."[7] Qfwfq, then, is an expression of this potential – a prophet of transcendence, an awed perceiver outside the horizon of the events connecting past and future – the very source of all sign.

Qfwfq is sure his sign will be unchanged by time because it is so pure, so simple, so permanently outside the Galaxy. That point in space is now gifted, endowed, elevated in value because Q has touched it, and his "sign was the thing you could think about and also the sign of the thing thought, namely, itself" (*C* 32). The sign not only marked the spot; it also marked Q because it "possessed him entirely" (*C* 30). That sign was truly the expression of Qfwfq himself.

Now, time-space passes, and Q mentally plays with his sign, "derive[s] other signs from it," puts these together in various combinations, compares and contrasts them, and, in his excitement, loses the exactness of the original sign, loses himself in thought, until only the generality of the original sign remains (*C* 33). Not the "why" but the "how" of his sign becomes important to Q, and he begins to try logic, then inductive reasoning, but he cannot reassemble his sign, since he has no original for comparison. "The sign-within-the-sign changed the sign itself" (*C* 34). This transcending universe is becoming very complicated, but all Q has to do is be patient. After all, the sign is out there just waiting for him, isn't it?

In fact, time does not pass quickly. Due to gravity oscillations, three times more time-space passes than Q had expected, and

---

7. See K. Sharpe, *David Bohm's World: New Physics and New Religion* (Lewisburg: Bucknell University Press, 1993), 51.

Qfwfq's anxiety about his sign increases proportionately. At last one revolution is completed and – his sign is gone. Only a "shapeless, scratched, a bruised, chopped abrasion of space" (*C* 35) is there in its place. Q has been violated; his sign, himself, has been erased, effaced, negated. Qfwfq is disconsolate.

Utopia, "the place where harmony, unity, and happiness are," is no more. His abused sign is a sign itself of a new experience:

> the movement from past to present always entails the passage from order to chaos, from unity to division, from happiness to misery – a passage whose emotional impact Qfwfq testifies to in his own 'person' and one which often brings with it his realization that he has been [self-]deceived, the victim of an impersonal con game, as it were.[8]

This thread weaves through all of Calvino's tales; it is an integral part of his philosophy of wholes and parts: "[Calvino] hopes always to find some pattern to [the unharmoniously moving world], a constant."[9] He uses his vision of Utopia as both a "verbal construction and an epistemological system."[10] Calvino expresses this vision further in the recurring themes of longing for the simplicity inherent in nothingness when all is potential, of his irritation with individualism and the proliferation of macro disorder which leaves behind only islands of order in the form of crystals and cells.[11] At the same time the universe is chanting its laws of thermodynamics: You can never win; you can only break even. You can only break even at absolute zero. You can never reach absolute zero. Absolute zero is the state of no disorder; at absolute zero is Perfection.

Meanwhile, Qfwfq notices a "square and careless and clumsily pretentious . . . counterfeit" (*t* 35) of his own sign right there in space. Kgwgk, in another part of the Galaxy, had seen Q's sign and had coveted it for himself. He rubbed out the original and shaped one of his own. Q was not flattered by this imitation; Q

---

8. Cromphout, 165.

9. Gore Vidal, "On Italo Calvino," *The New York Review* 32 (21 November 1985): 6.

10. Cromphout, 181.

11. See Italo Calvino, *t-zero*, trans. W. Weaver (Harcourt Brace Jovanovich, 1969), 28-38; hereafter cited parenthetically in the text as *t*.

was angry. This second sign was different because it was "spoken" by a different, a spiteful source. Did this fact alone make it inferior to Q's own? Or was it just the product of its maker, K (a constant) who is not spontaneously creative and does work (w) according to a different function (g) – a duller quasi-cyclic palindrome?

An idea takes shape in Q. He is moved to make a new sign that will make K even more jealous. With the practice he has had in signmaking, and, since the old is supposed to evolve into a better new, his second sign will be even more perfect than the original one. However, Q experiences only shame for that subsequent sign of himself; it is not even as perfect as his original sign, and he becomes concerned about what others will think of him. So the next time around, he erases the new sign in preparation for a reproduction of the first – only to discover he had completely forgotten it. The Utopian space had been spontaneously changed by Q's creative expression, and Q, who had projected his very identity by that sign, found his self deliberately changed by a force outside his control. He, in response, had provoked a greater change. "The sign that he has made makes him."[12]

Having forgotten that pure sign, Qfwfq decides to make false signs and let others copy them, let them expand on the idea of sign even to the fourth-dimension, time. In time, the world became crowded with hieroglyphics and ideograms and even eyes on peacocks' tails. Still Q longs for his own true sign and continues to look for the imprint of it, his self, in graffiti and skid marks and chromosomes, only to find instead a "general thickening of signs superimposed and coagulated, occupying the whole volume of space" (*C* 39).

Because the signs defined space, and "independent of signs, space didn't exist and perhaps never existed" (*C* 39), Qfwfq continues to look for himself. He is sure that, even though others have copied and modified it, his name is buried in some sign-heap under all those overlapping symbols. Space – chaotic, littered – still holds that perfect sign, that perfect Word, spoken by a Transcendent.

---

12. Cromphout, 174.

There is certainly a "being beyond the limits of experience and hence unknowable,"[13] a transcendent quality to the experiences of Q. He may look like a physical formulation of some objective reality, but he is his author's intuition of the possible. Calvino climbs into the uncharted, unmapped unknown, and pulls Q right along with him.

In "Games Without End" (*C* 63-68), we find Qfwfq intimately acquainted with each hydrogen atom in the universe. As a monad himself, an "invisible and impenetrable unit of substance viewed as a basic constituent element of physical reality,"[14] Q can identify with those univalent hydrogens – all proton and electron. He and his friend, Pfwfp, roll those atoms along the curve of space, trying not to lose them, trying not to knock them together to form deuterium (proton, electron, neutron) or trigger a thermonuclear reaction and get helium (2 protons, 2 electrons, 2 neutrons).

Pfwfp is a momentum (p) figure. He is another youngster about Q's age, whose name could well relate to Heisenberg's Uncertainty Principle: one cannot predict the momentum of a body (mass times velocity) and its position (x) at the same time. This poses a different way to look at work (w) which relates force and distance (x). Pfwfp, then, is an unpredictable figure relating momentum as a function of work. This palindrome is depicted as an opportunist, sly and predatory, greedy and vindictive. Nevertheless, P and Q dabble in transcendence as they play the game of galaxy-building.

To play this game, one has to know the effects of fields: gravitational, magnetic, and electric. If any collision brings about a change, the player has to forfeit a hydrogen atom to his opponent. The one who loses all his atoms, loses the game. Any new, bright and shiny hydrogens that might appear are to be shared equally.

But just as suddenly as hydrogen atoms begin to appear, they stop appearing, and Q and P begin to play their game with caution so as not to lose any atoms unnecessarily. This is when all fun goes out of the sport; this is when Qfwfq notices that Pfwfp is becoming

---

13. *The American Heritage College Dictionary*, s.v. "transcendence."
14. Cromphout, 181.

rather secretive and starts to forget to appear for his turn to shoot. This is also when a curious Q decides to follow P.

The fact is that P has found a wrinkle in space, a place where new atoms are formed, and has begun to haunt this spot, snatching up any shiny hydrogens as soon as they come into being. He hides the new atoms for future use by disguising them to look like old ones – even though a new one is worth three old ones in the game. It is this deceit that moves Qfwfq to decide to trap P, to punish him for being unsportsmanlike.

Out of "photoelectric radiation, scrapings from magnetic fields, [and] a few neutrons," all held together with a bit of saliva, Q constructs some false hydrogen atoms (*C* 65). He then substitutes his quasi-hydrogens for the real ones formed in their space pocket. Deceit for deceit gives Q new atoms for his game, while P collects and saves the false ones.

At this point, Qfwfq suggests a new game. He flings his good atoms into space, where they form a cloud, which condenses to form constellations that spiral away, an excited Q swept along with them. However, when Pfwfp tries to follow, his bad hydrogens sizzle and pop, leaving P spacebound, while Q proudly displays his latest, shiniest galaxy to the universe. P is not pleased.

Eventually, Pfwfp collects enough good hydrogen atoms to create his own galaxy. He chases Q until they enter a dimension with an edge that acts like a double mirror, splitting time so that P chases Q who chases P in an infinite series of reflections. Now neither can overtake the other as they become caught in a spacetime dilation. They have become mirror images of each other, trapped by their own game – which is now truly no fun at all.

Transcending matterenergy and spacetime, ordinary atoms evolve into galaxies of stars as Q and P enter their new space. Their new dimension holds a single event between past and future in a constant repetition of the present – certainly beyond the limits of experience, but, in a sense, perhaps not. In "t-zero," a story in which a more sophisticated, future Qfwfq dilates the present moment by freezing a pouncing lion as well as an arrow that has just been released at that lion, Q speculates on time lines which can branch and intersect, and on the myriad of possible, very personal, outcomes that could be experienced as a result (*t* 95-111).

Reliving such a moment when time seems to stand still is intensely human.

"Reading Calvino," his friend, Gore Vidal writes, "I had the unnerving sense that I was also writing what he had written; thus does his art prove his case as writer and reader become one, or One."[15] To this Calvino responded in a letter, ". . . and to close all my discourse and yours in a perfect circle, let us say that this One is All."[16] His closing statement exposes the philosophy which ties together his writings: The whole and its parts are inseparable. "It [time] can be described, instant by instant, and each instant, when described, expands so that its end can no longer be seen."[17]

"Each second is a universe. . . ." Inside t_0, I, Q_0, am not in the least determined by my past (Q_{-3}, Q_{-2}, Q_{-1}), nor have to worry about what will happen to Q_1, Q_2, Q_3, etc. (t 108). "To stay still in time I must move in time, to become objective I must remain subjective" (t 109). As P and Q reflect their shared experience, Qfwfq might wonder if the atomic toss was worth it.

In the three stories retold, the gaming spirit evokes chance: the luck of the shot, the toss of the atom, the release of the sign. Science says that energy (Q) was first, followed by matter (P), and that they remain interactive but separate entities until they approach the speed of light – hanging on to the tail of a galaxy, mirrored at the edge of infinity. At this point in the universe, the boundaries between matter and energy disappear, and matterenergy, the common element in each, is unmasked. Q and P have become joined in the mirror of light.

Yet another tale of Q, "How Much Shall We Bet?" (C 85-93), has to do with wagering and the logic linking a chain of events, predictability. This type of logic involves a series of feedback loops which give the individual events direction: gravity, centripetal force, nuclear interactions. Potential, Qfwfq, and the status quo, (k)yk (who later bestows on himself the title, "Dean") are the only characters involved in this probability adventure.

---

15. See Vidal, 8.

16. Italo Calvino, quoted in Vidal, 8.

17. Ibid., 10.

(k)yk is not quite symmetric or balanced. His head wears parentheses, but he lacks imagination to justify the emphasis. (k) has a determined or independent variable, y, giving him a "static sense of reality" (C 87). He is a good foil for the spontaneous Qfwfq, who is intuitive and bold enough to wager on transcendence.

In this story, Q feels a change coming on, a slight chill as though something were going to solidify into atoms, and so he bets (k) that a universe will appear – and it does. His winning proves to him that he exists. But, like searching for the sign in space, Qfwfq needs a further confirmation of his being, so he maneuvers (k) into an opposing position and continues to wager. Q wins again – and again – and again. Soon so many bets have been placed that Q and (k) invent signs to keep track of them. They then use these "words" for betting and tallying. The only numbers are "e," which is the base of the natural logarithmic system (2.718...), and "π," a transcendental number which relates the circumference of a circle to its diameter (3.141 . . .). (k)yk bets that stars will grow to "e" to the "π" power, but Q bets they will stop at "π," a natural circumference. Qfwfq wins again.

After numerous successes, Q "hypothesizes on the probability of forming an hypothesis" (*C* 87), and his imagination leads him to take greater and greater chances. He concludes from his results that imagination can be both an advantage and a disadvantage; (k), however, is not concerned. Once (k)yk understands a word, he cannot conceive of it having any other meaning. (k) is static.

One of Q's big losses, one which is ours today, involves the rarest of atoms, technitium (Tc), which he hoards in order to hedge his bets. The element was unstable, underwent nuclear change, and became something else of little value. All was lost because of a short half-life of 2.6 million years. This time (k) wins, but only because of Q's hedge and over-confidence.

The more Qfwfq projects, the more he understands the mechanisms involved. Once he can calculate in a rational manner, however, the game loses its appeal. To renew interest, Q begins to wager on the outcome of historical events, and as long as he uses combinations of concrete realities and macro conditions, he is highly successful and affirmed.

As Q and (k) race into the future, alternatives seem to predominate, and events become measured on a smaller scale. By this time Qfwfq is a compulsive gambler, giving the advantage to a conservative (k) – realizing he is doing so, yet unable to stop. His failures are primarily linked to events involving human decision-making, or caprice. Free will does not factor into any of Q's equations; and (k) doesn't realize why he is winning – only that he is.

For Q there is no certainty; chance seems to rule outcomes once again; corruption follows. (k), now Dean (k)yk, and still unable to figure out why Qfwfq is losing, is very busy crowing about his successes. There is a multimillion dollar funding agency to finance their game now and, for the Dean, the future is golden.

Indeed, transcendence is not always predictable. When free will became a moving force, the signs of the times became relative, became linked to each individual's lived experience. Simplicity succumbed to "progress." Calvino realizes this condition and uses a newspaper to represent the assembly of information or unformed matter. Reported events, while elating (k) who is winning just by wagering against Q, have become "intrinsically illegible" to Q (*C* 93). Like Calvino, he longs for a less complicated time. They both would like to go back to the beginning, in which simplicity would reign once again.

Each of the nine physical science stories which comprise *Cosmicomics*, as well as those which make up two-thirds of *t-zero*, is prefaced by a statement of the scientific basis for the tale. Current science may have reevaluated or modified or expanded some of the theories Calvino used, but they remained essentially true in his lifetime.[18] In a dynamic universe, changing perspectives are necessary for survival – (k) won't last, but Qfwfq is a survivor!

Paul Baumann, discussing Calvino, refers to his "labyrinthine schematic" which "posits the world as a system of systems, where each system contains the others and is contained by them." This is

18. See, e.g., I. Nicolson and P. Moore, *The Universe* (New York: Macmillan, 1985), chapter 26; W. Kaufmann, *Universe,* 3d ed. (New York: W. H. Freeman, 1985), 170-88; Zeilik/Gaustad, *Astronomy: The Cosmic Perspective,* 2d ed. (New York: J. Wiley & Sons, 1990), 225ff., 237-42.

the "mosaic in which man is set"; "geometric compositions modeled on the cosmologies of modern science" appear and disappear until "chance will win the battle."[19] Calvino, "the craft-conscious aesthete, [was] inspired to fashion transcendent beauty on the brink of the void" where "imagination participates in the truth of the world,"[20] and literature "gives speech to that which has no language." To him "relativism and the uncertainty of all things is a liberation. Even the self [Q] floats free."[21] Lovelock, who proposed the Gaia principle with its feedback systems for healing the whole Earth,[22] and Chardin, who envisioned an Omega point as the origin and destiny of all created beings,[23] would feel comfortable with Calvino.

Calvino once wrote that "a literary work can succeed in making us forget it as such, but it leaves its seed in us. We use the word 'classic' of a book that takes the form of an equivalent to the universe, on a level with the ancient talismans, [and] a classic is a book that has never finished saying what it has to say. We do not read the classics out of duty or respect, but out of love."[24] Calvino's own words designate *Cosmicomics* and *t-zero* as classic literature, and they have lost none of their character in translation.

When Italo Calvino died in 1985, at the age of 62, Europe regarded his death as a calamity. But Calvino was attuned to transcending, and left this message in words which Qfwfq, himself, might say some day when the universe finally collapses:

> First of all, you must not confuse being dead with not being, a condition that occupies the vast expanse of time before birth, apparently symmetrical with the other, equally vast expanse that follows it. In fact before birth we are part of the infinite possibilities that may or may

---

19. Bauman, 339.

20. Ibid., 340.

21. Ibid., 341.

22. See J. E. Lovelock, *Gaia: A New Look at Life on Earth* (New York: Oxford University Press, 1987), especially 48-63.

23. See Teilhard de Chardin, *Science and Christ*, trans. R. Hague (New York: Harper & Row, 1965), 48.

24. Italo Calvino, "Why Read the Classics?" *The New York Review* 33 (October 1986): 19.

not be fulfilled, whereas, once dead, we cannot fulfill ourselves either in the past (to which we now belong entirely, but on which we can no longer have any influence) or in the future (which, even if influenced by us, remains forbidden to us). A person's life consists of a collection of events, the last of which could also change the meaning of the whole. If time has an end, it can be described, instant by instant, and each instant, when described, expands so that its end can no longer be seen.[25]

With this sentiment Calvino/Qfwfq would seem to have wagered and won transcendence – the simplicity and purity of an unbounded eternity shared with the Transcendent One.

Author's Note:

The poet in Italo Calvino seems to enjoy papering the void of prehistory with signs and symbols, characters and covenants, which give expression to an emerging universe. The natural scientist in Calvino bets on the mysteries he imagines enfolded in his undefined Now. The communicator in Calvino provides a unique experience for future generations of time travellers.

Throughout his adventures, whether as author or as Qfwfq, Calvino is energized by the freedom associated with beginnings, where the desire for self-expression conflicts with the yearning for the predictably simple. This condition leads Q (and the reader) to ask the big questions: Where do I, spontaneous and creative, fit in the stream of space-time? What can possibly happen next to challenge my existence? Why is change so inevitable? How are freedom and order related? Whatever opportunity for progress occurs, is it worth the risk? And who holds the Master Plan? Who transforms, transmits, transcends?

P.A.O.

---

25. Italo Calvino, quoted in Vidal, 10.

Appendix A

In addition to the quantized, thermodynamic Qfwfq, Calvino populates his prehistory with other formulae who embody some important aspect of the dynamics of the tale, or who are apparently there for their own sake – like the sign in space. An interpretation of the symbols does not appear in the literature, so the author has taken the liberty to devise an identity for some of Calvino's many characters, in addition to those already mentioned in the body of this paper.

Uff is Q's father. Since internal energy (U) equals $q + w$, according to the first law of thermodynamics, this is a good name for the progenitor of Qfwfq. His father is the source of energy and functionality (f).

Q's mother is unnamed. She is described as "flighty" or nonscientific, in contrast to his father and Q himself. Perhaps she really represents the creative, intuitive side of Qfwfq.

Rwzfs is Q's brother. He is unsymmetric and a function of entropy or disorder (fs). The "z" could stand for atomic number, which could make "r" a radial distribution, as in atomic theory. Work (w) is related to matter as well. He likes to lose himself in the emerging matter nebula; he is very young and unformed as yet.

$G'd(w)^n$ is Q's sister, who is shy and creative and empowers or activates her environment. She could stand for gravity (G), which slopes (d) or directs work (w) in the environment. The degree of work is to the nth. She disappears into the heart of the elemental cloud, which eventually condenses into Earth or Gaia.

Granny Bb'b also belongs to Q's family, along with the twins and a female cousin, X/th/X. Granny comes from the era just after the Cosmic Event or Big Bang, when light, the first element of creation, was intensely experienced. Perhaps her name refers to coming shortly after the event or point A. The twins are unnamed, but the cousin could relate to the partitioning of a probability function, X.

Captain VhdVhd directs the moon mission and is a very earthy character. His name is linear and repetitive, like the rowing of a boat. It links velocity (v) with distance (d) through Planck's constant (h), or "h" could just refer to another symbol for a function.

In that case the Captain is indeed Earth-bound, because velocity is a function of distance. The name could also represent volume (V), with "h" representing height ($V = \pi r^2 h$, where d, diameter, equals 2r, or twice the radius). Volume would be appropriate for someone who works on water.

The feminine elements related to Qfwfq may have formulae softened with apostrophes, digraphs, diphthongs, or vowels. Of special interest is Ayl, his Earthly love, who is reminiscent of Ayla, in the Earth Children Series of novels by Jean Auel. Ayl may be the root for ayle (grandfather) and ayla (grandmother).

Mrs. $Ph(i)Nk_0$, in her orange dressing gown, is a warm and generous and nurturing being – and the object of Q's lust. As "energy-light-heat," her total knowledge of the individual radiates throughout space (k_0) from numerous starry locations (N). She is all heart (i), and movement (p, as in momentum) near the speed of light (h, as in Plank's constant, $h = E/f$).

In the last analysis, it could have been that Calvino simply leafed through a physics text until he found a combination of letters that pleased his eye or ear or was sufficiently interesting to tease his reader – like Mr. Hnw, who later in time became a horse, and Mr. Pber^t Pber^t (leadertee-leadertee), of the silver tooth and loud suspenders.

Appendix B

Not only is the imagery in Calvino's tales vivid, but the language is beautiful, even in translation. Following are free verse renditions of some of his passages, which indicate yet another aspect of Calvino's genius.

PROGRESS

And I think
how beautiful it was then,
through that void,
to draw lines and parabolas,
pick out the precise point,
the intersection
between space and time where

the event would spring
forth, undeniable
in the prominence of its glow;
whereas
now events came flowing down
without interruption . . .
intrinsically illegible. . . . (*C* 93)

FOSSILS

. . . looking
at the skeleton,
the Father,
the Brother,
my counterpart,
my self;
I recognized
my fleshless limbs,
my lineaments carved
in the stone,
everything
we had been
and were no longer,
our majesty,
our faults,
our ruin. (*C* 109)

ON THE RISING MOON

. . . it had become
much smaller, it kept
contracting, as if
my gaze were driving it away,
and the emptied sky gaped
like an abyss where
at the bottom, the stars
had begun multiplying
and the night
poured a river of emptiness

over me, drowned men
in dizziness and alarm. (*C* 12)

Works Cited

Bauman, Paul. "Mosaics, Magicians, and Mystery." *Commonweal* (2 June 1989): 339-41.

Calvino, Italo. *Cosmicomics.* Translated by W. Weaver. New York: Harcourt Brace Jovanovich, 1968. Cover Illustration, *Other World,* by Escher.

_____. *t-zero.* Translated by W. Weaver. New York: Harcourt Brace Jovanovich, 1969.

_____. "Why Read the Classics?" *The New York Review* 33 (9 October 1986): 19-20.

Chardin, Teilhard de. *Science and Christ.* Translated by R. Hague. New York: Harper & Row, 1965.

Cromphout, F. "From Estrangement to Commitment: Italo Calvino's *Cosmicomics* and *t-zero.* " *Science-Fiction Studies* 16 (July 1989): 161-83.

Kaufmann, W. *Universe,* 3d ed. New York: W. H. Freeman & Co., 1985.

Lovelock, J. E. *Gaia: A New Look at Life on Earth.* New York: Oxford University Press, 1987.

Nicolson, I. and P. Moore. *The Universe.* New York: Macmillan, 1985.

Sharpe, K. *David Bohm's World: New Physics and New Religion.* Lewisburg, PA: Bucknell University Press, 1993.

Stille, A. "An Interview with Italo Calvino." *Saturday Review* (March/April 1985): 37-39.

Vidal, Gore. "On Italo Calvino." *The New York Review* 32 (21 November 1985): 3-10.

Zeilik, M. and J. Gaustad. *Astronomy: The Cosmic Perspective,* 2d ed. New York: J. Wiley & Sons, 1990.

III.

Time and Space

Chapter Six

Czeslaw Milosz and the Many Aspects of Time

Mary Hester Valentine, S.S.N.D.

Admirers of the work of Czeslaw Milosz, whom Joseph Brodsky classifies as one of the greatest poets of our time, perhaps the greatest,[1] have been distressed by the fact that there has been relatively little appraisal of this Nobel prize-winning poet by American critics. I belong to that number, although writing this essay has helped me to understand somewhat the reason for the neglect. The author's interests are so wide, his philosophical probing so deep, his education – both academic and life-developed – so solid, his biography almost a personal history of our troubled century, his writing, both prose and poetry, such a rich body of work, that it is difficult to do justice to even a limited area of study, or even to decide upon an area for analysis. Add to this the fact that as of late 1996, Milosz seems to be still vigorously writing.

The fact that Milosz's poetry, even today, is written in Polish is not, in itself, a deterrent, for while usually the reader may wonder to what an extent a translation expresses the poet's original, that is not the case with translations of Milosz. His is the unique case of a poet who either translated himself, or actively collaborated with his translators. As his friends and cotranslators, Leonard Nathan and Arthur Quinn point out, the English versions of his work give a rare opportunity of dealing with translations which, even though they differ to some extent from the original, for natural

---

1. Joseph Brodsky, quoted in Leonard Nathan and Arthur Quinn, *The Poet's Work. An Introduction to Czeslaw Milosz* (Cambridge, Mass.: Harvard University Press, 1991), vii; hereafter cited parenthetically in the text as *PW*.

linguistic and cultural reasons, are still texts for which Milosz assumed total responsibility (*PW* 10).

The wide range of Milosz's interests is an embarrassment of riches for anyone embarking on an analysis of the work of this extraordinary man. His Nobel lecture gives some hint of what he himself considers important: the choice is never between ideas, world views or philosophies, although they may provide a background for his statements. For him the "moral obligations are to people," and he questions how we are to exercise those responsibilities to those no longer alive: "those who are alive receive a mandate from those who are silent forever."[2] With Einstein he believes time is always relative to the measurer.

Milosz's preoccupation with the mystery of time and its frozen counterpart, memory, reality and the eternal values, with responsibility and guilt – dark, sinister shadows in the background – rests upon God as base. There are other issues that absorb him, but these are the major ones, none of which is handled superficially, for this man is not only a sensitive participant in history, but a seer whose insights probe deep into the causes and results of what he has experienced.

To cover Milosz's treatment of time in all its implications would require a book, and I am reminded of C. S. Lewis' comment that all women and mostly old women like gnomic poetry, and thus very literally a comment on life. They use it rather as their grandmothers would have used proverbs or biblical texts. But Lewis also has hard things to say of the sophisticated literary reader who sometimes *uses* poetry instead of receiving it. I have elected to be Lewis' old woman, and to follow his later recommendation that the reader enjoy the poems in themselves.

The mystery of time has fascinated human beings from the earliest philosophers to contemporary humans. Milosz appears to have brooded on the various definitions, and his awareness of their complexity has frequently found form in poetry. Not all of it is cheerful, but that is to be expected, for someone has said that time, divided by life, equals death; it is the deadly equation with time as the unknown. Milosz himself experienced the underside of the

---

2. Czeslaw Milosz, *Nobel Lecture* (New York: Farrar Straus Giroux, 1980), 138.

world, living as a forced worker during the Nazi invasion of Poland and the later Communist takeover under Stalin. But what is remarkable is his awareness of the top side, too, where there is wonder, ecstasy, love and friendship. He himself recognizes this duality; at Berkeley he said that nothing could stifle his inner certainty that a shining point exists where all lines intersect. He repeats the idea in "Treatise":

> . . . here at the edge
> Of what lasts and what does not, two lines intersect.
> Time lifted above time by time. (*PW* 55)

It is interesting to see how all the philosophical and linguistic analyses of time are assessed and assimilated in the poems. Philologists trace the word *time* to an old Teutonic root denoting "to extend."[3] Milosz in "The Year" says, "I looked around in the unknown year, aware that few are those / who come from so far. I was saturated with sunlight as a plant with water. / . . . At the very border of inhabited time the same lessons were being learned, how to walk on two legs and to pronounce the signs traced in the always childish book of our species."[4]

The Romans and Greeks derived their word *time* from Sanskrit roots meaning light and burning, and there are echoes of that definition in "A Legend":

> For a country without a past is nothing, a word
> That, hardly spoken, loses its meaning
> A perishable wall destroyed by flame. . . .
> The ashes of centuries mixed with fresh blood.
> (*CP* 103-4)

According to Plato, time is the moving image of eternity, or the everlasting image of revolving.[5] Milosz plays with this idea, whether consciously or unconsciously, when he says, "Without time we are nothing; we require a temporal eternity" (quoted in *PW* 55). Reflecting further, he writes in "Dithyramb,"

---

3. *Oxford English Dictionary*, 2d ed., s.v. "time."

4. Czeslaw Milosz, *The Collected Poems 1931-1987* (New York: Ecco Press, 1988), 183; hereafter cited parenthetically in the text as *CP*.

5. See *Plato*, Timaeus, in *Plato with an English Translation*, ed. Rev. R. G. Bury (Cambridge, Mass.: Harvard University Press, 1942), 37C; 39E; 47B; 49C.

A new ordering
Of forms reborn, expressing avidly
the truth that should make continents tremble;
it arrives silently. . . .

But then he adds a strictly new, non-Platonic interpretation:

For now a flame descends and cleaves the earthly house,
God is here, and evil is here. And immortality is given.[6]

For St. Augustine, if time is a measure of change, it demands a present beyond the fleeting instant and above bodily motion.[7] Time is a distention of the soul, with future and past segments stretching bilaterally from the distended present of attention. In his Nobel lecture, Milosz echoes Augustine with twentieth-century insights when he says,

And how to be above and simultaneously to see the earth in every detail? And yet, in a precarious balance of opposites, a certain equilibrium can be achieved, thanks to a distance introduced by the flow of time. *To see* means not only to have before one's eyes. It may also mean to preserve in memory. . . . A distance achieved, thanks to the mystery of time, must not change human figures into a tangle of shadows growing paler and paler. On the contrary, it can show them in full light, so that every event, every date becomes expressive and persists as an eternal reminder of human depravity and human greatness.[8]

Kant transplants absolute time into human sensibility. To him a time cut off from events is a preposterous void, for the fact is that awareness of motion precedes awareness of time. Czeslaw Milosz echoed this idea with a personal shade of distinction in "The Year," when he wrote, "I looked around in the unknown year, aware that few are those / who come from so far. . . ." (*CP* 183) and in "With Trumpets and Zithers,"

---

6. Quoted in Edward Możejko, *Between Anxiety and Hope: The Poetry and Writing of Czeslaw Milosz* (Alberta: The University of Alberta Press, 1988), 60.

7. *Confessions of St. Augustine,* trans. F. J. Sheed (New York: Sheed and Ward, 1945), 11, 14, 17, 28, 39.

8. Czeslaw Milosz, *Nobel Lecture,* 252.

And on the roads of my terrestrial homeland / turning round with the music of the spheres / I thought that all I could do would be done better one day. (*CP* 196, 202)

To Bergson, one recovers real time in the primacy of change. For him each state of unceasingly changing psychic life melts into its neighbor as an unbreakable flood. Milosz has parallel intuitions, but they bear the mark of his personal history and Christian orientation. For example, again and again he links his individual experiences with that of all humanity, with special emphasis on contemporary history, that bitter history of which he is a survivor. He says of poetry and its relation to life and time: "Whoever commits himself to movement alone will destroy himself. Whoever disregards movement will also destroy himself, but in a different way. This, I said to myself, is the very core of my destiny – never to be satisfied with one or the other, only at moments to seize the unity of these opposites."[9] For him, "We must not forget the unchanging element that allows us to make contact with the peoples of past civilizations."[10]

Milosz admits that as an eyewitness to the crime of genocide he was deprived of the luxury of innocence. "I am prone to agree with the accusations brought against myself and others. In reality, however, it is not so easy to judge, because the price of aiding the victims of terror was the death penalty" (*NR* 105). His colleagues, Nathan and Quinn, analyze the poem "To Raja Rao" in terms of its relationship to Eastern Nirvana, but to me it is equally Milosz's personal response to our century's guilt.

Raja, this did not cure me
of my guilt and shame.
A shame of failing to be
what I should have been.

The image of myself
grows gigantic on the wall

---

9. Czeslaw Milosz, *Native Realm: A Search for Self-Definition* (Berkeley: University of California Press, 1981), 276; hereafter cited parenthetically in the text as *NR*.

10. Czeslaw Milosz, *Beginning with my Streets* (New York: Farrar, Straus, Giroux, 1991), 185; hereafter cited parenthetically in the text as *BWMS*.

and against it
my miserable shadow.

That's how I came to believe
in Original Sin
which is nothing but the first
victory of the ego. . . . (*CP* 227)

In his analysis, the individual is stretched between two poles
in time – the contemplation of the motionless point and the
command to participate actively in history – in other words,
between transcendence and becoming. He acknowledged that he
did not manage to bring those extremes into a unity, that he did
not want to give either of them up. In this he speaks to the guilt
of all of us, the survivors, of the subterranean distance where
history weighs secretly upon us:

We needed God loving us in our weakness
And not in the glory of beatitude.

No help, Raja, my part is agony,
struggle, abjection, self-love and self-hate. . . .
(*CP* 227-28)

Ruminating on Bergson's primacy of change, Milosz remembers in
"Café,"

Of those at the table in the café
where on winter noons a garden of frost glittered on
window panes
I alone survived.
I could go in there if I wanted to
. . . .
With disbelief I touch the cold marble,
with disbelief I touch my own hand.
It – is, and I – am, in ever novel becoming,
while they are locked forever and ever
In their last word, their last glance,

. . . .
. . . The waiter whirls with his tray,
and they look at me with a burst of laughter
for I still don't know what it is to die at the hand of man,
they know – they know it well. (*CP* 62-63)

In "Dictionary of Wilno Streets" he returns to his version of Bergson's psychic life in time. "Here there is no earlier and no later; the seasons of the year, and of the day are simultaneous" (*BWMS* 51).

One such moment is captured in a poem:

We were riding through frozen fields
in a wagon at dawn.
A red wing rose in the darkness.
And suddenly a hare ran across the road.
One of us pointed to it with his hand.
That was long ago. Today neither of them is alive.
Not the hare, not the man who made the gesture.
O my love, where are they, where are they going?
The flash of a hand, streak of movement, rustle of pebbles.
I ask not out of sorrow, but in wonder. (*CP* 27)

and in another:

Between the moment and the moment I lived through
much in my sleep. / so distinctly that I felt time dissolve
/ and knew that what was past still is, not was. (*CP* 150)

Heidegger's theories fascinated Milosz for a while, but he finally rejected them, or rather, as he did so often, changed them to accord with his own perceptions. Heidegger derives his conception of time through noting that *Dasein* or a human being is a being traveling toward death; for him the future is primary in primordial time. Humans become fully human by projecting themselves into the future to illumine the banal present and transfigure the inertial past. For him the primitive-lived time, or the "I-time" is the felt sense of duration in the person as shaped by his past and advancing toward his future. Echoes of Heidegger's thought, the more universal, slipped into Milosz's poetry.

Milosz had lived through the ever-present threat of immediate death, not the universal, inevitable death sentence passed on every person at birth, but the violent shattering of life which time has always seen as a dominant reality. In "Sons of Adrian Zielinski" he says,

. . . What are centuries,
What is history? I hack out each day
And it's a century to me. (*CP* 68)

In "City Without a Name," he elaborates:

> Unexpressed, untold
> But how?
> The shortness of life,
> The years quicker and quicker,
> not remembering whether it happened in this or that
> autumn. (*CP* 188)

He is even more emphatic in "From the Rising of the Sun, VII: Bells of Winter":

> Yet, I belong to those who believe in *apokatastasis,*
> That word promises reverse movement.
> Not the one that was set in *katastasis,*
> and appears in the *Acts,* 3, 21.
> It means: restoration. So believed St. Gregory of Nyssa.
> . . . .
> For me, therefore, everything has a double existence.
> Both in time and when time shall be no more. (*CP* 310)

For Milosz the contemplation of time becomes eschatological. In fact, he does not believe that a noneschatological poetry is possible, for it would be a poetry indifferent to the existence of the Past-Future axis, and to the last things: Salvation and Damnation, Judgment, the Kingdom of God, the goal of History, in other words, to everything that connects the time assigned to one human life with the life of all humanity.

Milosz insists, "This goes against the grain of our civilization, shaped as it is by the Bible, and for that reason, eschatological to the core."[11] There is, inevitably, the human questioning, "Why all this ardor if death is so close?" (*CP* 363):

> You, God, have mercy on me.
> From the earth's greedy mouth deliver me,
> cleanse me of her untrue songs" (*CP* 8)

Milosz turns the anonymity of death to:

> . . . I, a faithful son of the black earth shall return to the
> black earth.

---

11. Czeslaw Milosz, *The Witness of Poetry: The Charles Eliot Norton Lectures* (Cambridge, Mass.: Harvard University Press, 1983), 37.

as if my life had not been,
as if my heart, not my blood,
not my duration
had created words and songs,
but an unknown, impersonal voice. . . . (*CP* 13)

Personal grief in the death of those long loved is expressed in "To Joseph Sadzik":

The Living is too closely bound to the living
For me to recognize the power of closed borders,
And to consent to leave you, alive,
By an underground river, in the realm of shadows. . .

But Milosz transforms that grief into triumphant faith:

Let the Communion of the Saints triumph,
And a purifying fire, here and everywhere
Together with our common rising from the dead
Toward Him, who is, was, and will be. (*BAH* 110)

In the beautiful poem to his mother, Milosz forces on us literal fact and poetic counterpoint to grief:

Those poor, arthritically swollen knees
Of my mother, in an absent country.
I think of them on my seventy-fourth birthday,
As I attend early Mass at St. Mary Magdalen in Berkeley.
A reading this Sunday from the Book of Wisdom.
About how God has not made death
And does not rejoice in the annihilation of the living.
A reading from the Gospel according to Mark
About a little girl to whom He said, "Talitha, cumi!"
This is for me. To make me rise from the dead
And repeat the hope of those who lived before me,
In a fearful unity with her, with her pain of dying
In a village near Danzig, in a dark November,
When both the mournful Germans, old men and women,
And the evacuees from Lithuania would fall ill with typhus.
Be with me, I say to her, my time has been short.
Your words are now mine, deep inside me;
"It all seems now to have been a dream." (*CP* 453)

Compassion, which Milosz calls that "ache of imagination," permeates his poem "Old Women," and with the compassion is the perception of the hidden glory linked with their personal time span.

Arthritically bent, in black, spindle-legged,
They move, leaning on canes, to the altar where the Pantocrator
In a dawn of gilded rays lifts his two fingers.
The mighty, radiant face of the All-Potent
In whom everything was created, whatever is on the earth and in Heaven,
To whom are submitted the atom and the scale of galaxies,
Rises over the heads of His servants, covered with their shawls,
While into their shriveled mouths they receive
His flesh . . .
He, who has been suffering for ages rescues
Ephemeral moths, tired-winged butterflies in the cold,
Genetrixes with the closed scars of their wombs,
And carries them up to His human Theotokos,
So that the ridicule and pain change into majesty
And thus it is fulfilled, late without charms and colors,
Our imperfect, earthly love. (*CP* 454)

Milosz's poetry keeps returning to that moment of time which St. Catherine called "the point of the needle," the moment of our individual death, when our personal span of time crumbles into the unknown dimensions of eternity. One can see it on the horizon as age begins the slow process of diminishment, and Milosz captures that personal awareness in a number of strong poems. He acknowledges that "there is a certain amount of grief when you are in advanced age, because you are accustomed to look forward, to plan for the future, and you realize that you have little time – many plans will probably have to be suspended, though, of course, we never know the day or hour of our death" (*BWMS* 146). He remembers that old people of traditional religion yearn for a day of comprehension; they wonder when we all will finally reach "that shore . . . from which at last we see how all this came to pass, and for what reason" (see *PW* 112). He struggles to remember, to call up his mother, but the memory has faded, and he laments: "O what happened and when to *principium individuationis*?" (see *PW* 115).

He notes that "the sick man constantly sees time as an hour glass through which states, systems, and civilization trickle like sand; his immediate surroundings lose the force of reality; they do not last at all; they disintegrate; in other words, being is unreal, only movement is real" (*NR* 261-62). The paradox is that in all this dwelling upon death there are strong elements not only of faith-based hope for the future, but a joyful recognition of the sun shining in the now-time. In "A Mistake" he says, .

> I thought: all this is only preparation
> For learning, at last, how to die.
> . . . .
> . . . We have a beautiful time
> As long as time is time at all. (*CP* 222)

Milosz provides a partly amused and wholly rueful assessment of his place in world history.

> THE ACCUSER
> Oh yes, not all of me shall die, there will remain
> An item in the fourteenth volume of an encyclopedia
> Next to a hundred Millers and Mickey Mouse. . . .
> (*CP* 301, 307)

Of Milosz, for whom time is both tangible and elusive, Cardinal Myszynski, the late Primate of Poland said, on awarding him an honorary degree, "In the effort of lonely navigation through history the man named Czeslaw Milosz is supported by a vision of God Incarnate, which exists in each deliverance of man from bondage" (*BAH* 18). Milosz corroborates this in "Bells in Winter," when he says,

> For me, . . . everything has a double existence.
> Both in time and when time shall be no more. (*CP* 310)

and in his paraphrase of the prophets,

> For God himself enters Death's Door always with those
>   that enter
> And lies down in the Grave with them, in Visions of
>   Eternity
> Till they awake and see Jesus and the Linen Clothes lying
> That the Females had woven for them, and the Gates of
>   their Father's House. (*CP* 313)

There is personal linking of past and present and the potential future in the poem "1913": "Young again, yet identical with my older self" (*CP* 313).

Because Christ entered Death's door, and in doing so broke the chains of time, Milosz was able to write: " 'Christ has risen.' Whoever believes that / should not behave as we do" (*CP* 490). In "Lecture VI" he explores the Divine-time relationship:

> Boundless history lasted in that moment
> When he was breaking bread and drinking wine.
> They were being born, they desired, they died.
> My God, what crowds! How is it possible
> That all of them wanted to live and are no more?
> . . . .
> Simultaneously, now, here, every day
> Bread is changed into flesh, wine into blood,
> And the impossible, what no one can bear,
> Is again accepted, and acknowledged. (*CP* 492)

In "Throughout Our Lands" he notes the passage of time:

> Between the moment and the moment I lived through
> much in my sleep
> so distinctly that I felt time dissolve
> and knew that what was past still is, not was. (*CP* 149)

For Milosz, what really counts is today, or rather, what we are going to do today with any inheritance we have, which exemplifies the belief that present and past are inextricably bound so long as time exists. He is even conscious that time may exist in eternity;

HOW IT SHOULD BE IN HEAVEN

> . . . But where is our, dear to us, mortality?
> Where is time that both destroys and saves us?
> This is too difficult for me. Peace eternal
> Could have no mornings and no evenings,
> Such a deficiency speaks against it.
> And that's too hard a nut for a theologian to crack. (*CP* 455)

After having questioned the alternatives, he has recourse to traditional theology to make his point. "There have always been schools that sought to achieve the immutable. But when it came to discussing an eternity entirely devoid of the flow of time, the theologians concluded that there still must be some sort of time and an eternity conceived as paradise, heaven; so they introduced the concept of *aevum* instead of *aeternum,* a time different from the earth's, but still a variation on it, because man cannot imagine anything outside of time, nothing can exist without developing" (*PW* 55).

Milosz summarizes this conviction in a single sentence, "First, time is only a biological continuity, then comes historical time, connected with memory, and then – I don't know – contact with God, the acquiring of lasting immutable values, but through a rootedness in time" (quoted in *PW* 55). "For God, the most subjective of subjects, because although unseen Himself, He sees – has been embracing with his vision all the moments of time which lie spread out before him like a deck of cards, for they are simultaneous beyond any was, is, will be" (*BWMS* 105).

Paradoxically, because Milosz's work is so personal and private, it has become universal, and every reader relates to the poet who cries, in his conclusive evaluation of time in "Thankfulness,"

> You gave me gifts, God-Enchanter,
> I give you thanks for good and ill.
> Eternal light in everything on earth.
> And now, so on the day after my death. (*CP* 438)

In Milosz's poems we share the universal tension between our existence in time and our inability to cope with it, other than metaphysically. Its reality eludes us; we are immersed in it as we are in the air which surrounds us, and upon which we depend. As Milosz himself repeatedly demonstrates: the contemplative individual experiences simultaneously past, present and future, because sharing God, he is above time even while he is a part of it.

Author's Note:

It was the man Czeslaw Milosz to whom I was first drawn when I met him, some years ago, at a consortium of Nobel Prize winners. Among those giants, he stood out, a solid, craggy embodiment of our tormented century, wearing visible peace and hard-won integrity. His poetry, reflective of what the young man experienced as a forced laborer in his Nazi-dominated country, and later under Stalin's Communism, illustrates the power of the human spirit to transcend the darkness, to experience and to expand in the glow of small natural beauty and the warmth of friendship and love.

His poems probe the point of time which is personal, both remote and immediate, as he reflects, a bit ruefully, that that is all we have: past and future. What does the present really mean? Do we ever live in the present moment? Does the awareness of the awesomeness of our condition – balanced against our personal unimportance as but one of uncounted millions – lead to despair, or can it lead to the larger Reality, the great Mystery in whom we live and move and have our being?

M.H.V.

Works Cited

Augustine. *Confessions of St. Augustine.* Translated by F. J. Sheed. New York: Sheed and Ward, 1945.

Milosz, Czeslaw. *Beginning with my Streets.* New York: Farrar, Straus, Giroux, 1991.

_____. *The Collected Poems 1931-1987.* New York: Ecco Press, 1988.

_____. *Native Realm: A Search for Self-Definition.* Berkeley: University of California Press, 1981.

_____. *Nobel Lecture.* New York: Farrar, Straus, Giroux, 1980.

_____. *The Witness of Poetry: The Charles Eliot Norton Lectures.* Cambridge, Mass.: Harvard University Press, 1983.

Możejko, Edward. *Between Anxiety and Hope: The Poetry and Writing of Czeslaw Milosz.* Alberta: The University of Alberta Press, 1988.

Nathan, Leonard and Arthur Quinn. *The Poet's Work: An Introduction to Czeslaw Milosz.* Cambridge, Mass.: Harvard University Press, 1991.

Plato. *Plato with an English Translation.* Edited by Rev. R. G. Bury. Cambridge, Mass.: Harvard University Press, 1942.

Chapter Seven

Osip Mandelstam, Seamus Heaney and the Language of Place

Catharine Malloy

I became aware of the poetry of Osip Mandelstam when I first read an essay Seamus Heaney wrote about him in his prose collection *Preoccupations*, and it never occurred to me then that there could be a link between the Russian poet and the Irish one that went beyond their vocations as lyric poets. Born nearly fifty years apart in countries not even sharing the same language, Mandelstam to Jewish parents in Warsaw, Heaney to Catholic parents in County Derry, these two writers could not be coming from – and writing about – two more disparate places. And yet, more similarities than differences began to surface from my readings. The Russian respected the "word as such" and passes this on to us with a "pure voice shot through with love, terror, memory, culture, faith – a voice trembling . . . [as Joseph Brodsky writes] like a match burning in a high wind, yet utterly inextinguishable."[1] His love of the word – his "fascination with verbal texture, phonology, sound harmony, and the relationship of the impulse to the text"[2] – is one of several strong links to Heaney who wrote of language in *Preoccupations* that he is "in love with words themselves . . ." and "that whole creative effort of the mind's and body's resources to bring the meaning of experience within the jurisdiction of form."[3] In addition,

1. Joseph Brodsky, *Less Than One* (New York: Farrar, Straus, Giroux, 1988), 144.
2. J. G. Harris and Constance Link, eds. and trans., *The Complete Prose and Letters of Osip Mandelstam* (Ann Arbor: Ardis, 1979), 42.
3. Seamus Heaney, *Preoccupations: Selected Prose 1968-1978* (New York: Farrar,

both poets consider themselves inner *emigrés* – for Mandelstam the reference is to his exile in the Russia he loved and, in Heaney's case, the term refers to the persona in his poem "Exposure" and relates to Heaney's decision to move to the South. Both Mandelstam and Heaney are devoted to the "earth" of place as well as to the words of place, creating poetry that resists the erosion of time. The hallowed space silence offers, the sacred place language creates, serve both poets as stations of indwelling from which they mark their separate, but coterminous ways.

Osip Mandelstam, considered by many to be one of the great lyric poets of this century, was born in Warsaw in 1891, died in 1938 in one of Stalin's labor camps, and was for twenty years after his death considered a "non-person."[4] From about 1923 on, he was followed, watched, deprived of clothing and of a place to live, accused falsely of plagiarism, plagued by "Stalin's prescription for correct writing"[5] until his first arrest on May 13, 1934, when an informer reported him for writing a derogatory poem about Stalin. After he spent three years of exile in Cherdyn, Mandelstam's already poor health deteriorated, and upon completion of his exile he was sent to a sanitorium for treatment. His final arrest for counterrevolutionary activities took place in May of 1938, and he was sent to a camp near Vladivostok where his official date of death is listed as December 27, 1938.

Mandelstam, defining himself as a *raznochinets,* a "classless or 'upstart' intellectual with no clearly defined social or official rank"[6] was devoted to the word, to language, from childhood, and this devotion informs all of his work. As a child, he became aware of the arrangement of books in the family bookcase: his father's Hebrew books, his mother's Russian ones. Although his parents encouraged Osip to read about the Judaic traditions and culture found in the paternal section of the Mandelstam "library," he found

---

Straus and Giroux, 1980), 45; 47; hereafter cited parenthetically in the text as *P.*

4. See Clarence Brown, *Mandelstam* (Cambridge, England: Cambridge University Press, 1973), 3.

5. Ibid., 125.

6. See Osip Mandelstam, *Stone,* trans. Robert Tracy (London: Collins Harvill, 1991), 13.

the Russian books on the "maternal" shelf more to his liking. Both shelves influenced him: "the speech of the father and the speech of the mother – does not our language feed throughout all its long life on the confluence of these two, do they not compose its character?"[7]

The in-betweenness he may have experienced when first reading his parents' books became a way for Mandelstam to circumscribe both parental traditions, and it may be the back and forthness of his exploratory endeavors early on that prepared him for the power language could offer to him as a resource for transcendence.

Influenced by the assemblage of his parents' books, as well as committed to the liberal and human values of the intelligentsia, Mandelstam, from his earliest Acmeist poems to his later visionary ones, constructed verse rich in the representation of human values. He created, for example, word monuments praising the medieval and Gothic architecture of famous basilicas and of the human hands that made them as places in which to pray and praise. As early as 1912, in his poem "Notre Dame," he illustrated his impulse for structuring versions and visions of place. Aware of the enclosure the Gothic structure represents, he is also sensitive to the man-made "flying buttresses [that] ensure / That cumbersome mass shan't crush the walls."[8] With its real and allegorical "elemental labyrinth, unfathomable forest . . . Oak together with reed," the basilica becomes a word, a "stronghold . . . never unnerved" or changed, immutable in its solidity, created by the work of human hands. Placing words like a stonemason sets bricks, Mandelstam is cognizant of heft, pitch, balance, the "ribs" of Notre Dame seen from the outside as the "bones" that "betray the plan" but not the poem, its rising handiwork capable of "one day . . . creat[ing] / Beauty from cruel weight." The Gothic cathedral in its poetic configuration is an enduring monument, perhaps more enduring, Mandelstam seems to be saying, than the stone basilica that inspired it. The poem itself becomes a dwelling place.

---

7. Mandelstam, *The Complete Prose and Letters*, 89, 90.

8. Osip Mandelstam, *Selected Poems*, trans. James Greene (New York: Penguin, 1991), 17; hereafter cited parenthetically in the text as *SP* [OM].

Not all the early poems are concerned with monumental structures, although "Notre Dame" and "Hagia Sophia" stand as important examples of Mandelstam's gift for turning words into places. What Mandelstam wants is for the equilibrium found in the stasis of the buildings themselves to be available to him in the fleetingness of the language that constructs them. It is noteworthy that both Hagia Sophia and Notre Dame were well-known as places of worship, and that Mandelstam, in writing about them, creates that sense of equilibrium and centeredness one is supposed to find within their walls. He refers to "Hagia Sophia," that "splendid temple . . . a festival of light from forty windows" *(SP* [OM] 16), and transforms his words into a spiritually habitable place, a temple of the mind and a representation of the solidarity he yearned for, but could never enjoy under an oppressive political system.

By 1928 Mandelstam had survived some of the most significant events in twentieth-century Russian history: the First World War, the revolutions of 1917, the civil war of 1918-1920, "and the gradual tightening of Soviet control in all areas of life, including literature, [that] occurred between 1913 and 1928."[9] As early as 1918, however, Mandelstam began to reach toward the concept of creating a place with language, moving to and through places of entrance and departure, boundaries and gates, pondering their questionable security, their ability to reveal and conceal space at the same time. He writes of "city walls," and compares the light burning "in the acropolis" to the vision of a brighter dawn in another province or place:

> Who can know from the word *goodbye*
> What kind of parting is in store for us,
> What the cock's clamour promises
> When a light burns in the acropolis,
> And at the dawn of some sort of new life
> When the lazy ox chews in his stall
> Why the rooster, herald of new life,
> Flaps his wings on the city walls?
> (*SP* [OM] 30)

---

9. See Osip Mandelstam, *Stone,* trans. Robert Tracy (London: Collins Harvill, 1991), 9.

Both lamenting and rejoicing at the promise of the cock's crowing in the "last hour," the poet imagines the winged herald and questions where the possibilities for wholeness might exist. Buildings, walls, basilicas, mosques, even spaces, all are visible places created with language, but within which one may dwell. And he creates places from absence or lack, as well, rising to the more difficult challenge of forging a place from utter loss. Mandelstam rises to it, disentangling himself from the assaults of the ongoing intimidations of the political regime attempting to silence him. His poetry is evidence he accepts each challenge, continuing to write, for it is in the writing of it that his freedom lies. It may be that, for Mandelstam, the ultimate creation, the place that "hold[s] in a single thought reality and justice," as Yeats suggests, may reside in the poetic forms that language takes.[10]

By the end of the 1920s, Mandelstam's wayfaring in body, spirit, and language, reached out farther, his imagination mapped more heavily now with destinations deeply imbued with "silences" and "meekness," "faith," "air," "light," than with buildings made of brick or city walls made of stone. Resisting the oppression imposed on writers and others during the Stalin regime, he moved farther and farther away from using the "word as such" to represent things and their essences, while continuing to construct shelters made of words, word-places parleying poetic impulses towards transcendence:

> I like the grey silences under the arches:
> Public prayer, funeral processions,
> The affecting obligatory rites and requiems at Saint Isaac's.

And he continues:

> Hagia Sophia and Saint Peter's – everlasting barns of air
>   and light,
> Storehouses of universal goods,
> Granaries of the New Testament.

Not to either of you is the spirit drawn in years of grave disaster:

---

10. Seamus Heaney, *The Government of the Tongue* (New York: The Noonday Press, 1990), 108.

Here, up the wide and sullen steps,
The waves of tribulation slink; we'll never betray their
    tracks.
For the slave is free having overcome fear,
And in cool granaries, in deep bins,
The grain of whole and perfect faith is stored.
(*SP* [OM] 124)

The realization of his themes begins to unfold gradually, and in this poem recognition of the "everlasting barns of air and light" precedes but does not overshadow the reigning impulse of the poem. Fear, Mandelstam writes, is what enslaves, emphasizing that writing for him is an act of courage, of stealth, securing for him all the freedom he would ever need or know.

By 1930 Mandelstam was deliberately displaced, *persona non grata,* limited to certain marginal and restricted forms of writing granted to undesirables. Continually watched, he integrated into his own work his desperate search for a home, writing in 1931 of his "constant searching for some shelter, [and of his] unsatisfied hunger for thought."[11] By May of 1934, he was arrested for writing a poem critical of Stalin. Sentenced first to hard labor and then to exile in Cherdyn, where he had a breakdown and attempted suicide, he was ultimately sent to Voronzeh. Neither destroyed nor defeated, Mandelstam continued to construct poetry from the negative space of his existence, muttering words, writing poems to affirm a place without borders or restrictions.

You took away my seas and running jumps and sky
And propped my foot against the violent earth.
Where could this brilliant calculation get you?
You couldn't take away my muttering lips.
(*SP* [OM] 307)

The moral force of Mandelstam's poetry survives, his places of language monuments to freedom where the "theme of the creative consciousness in an alien environment" stands firm.[12] Mandelstam's places of language span the decades of his life, changing to suit and to accommodate his imagination, providing

---

11. Mandelstam, *Stone,* 11.

12. Mandelstam, *The Complete Prose and Letters,* 22.

stations for contemplation and reflection as he journeys. From religious and historical buildings, to spaces without discernible boundaries or dimensions, he creates places with words; in 1937, just two years before his death he wrote, for example, of "a ray of light spun by a spider," and of the "columns of grateful pure lines/ . . . Like guests with an open countenance" (*SP* [OM] 81), replacing constructions of brick and mortar with structures of obstinate space, less weighted and girded, more fused with sound and light, more integral to his Dantean vision of home. No need for historical buildings to lend their architecture to the poet for reconfiguration, his inspiration is now of another order. "To build," Mandelstam wrote, "means to contend with the void, to hypnotize space . . . the beautiful shaft of the Gothic bell tower is angry, for the entire meaning of it is to stab the sky, to reproach it because it is empty."[13]

In his introduction to the *Moscow Notebooks,* Professor McKane wrote that Mandelstam "has transcended the constraints of time and place which he so bitterly resisted." And that "One hundred years after his birth we can read, in English, his prophetic words: 'Yes, I am lying in the ground, but my lips are moving.' "[14] And yes, we can still hear the echoes. Osip Mandelstam *has* transcended historical time and place with language, and in his wayfaring creates shelters in which to dwell, if only temporarily.

Like Osip Mandelstam, Seamus Heaney wrote of the early influences of language. In *Preoccupations,* for example, one need read only the titles of some of the essays to realize that place is important to Heaney. There is the "country of convention," and "Englands of the Mind," "Mossbawn," "Belfast," even an essay called, simply, "The Sense of Place." Heaney's interest in place is woven throughout his writings and, when asked to inaugurate the Richard Ellmann Memorial Lectures at Emory University in 1988-89, he focused on the importance of place in the imagination and suggested, as in the case of W. B. Yeats, for example, that Yeats created in his later writings "a country of the mind rather than the

---

13. Mandelstam, quoted in *Stone*, 28.

14. *The Moscow Notebooks,* trans. Richard and Elizabeth McKane (Newcastle Upon Tyne: Bloodaxe Books, 1991), 11.

other way round, (and the more usual way) where the country has created the mind which in turn creates the poems."[15] Underscoring the importance of place for the imagination, Heaney wrote in the same essay that "we are more and more aware of writing as a place in itself, a destination in art arrived at by way of art. And yet an urge persists," he goes on, "to enquire into the inspiration and foundation which place affords in the creative process."[16] Heaney's discussion of place is foregrounded on two crucial points concerning it: "that the poetic imagination in its strongest manifestation imposes its vision upon a place rather than accepts a vision from it; and that this visionary imposition is never exempt from the imagination's antithetical ability to subvert its own creation."[17] Like Yeats, like Mandelstam, Heaney constructs places of the mind which transcend the longitude and latitude of their geographic inspirations, aspiring to their own perch, their own space, apart from, yet fueled by, the quotidian.

Places from Heaney's childhood figure in numerous poems, affirming the imagination's role in the creation of a location that exists both in the poet's mind and in the realm of the poem, in its language and form, its rhythms and cadences, as well as in a geographic site such as a country, a province, a parish, a farm. In "The Peninsula," for example, an early poem where the speaker who has "nothing more to say, just drive[s] / For a day all round the peninsula" only to return "back home still with nothing to say / Except that now [he] will uncode all landscapes / By this,"[18] may be saying that what he learned on his motoring excursion to a place – the peninsula – provides the key to all the other landscapes of place and mind and daily grind he may encounter and be challenged by. Forming the place the poet shapes with language, the four quatrains become more tangible than "the land without marks" he passes through, more insistent than the "whitewashed gable" swallowed up by "the ploughed field," and the driver becomes an

---

15. Seamus Heaney, *The Place of Writing* (Atlanta: Scholars Press, 1989), 21.

16. Ibid., 19, 20.

17. Ibid., 20.

18. Seamus Heaney, *Selected Poems* (New York: Farrar, Straus and Giroux, 1990), 16; hereafter cited parenthetically in the text as *SP* [SH].

informer and travel guide, telling himself to "recall / The glazed foreshore" and "breakers [and the] Islands riding themselves out into the fog" because they are the key to "uncod[ing] all landscapes," even the most formidable, even the most interior, even the most resistant. Poetry, writing, language, Heaney seems to be saying, provides the bridge – is the bridge – the place between where we are and where we want to be.

Like Mandelstam's places, Heaney's are as much structures of language as they are constructs that have architectural or geographical dimensions. But while language serves to map out and claim and blueprint his place, the forms poetry takes are non-restrictive; poetry enables and "poetry," as Helen Vendler wrote recently, is associative,

> is language used in a special way – not merely to convey emotion or to purvey information or to facilitate conversation or to sum up an argument. It is language used with particular attention to binding phrases together by sheer interior association. These associations need to be emotional, logical, allusive, symbolic, phonetic, syntactic and rhythmic, or at least a combination of several of these . . . [for in the language of poetry] many associative patterns are at work at the same time. . . .[19]

Employing the associative patterns of claiming a childhood place by naming it, Heaney writes in "Anahorish," a poem from his collection *Wintering Out* (1972), of the local, and of possession of it by language: "Anahorish," his "place of clear water." While transforming place into words, he becomes its owner, using poetry to define his claim with words. He blesses place and gives it permanence while marking it as his own: the remembered earth becomes a "soft gradient / of consonant, vowel-meadow" recalling an image of "lamps / swung through the yards on winter evenings" (*SP* [SH] 29). From patterns of language that are heard with the ear and seen with the eye, Heaney creates a place for the moment.

And these brief moments inspired by place are evident throughout his work, giving off a decided sense of being both earth

---

19. Helen Vendler, Review of *The Language of Life: A Festival of Poets* by Bill Moyers. *The New York Times Book Review* (18 June 1995): 15.

and heaven-bound at the same time. Poems like "The Strand at Lough Beg," "Station Island," "The Disappearing Island" and others, offer places pulled as much by gravity as by grace. And following the path set by the language of place in some of his earlier work, Heaney, in his later collection, *Seeing Things*, continues his exploration of ways to transcend time and space with language. In these more recent poems, while he continues to set up domiciles made of verse, he rediscovers, reconfigures, re-sees, measuring the distance between past and present, but increasingly aware that time is fleeting, place is transient; he is astonished that he has waited "until [he] was nearly fifty / To credit marvels."[20] Cognizant of "time's winged chariot," he knows both the permanence and the possibility of art, the potential a poem has to stay confusion as well as to restore what is good. Heaney is poised between settling for that permanence and wagering on the transcendence that language and his poetic art have come to insist upon.

In the collection *Seeing Things,* Heaney often returns to places from his past, traveling back, retrieving memories, measuring with language the distance he has come from then until now. In poem xxxi of *Seeing Things*, for example, he moves back to a place where he "drive[s] into a meaning made of trees" which translates, perhaps, to a meaning made of trees that are made of language. In this place where he has a sense of "running through and under without let," he is free, if fleetingly, in a space he creates with words. One wonders if these places made of language, in the end, represent Heaney's choice, reaffirming his belief that poetry purifies possibilities again and again and that the *process* of poetry writing is itself redemptive.

Both Mandelstam and Heaney are wayfarers, using language to create places *en route.* Heaney often returns to a place to rediscover and re-see a remembered past, and in writing about it reconfigures the memory in the form of a poem. A place becomes an "Unroofed scope" (*ST* 55), or a "throne-room of [the] mind" (*ST* 79), or "drifts of sleep" (*ST* 45), or a "whole world [that] was a farm" (*ST* 32). Heaney reclaims these places as parts of a continuum,

---

20. Seamus Heaney, *Seeing Things* (London: Faber and Faber, 1991), 50; hereafter cited parenthetically in the text as *ST.*

shores them up, proves language's potential to create anew a place that is self-contained within a poem and yet connected to the scrapbook of memories in his mind.

Masters of the imagination and of using language to create place, both Osip Mandelstam and Seamus Heaney transcend geographic place on their way to another, more spiritual, realm. Both poets utilize place as a transitory dwelling for the imagination: for Mandelstam, each place created with language is part of the continuum that constitutes his search for a home; for Heaney, place is where one returns in order to re-see and to become whole yet again.

Author's Note:

One of the most memorable times of my life is a brisk, March day in 1990, in Cambridge, Massachusetts, where Seamus Heaney talked to me about his poetry. During the conversation he referred to Dante's Commedia, *calling it "a housing place." Heaney's deep respect for place, and for the power of language to create place, is what first led me to explore the connection to Mandelstam, whose poetry Heaney admired and wrote about. Like Dante, Mandelstam, too, employed language to create place and, like his Irish admirer, he used imaginative language to define and mark his ongoing quest for wholeness via the in-placeness of poetry. Mandelstam's and Heaney's searches for meaning are, ironically, found in the still poems of place.*

Can poetry provide places that are stopping off stations, spots of refuge where history goes on around you with a sense of your being apart from it as well as a part of it? And do these places of the imagination prefigure a timeless place that awaits us?

C.M.

Works Cited

Brodsky, Joseph. *Less Than One.* New York: Farrar, Straus, Giroux, 1988.

Brown, Clarence. *Mandelstam*. Cambridge, England: Cambridge University Press, 1973.

Heaney, Seamus. *The Government of the Tongue*. New York: The Noonday Press, 1990.

_____. *The Place of Writing*. Atlanta: Scholars Press, 1989.

_____. *Poems (1965-1975)*. New York: Farrar, Straus, Giroux, 1985.

_____. *Preoccupations: Selected Prose 1968-1978*. New York: Farrar, Straus, Giroux, 1980.

_____. *Seeing Things*. London: Faber and Faber, 1991.

_____. *Selected Poems*. New York: Farrar, Straus, Giroux, 1990.

Mandelstam, Osip. *The Complete Prose and Letters of Osip Mandelstam*. Translated and edited by J. G. Harris and Constance Link. Ann Arbor: Ardis, 1979.

_____. *The Moscow Notebooks*. Translated by Richard and Elizabeth McKane. Newcastle Upon Tyne: Bloodaxe Books, 1991.

_____. *Selected Poems*. Translated by James Greene. New York: Penguin, 1991.

_____. *Stone*. Translated by Robert Tracy. London: Collins Harvill, 1991.

Vendler, Helen. Review of *The Language of Life: A Festival of Poets* by Bill Moyers. *The New York Times Book Review* (18 June, 1995): 14-15.

IV.

Transcendence and the Human Story

Chapter Eight

Buechner's Concrete Evidence of the Transcendent

Heidi N. Sjostrom

Presbyterian minister and writer Frederick Buechner has made a career of calling attention to the quiddity of life on this earth – the pleasant details and the unpleasant details. Buechner wagers that "If God speaks to us at all other than through such official channels as the Bible and the church, then I think that he speaks to us largely through what happens to us. . . . God speaks to us [in] always an incarnate word – a word spelled out to us not alphabetically, in syllables, but enigmatically, in events."[1] Buechner has learned from the dark and light of the incarnate events in his own and his characters' lives that the Transcendent is present, and he has stated his central message unequivocally: "If I were called upon to state in a few words the essence of everything I was trying to say both as a novelist and as a preacher, it would be something like this: Listen to your life. See it for the fathomless mystery that it is. In the boredom and pain of it no less than in the excitement and gladness: touch, taste, smell your way to the holy and hidden heart of it because in the last analysis all moments are key moments, and life itself is grace" (*N&T* 87). Buechner believes that God is made known in the ordinary, five-senses world in which we live. As a writer and minister, Buechner uses words as tools to evoke concrete images that communicate the Transcendent.

---

1. Frederick Buechner, *Now and Then* (San Francisco: HarperCollins, 1991), 3; hereafter cited parenthetically in the text as *N&T*. Buechner pronounces his name "*Beek-ner.*"

Words Grounded in Concrete Experience Can Communicate the Transcendent

Buechner's ministry is in showing that transcendent truths are expressed in the incarnate words of our experiences – both joyful and painful. He writes, "Transcendent as God is – of another quality entirely from the world that he transcends – he nonetheless makes himself known to the world."[2] As a writer, Buechner evokes the presence and message of the Transcendent by writing scenes and dialogue. His stance is supported by George Steiner, professor of English at Cambridge and the University of Geneva, who argues in his book *Real Presences* that "the wager on the meaning of meaning, on the potential of insight and response when one human voice addresses another . . . is a wager on transcendence."[3] Later, Steiner clarifies his point about artists who wager that they can indeed create art that is meaningful to another person when he writes that "there is in the art-act and its reception, . . . a presumption of presence."[4] Steiner's view that words are real presences with meanings that resist deconstruction is based on his belief that humans share a common Creation "out of which, inexplicably, have come the self and the world into which we are cast."[5] Transcendent truths and our ability to recognize them affirm the spiritual bonds among humans. Frederick Buechner wagers that poet and author Natalie Goldberg is right: "But we should never underestimate people. They do desire the cut of truth."[6] In Buechner's work, words evoke the quiddity and thus the true meaning of Creation.

Buechner admits that the events of our lives – the incarnate words of God – speak to different people in different ways: "The meaning of an incarnate word is the meaning it has for the one it is spoken to, the meaning that becomes clear and effective in our lives only when we ferret it out for ourselves."[7] If we each ferret

---

2. Frederick Buechner, *A Room Called Remember* (San Francisco: HarperCollins, 1992), 59; hereafter cited parenthetically in the text as *RCR*.

3. George Steiner, *Real Presences* (Chicago: University of Chicago Press, 1989), 4.

4. Ibid., 214.

5. Ibid., 215.

6. Natalie Goldberg, *Writing Down the Bones* (Boston: Shambhala, 1986), 122.

7. Frederick Buechner, *The Sacred Journey* (San Francisco: HarperCollins, 1991),

out a slightly different meaning for our lives, that does not mean no life has any meaning.[8] Buechner does not even desire for all readers to find the same meaning in his work. He cautions preachers and writers that if they "have to choose between words that mean more than what you have experienced and words that mean less, choose the ones that mean less because that way you leave room for your hearers to move around in" (*N&T* 93). Buechner knows he leaves room for his readers to move around and see their own stories in the books he writes, so if individuals ferret out different meanings in Buechner's writings, that does not mean that the Transcendent was not portrayed. Steiner rephrases this idea thus: "But the fact that there cannot be, in Coleridge's macronic phrase, any *omnium gatherum* of the context that is the world, does not mean that intelligibility is either wholly arbitrary or self-erasing."[9] Steiner states that, if the reader is open to them, transcendent truths about the human condition and mystical experiences are available in good literature.[10]

Buechner also affirms the power of words to bring us the experience of the transcendent: "The final mystery as well as the final power of words [is] that not even across great distances of time and space do they ever lose their capacity for becoming incarnate. And when these words tell of virtue and nobility, when they move us closer to the truth and gentleness of spirit by which we become fully human, the reading of them is sacramental" (*RCR* 181). Because of this power of words to evoke the transcendent, Buechner has made them his life's work. Still, he advises homiletic students to find "not the poetic word, but the *right* word, the word true to one's own unique experience."[11] Buechner does not advo-

---

4; hereafter cited parenthetically in the text as *SJ*.

8. Individual readers will have different experiences of a single piece of literature, but taking a deconstructionist approach to literature in order, as deconstructionist scholar Jonathan Culler says, to "show how it undermines the philosophy it asserts" and to claim, therefore, that the writer had no real meaning or truth to communicate is tantamount to claiming that there is no such thing as white light because a prism can split it into colors which "undermine" the clear white light. See Jonathan Culler, quoted in Steven Lynn, "A Passage into Critical Theory," *College English* (March 1990): 263.

9. Steiner, 163.

10. Ibid., 187.

cate leaving so much room in the words he writes that they are empty of meaning; his antidote against preachy, easily misinterpreted writing is to ground that writing in events, in incarnate experience.

Buechner continually emphasizes the spiritual ground and importance of events. Often the events of experience defy explanation in words, and he admits that "To try to express in even the most insightful and theologically sophisticated terms the meaning of what God speaks through the events of our lives is as precarious a business as to try to express the meaning of the sound of rain on the roof or the spectacle of the setting sun" (*SJ* 4). If God could have told the whole story in words, the incarnation – Jesus – would not have been necessary.

Buechner's own fiction arises not from a word-dependent, cerebral idea but from "a lump in [his] throat" (*N&T* 59), like any other artist's ideas, he says, and he is most concerned with capturing the truth of the moment that "unaccountably brings tears to your eyes; that takes you by crazy surprise; . . . that haunts you with what is just possibly a glimpse of something far beyond or deep within itself."[12] What Buechner notices are not words, but experiences. Then he must find words to express those experiences so that they seem true to life and true to the transcendent, also. Like poet Adrienne Rich, Buechner looks in literature for "language that bears its own witness in the world, whose charge is never to trivialize my or any life; language located in the pulse, ordinary pungent speech, music, desire, anger, risk."[13] Buechner says that even in preaching, he tries to remain grounded in experience: "preaching is . . . to proclaim a Mystery before which, before whom, even our most exalted ideas turn to straw. . . . It is to try to put the Gospel into words not the way you would compose an essay but the way you would write a poem or a love letter – putting

---

11. Frederick Buechner, quoted in Kenneth Gibble, "Listening to My Life: An Interview with Frederick Buechner," *The Christian Century* (16 November 1983): 1043.

12. Frederick Buechner, *The Clown in the Belfry: Writings on Faith and Fiction* (San Francisco: HarperCollins, 1992), 15; hereafter cited parenthetically in the text as *CB*.

13. Adrienne Rich, "Poetry for Daily Use," *Ms.* (September/October 1991): 71.

your heart into it, your own excitement, most of all your own life" (*TS* 61).

Marjorie Casebier McCoy, author of *Frederick Buechner: Novelist/Theologian of the Lost and Found* – a book of biography and criticism – states that "His writing has a compelling quality for me and many others because it emerges from those times in his life that have forced him to listen. Before we know it we find ourselves paying attention first to him and then to our own experience."[14] In those experiences, we see glimmers of the transcendent. Buechner has taken seriously the importance of developing a language that describes the human condition as he has experienced it. James Baldwin – in his famous essay "If Black English Isn't a Language, Then Tell Me, What Is?" – makes the same point: "People evolve a language in order to describe and thus control circumstances or in order not to be submerged by a situation that they cannot articulate."[15] Finding the right words becomes a wager on transcendence and a truth-telling tool.

As a Presbyterian – those people associated with the doctrine of predestination – Buechner might be expected to see God as someone who has planned all the informing events of our lives – written out the whole plot – ahead of time, leaving us no room in the script for reinterpretation or new insights. But Buechner explains predestination a bit differently: "The fact that I know you so well that I know what you're going to do before you do it does not mean that you are not free to do whatever you damn well please."[16]

In another explanation, Buechner uses the concrete image of the theater to explain how God works in the events of our lives: "God acts in history and in your and my brief histories not as the puppeteer who . . . works the strings but rather as the great director

14. Marjorie Casebier McCoy, with Charles S. McCoy, *Frederick Buechner: Novelist/Theologian of the Lost and Found* (San Francisco: Harper and Row, 1988), 1.

15. James Baldwin, "If Black English Isn't a Language, Then Tell Me, What Is?" in *Major Modern Essayists,* 2d ed., ed. Gilbert H. Muller and Alan F. Crooks (Englewood Cliffs, N.J.: Blair Press, 1994), 150.

16. Frederick Buechner, *Wishful Thinking: A Theological ABC* (New York: Harper and Row, 1973), 72; hereafter cited parenthetically in the text as *WT.*

who no matter what role fate casts us in conveys to us . . . how we can play those roles in a way to enrich and ennoble and hallow the whole vast drama of things" (*TS* 32). Buechner wants us to notice that life does have a plot and then, most importantly, to notice that the memorable events forming the plot reveal God working for good all along. He has noted, "I developed through the writing [of novels] a sense of plot and, beyond that, a sense that perhaps life itself has a plot – that the events of our lives . . . are seeking to show us something, lead us somewhere. . . . [In] the midst of our freedom, we hear whispers . . . whose plot it is . . . to make us truly and everlastingly human" (*SJ* 95).

Buechner's writing attempts to make those whispers audible, to show the presence of the Transcendent in life's experiences. He sees the Bible and its stories as saying the same thing. He considers the Bible a book with "a plot that can be readily stated. God makes the world in love. For one reason or another the world chooses to reject God. God will not reject the world but continues his mysterious and relentless pursuit of it to the end of time" (*N&T* 20). That pursuit can be glimpsed if we look at the quiddity of life.

The Transcendent Made Present in Events

Between 1950 and 1965, Frederick Buechner wrote three novels that met with varying degrees of success. Then after his graduation from Union Theological Seminary and his 1958 ordination as a Presbyterian minister, Buechner again dealt, in his fourth novel – *The Final Beast* – with the search for the Transcendent. In that novel, published in 1965, a young minister travels to retrieve a lost lamb – a woman in his congregation who has fled after a brief adultery. Finding no trains or buses going to his destination, Rev. Nicolet hitchhikes, reflecting that "It was good to be going and not to know why; if you waited until you knew why, you would never go anywhere. It was faith, after all: simply to go."[17] A car speeds past and sends him spinning so that "He ended by catching hold of the telephone pole in the crook of his arm and swinging once

---

17. Frederick Buechner, *The Final Beast* (New York: Atheneum, 1965), 45; hereafter cited parenthetically in the text as *FB*.

around it to stop with his cheek pressed against the rough, dry wood" (*FB* 45). As much as in the theological reflection about his reasons for going on the trip, God's helping presence is seen in the texture of the telephone pole – the quiddity of creation. Nicolet's experience of the rough wood is reminiscent of a day in the Army when Buechner suddenly perceived the goodness of creation – by eating a turnip a fellow recruit had thrown to him: "I missed the catch, the turnip fell to the ground, but I wanted it so badly that I picked it up and started eating it anyway, mud and all. . . . I saw suddenly, almost as if from beyond time altogether, that not only was the turnip good, but the mud was good too, even the drizzle and cold were good, even the Army" (*SJ* 85). The taste of mud and the rough surface of a telephone pole are concrete enough to incarnate a spiritual truth for Buechner.

Near the end of *The Final Beast*, Buechner has Nicolet again experience the transcendent through an unspectacular physical sign. He is lying in the summer grass, dreamily planning a sermon, when he "no longer [dares] not to dare" – he asks God to become present to him (*FB* 176). He raises his arms to a "superbly humdrum stand of neglected trees" and whispers, "Please come" (*FB* 176). Nicolet lies waiting for shafts of light, voices, or some other magnificent sign. Nothing happens. Finally, "Two apple branches struck against each other with the limber clack of wood on wood. That was all – a tick-tock rattle of branches – but then a fierce lurch of excitement . . . oh Jesus, he thought, with a great lump in his throat and a crazy grin, it was an agony of gladness and beauty falling wild and soft like rain" (*FB* 177). Buechner based Nicolet's concrete, subtle experience of the transcendent on an autobiographical incident (*RCR* 146), but it stands for all those times each of us has longed for a grand sign and gotten only our own lives to look at. Buechner says that this is enough; indeed, it's all we can understand or withstand now. Nicolet says in the novel, "If we saw any more of [the] dance than we do, it would kill us sure. . . . The glory of it. Clack-clack is all a man can bear" (*FB* 182). Clack-clack is how God speaks in the lives of humans on earth, in the most secular of incarnate experiences. No part of life is removed from the influence of the divine. Biographer and critic Marjorie Casebier McCoy agrees that Buechner's work shows that "There is no sector that is secular; every part is sacred and may become in any moment and in unexpected ways a window through which we see God or a hand with which the divine reaches out to grasp us."[18]

Buechner has listed the mundane life experiences that tell you whether you've been living your life or existing in a cramped living death, not aware of the presence of the Transcendent in this life on earth. He asks,

> Have you wept at anything during the past year?
> Has your heart beat faster at the sight of young beauty?
> Have you thought seriously about the fact that someday you are going to die?
> More often than not do you really *listen* when people are speaking to you instead of just waiting for your turn to speak?
> Is there anybody you know in whose place, if one of you had to suffer great pain, you would volunteer yourself?
> If your answer to all or most of these questions is No, the chances are that you're dead. (*WT* 51)

Buechner gives a similar checklist to preachers, who should "keep a journal not of 'interesting things,' but of experiences that some-how – even if they can't say how – seem to illumine, or be illumined by, religious truth. I tell them to pay special attention to those times when they find tears in their eyes, even if they don't know why the tears are there."[19] These inexplicably emotional experiences may be moments of transcending the boundaries between the divine and the human.

Buechner notes elsewhere that "every once in a while in the world . . . something like peace happens, love happens, light happens. . . . And when they happen, we should hold on to them for dear life, because of course they are dear life. They are glimpses and whispers from afar: that peace, light, love are where life ultimately comes from" (*RCR* 20). God is present in our experience, and Buechner searches for the words that evoke that presence.

Buechner's novel *Godric*, published in 1980 and nominated for a Pulitzer Prize, demonstrates Buechner's ability to evoke the

---

18. Marjorie Casebier McCoy, with Charles S. McCoy, 101.

19. Frederick Buechner, quoted in Gibble, 1043.

transcendent in life's experiences. Even the choice of this medieval saint as a main character for his novel seemed inspired by the Holy Spirit: "I picked up a small paperback book of saints and opened it, by accident, to the page that had Godric on it" (*N&T* 106). Here was a concrete life filled with events of just the sort that resonated for Buechner: "[Godric] had been a peddler before he turned hermit, and master of a merchant ship. He had tried his hand at piracy for a while. He had rescued Baldwin the First, King of Jerusalem, at the time of the First Crusade. He had not considered himself a saint at all" (*N&T* 106). The grit of life in the Middle Ages fills *Godric*, and so do the grace and compassion of the transcendent. Of his pirate-days friend, Roger Mouse, who liked the ladies, Godric says, "What a sinner too was Mouse, but . . . what with all the man's great mirth, there was [little] room left in him for truly mortal sin. . . . Mouse's sin smacked less of evil than of larkishness the likes of which Our Lord himself could hardly help but wink at when he spied it out in whore and prodigal."[20] Here is a real life "sinner" and a real life Jesus with a sense of humor.

Saint Godric's first experience of the living Christ is also in a real life, or death, event. He almost drowns when, unaware, he is caught stranded on a sandbar by high tide. That day he learns not only to "keep an eye cocked on the waves' salt treachery" but also that Jesus has spoken to him and indeed saved him from drowning. He says that it was Jesus' porpoise-like "voice he'd heard beneath the waves and [his] eye that gazed at [me] so merrily. . . . Jesus saved [me] from the sea" (*G* 16). Throughout his life, it is in water, with its liquid texture and many moods, that Godric finds the divine manifested.

Godric ends up in Jerusalem the day he quits pirating, and he visits the holy places in the city. At sunset, he comes to the Jordan River and wades in for no special reason. Again, in texture, sound, and sights, Godric experiences the divine.

> Oh Lord, the coolness of the river's touch! The way it mirrored back the clouds as if I bathed in sky . . . the water reached my neck, my beard outspread, my garments

---

20. Frederick Buechner, *Godric* (New York: Atheneum, 1980), 4; hereafter cited parenthetically in the text as *G*.

floating free. . . . I felt I had, myself, no weight at all . . .
the untold weight of sin upon my heart was gone. I ducked
my head beneath, and in the dark I thought I heard that
porpoise voice again that spoke to me the day I nearly
drowned. . . . "Take, eat me, Godric, to thy soul's delight.
Hold fast to him who gave his life for thee and thine." (*G*
104)

It is the quiddity of the water on his skin that brings the voice of
salvation to Godric.

This willingness to see the divine presence in experiences of
the flesh corresponds with a crucial tenet espoused by many
feminist theologians, including Stephanie Demetrakopoulos,
whose position is described in this way: "When she speaks about
her own experience of nursing she describes it as a 'total sense of
flowing out of self.' The intriguing expression she uses is 'transcending downward.' The psyche renews and discovers itself in
this kind of transcendence, she says, not by going beyond the body,
but by immersing itself in it."[21] Buechner immerses us in Godric's
bodily experience so that we can see the Transcendent in our own
lives' events.

In the hermitage of his old age, Godric lives beside a river
called Wear, and this river brings more experiences of the transcendent. With a scene of lying in the grass – much like the
clack-clack scene in his earlier novel – Buechner tells how Godric
experiences Christ's love.

I'd sinned, no matter how, and in sin's wake there came
a kind of drowsy peace so deep I hadn't even will enough
to loathe myself. I had no mind to pray . . . just flesh to
feel the sun.

A light breeze blew from Wear that tossed the trees,
and . . . they formed a face of shadows and of leaves . . .
he opened up his mouth to speak. No sound came from
his lips, but by their shape I knew it was my name.

His was the holiest face I ever saw. My very name
turned holy on his tongue. If he had bade me rise and

---

21. Stephanie Demetrakopoulos, quoted in Sherry Ruth Anderson and Patricia
Hopkins, *The Feminine Face of God: The Unfolding of the Sacred in Women*
(New York: Bantam Books, 1992), 77.

follow to the end of time, I would have gone. . . . When
I deserved it least, God gave me most. (*G* 143-44)

Into this scene filled with the textures of earthly life – the feeling
of breezes and sun on skin, the sins of the flesh, the leaves of trees,
and the nearby river – Buechner brings the compassionate love of
God. This scene is reminiscent of the scene in C. S. Lewis' portrait
of heaven, *The Great Divorce*, in which the visitor sees a waterfall
that "itself was speaking: and I saw now (though it did not cease
to look like a waterfall) that it was also a bright angel who stood,
like one crucified, against the rocks and poured himself perpetually
downward towards the forest with loud joy."[22] For Buechner, also,
the leaves, sun, and water are the words through which God chose
to speak to his character Godric. As critic Stephen Kendrick notes,
"In figures such as Godric . . . , Buechner tells us that salvation is
unexpected, like a punch line in the black comedy of our lives."[23]
These unexpected moments of grace come with texture and clarity
in Buechner's work.

In his novel published in 1994, *Son of Laughter*, Buechner
again uses earthy terms, this time to describe the father of the
Judeo-Christian world: "[Abraham] had a habit, when he spoke, of
putting his hands on your shoulders and of drawing you gradually
closer and closer as the words flowed until at the end his great
nostrils were almost in your face like twin entrances to a cave. . . .
I pictured him breaking wind, groaning, as he heaved himself out
of the pit of sleep at sundown to lead his precious train of kin,
beasts, baggage, mile after moonlit mile."[24] This is the flesh and
blood man who will father the nation of Israel, and how much
more real he seems now that Buechner has put some meat on his
bones.

Son of Laughter is actually about Jacob, the son of Isaac –
which means "laughter." Even in seminary, Buechner's imagination
was captured by Jacob, of whom he writes, "Jacob betrays his

---

22. C. S. Lewis, *The Great Divorce* (New York: Macmillan, 1946), 52.

23. Stephen Kendrick, "On Spiritual Autobiography: An Interview with Frederick
Buechner," *The Christian Century* (14 October 1992): 900.

24. Frederick Buechner, *The Son of Laughter* (San Francisco: HarperCollins, 1994),
10-11; hereafter cited parenthetically in the text as *SL*.

brother [Esau], dupes his father, all but chokes on his own mendacity, yet the smell of him is the smell of blessing. . . . Jacob reeks of holiness. His life is as dark, fertile, and holy as the earth itself. He is himself a bush that burns with everything, both fair and foul, that a man burns with" (*N&T* 19-20). Clearly, Buechner is able to imagine the details of this man's life. He is also intrigued by Jacob's home life. Jacob was the one who fathered a daughter, Dinah, and the twelve men who would lead the twelve tribes of Israel. In *Son of Laughter*, Buechner invites us to feel what it was like to be the father of so many children: "One boy was pounding another boy's head against the hard-packed floor. Another was drowsing at his mother's teat. Three of them were trying to shove a fourth into a basket. Dinah was fitting her foot into her mouth. The air was foul with the smell of them" (*SL* 127).

Here are concrete details aplenty shouting, not just speaking, in the midst of Jacob's life. He gets the message. Jacob says, "I started to weep. Just a trickle at first. . . . Then it was as if I couldn't catch my breath for weeping. Laban came over and pounded me between the shoulders. He thought I was choking to death. . . . A deep hush fell over the children. . . . 'You are so – so noisy,' I choked out at them. They were the Fear's [God's] promise to Abraham, and I had forgotten it. . . . 'You are so hopeless,' I said. 'So important'" (*SL* 127-28). Jacob listens to his children and through his experience of them is reminded of the transcendent promise that God made to Abraham.

The Transcendent in Buechner's Own Life

Despite Nicolet's happy satisfaction with the clacking branches he heard and Jacob's lust for life, Buechner and his characters have not ignored those searches for God that seem to end in silence and pain, with not even the clacking of branches to ease the forsakenness. When Buechner was ten years old, his father committed suicide. Forty years later, one of his three daughters almost died of anorexia nervosa – self-starvation. Of his own struggles during that time of terrifying illness, Buechner writes,

> My anorectic daughter was in danger of starving to death,
> and without knowing it, so was I. . . . She had given up

food. I had virtually given up doing anything in the way of feeding myself humanly. To be at peace is to have peace inside yourself more or less in spite of what is going on outside yourself. In that sense I had no peace at all. If . . . she took it into her head to have a slice of toast, say, with her dietetic supper, I was in seventh heaven. If . . . she decided to have no supper at all, I was in hell. (*TS* 25)

The details of Buechner's suffering show the depth of his longing for the Transcendent and the depth of his feelings of abandonment. During his daughter's illness, Buechner began to realize how much like the elder son in the parable of the Prodigal Son he was. The elder brother never noticed that God loved him generously all along because, as Buechner says, "it was never love he was bucking for but only his due . . . he never thought to ask for [a party] because he was too busy trying cheerlessly and religiously to earn [it]."[25] The transcendent truth that glared at Buechner from this story was how cheerlessly he had been trying to earn God's love – and exert the control that would prevent further disasters like his father's death. Buechner imagines that the sound "of the hoedown reaches [the elder brother] out in the pasture among the cow flops. . . . [He] is Pecksniffe. He is Tartuffe. He is what Mark Twain called a good man in the worst sense of the word. . . . The fatted calf, the best Scotch, the hoedown could all have been his, too, any time he asked for them except that he never thought to ask for them" (*TT* 68-69). In Buechner's own time of pain and feeling that God did not love him, he learned that "earning" God's love is not necessary. Accepting it is.

Buechner discovered in this terrifying experience that God was present in silence: "When the worst finally happens, or almost happens, a kind of peace comes. I had passed beyond grief, beyond terror, all but beyond hope, and it was there, in that wilderness, that for the first time in my life I caught sight of something of what it must be like to love God truly. . . . Though God was nowhere to be clearly seen, nowhere to be clearly heard, I had to be near him. . . . I loved him because there was nothing else left. I loved

---

25. Frederick Buechner, *Telling the Truth: The Gospel as Tragedy, Comedy, and Fairy Tale* (New York: Harper & Row, 1977), 69; hereafter cited parenthetically in the text as *TT*.

him because he seemed to have made himself as helpless in his might as I was in my helplessness" (*RCR* 42). His father's suicide and daughter's anorexia would appear to be events devoid of the Transcendent, yet Buechner felt God's presence speaking in even these experiences.

By 1984, his daughter was regaining her health, and Buechner had started to heal the brokenness of his own childhood family that lived by the universal dysfunctional rules "Don't talk, don't trust, don't feel" (*TS* 10). He had finished writing *Godric* and learned much about how his daughter's anorexia was a manifestation of the unhappiness of his own childhood. It was to the main character of the four novels written before *Godric* that he now referred to explain what he had learned. The character Leo Bebb – so filled with abundant life – had a "narrow-brimmed hat, dimly Tyrolean, on the top of his head" and a disconcerting wink – "It was involuntary, just a lazy eyelid that slid partly shut sometimes."[26] The fat man so caught Buechner's fancy that "Instead of having to force myself to go back to it every morning as I had with novels in the past, I could hardly wait to go back to it" (*N&T* 98).

Bebb was a big man who lived life to the hilt. He was unlike anyone Buechner had ever known, saying things like "I've probably ordained [through the mail] all kinds of crooks and misfits – pimps, sodomites, blackmailers, and pickpockets for all I know, you name it – I say judge not that ye be not judged."[27] Bebb taught Buechner much about the pain of secrets. Buechner said in an interview, "Bebb is a man who does time for exposing himself – in a sexual way, but in other ways too. Bebb's power is that he tells it the way it is about himself, and I think in some ways I've learned from him. I've now become an exposer of myself."[28] After finishing the four books that Bebb seemed to require to tell his story, Buechner began his series of three autobiographies. He had learned for himself to look for the incarnate words that God had spoken in the events of his own life.

---

26. Frederick Buechner, *The Book of Bebb* (New York: Atheneum, 1979), 3.

27. Ibid., 5.

28. Frederick Buechner, quoted in Gibble, 1042.

Buechner had learned that the only way to loosen his strangle hold on happiness, the grip that made him believe that "I had no right to be happy unless the people I loved – especially my children – were happy too" (*TS* 102) was to remember all he could of his past and tell those secrets that had restrained him so long. Therapy taught him this and so did twelve-step groups like Alcoholics Anonymous and Al-Anon. He brings that experience to life for us in details – details through which he experienced the love and acceptance of God and of fellow human beings: "people very much like you and me . . . are sitting in the basement of a church or an American Legion post or an after-hours hospital cafeteria. Fluorescent lights buzz overhead. There is an urn of coffee. There is a basket which is passed around at some point which everybody who can afford to puts a dollar in" (*TS* 89). In this leveling atmosphere, Buechner learned to be like these recovering people who "try to follow a kind of spiritual rule, which consists basically not only of uncovering their own deep secrets but of making peace with the people they have hurt and been hurt by" (*TS* 91). Buechner found that uncovering his secrets – remembering – and having those secrets accepted by others and by God brought great healing.

Around this time, Buechner had a dream in which he stayed in a lovely, light-filled hotel room. He left for a while and came back to find that he had been assigned a different room, but he longed to be back in the bright room, so he described it to the desk clerk and asked what the room's name was. "The name of the room is Remember – the room where with patience, with charity, with quietness of heart, we remember consciously to remember the lives we have lived" (*RCR* 6). The name of the room was Remember, and this concrete image contains much of what Buechner learned about the healing power of telling our stories, reciting the details of how God has spoken in our lives.

With remembering those details comes an understanding of God's presence and purpose in our lives. Buechner writes, "memory makes it possible for us both to bless the past . . . and also to be blessed by it. . . . [When I aired] my crippling secret . . . then, however slowly and uncertainly, I could start to find healing. It is in the experience of such healing that I believe we experience also God's loving forgiveness of us, and insofar as memory is the doorway to both experiences, it becomes not just therapeutic but sacred" (*TS* 33-34). To illustrate the sacred importance of sharing one's story – however painful – Buechner uses the parable of the steward who was rebuked for hiding his share of his master's money in the ground while his fellow stewards were out trading with their shares and increasing them. Buechner writes that the parable means that "the buried pain in particular and all the other things we tend to bury along with pain, including joy, . . . is itself darkness and wailing and gnashing of teeth and the one who casts us into it is no one other than ourselves" (*CB* 97). Buechner admonishes us to be good stewards of our pain and of our joy – "taking the risk of being open, of reaching out" (*CB* 99).

Having learned the value of talking about his secret, Buechner wrote a book that tells the story of his father's suicide, thinly disguised in fiction, for child readers and for the child in himself. However, this time he lived it *right*, he says (*TS* 34). The difference was that the little boy speaks the *right* word near the end of the book. Instead of covering up his suffering and even the fact that he had had a father, the way Buechner's own family did, this little boy explains to his younger sister that Christmastide – the tide of Christmas – is the Wizard's tide, whose goal is to carry you back to shore, to carry you home. His sister asks if this applies to everybody. Teddy assures her this Wizard of Oz tide is for every-body, "Even Daddy."[29] The word "Daddy" is the word that breaks the silence and will bring the healing of memory for both children.

Buechner has experienced in the events of his own life that "way beyond all those [disturbing memories], at the innermost heart, at the farthest reach of our remembering, there is peace. The secret place of the Most High is there. Eden is there, the still waters, the green pastures. Home is there" (*TS* 66). Through tidal images and a written conversation between two grieving children, Buechner generously shares the way he found to peace and grace: Remember, and share words about what experience has taught you.

---

29. Frederick Buechner, *The Wizard's Tide* (San Francisco: HarperCollins, 1993), 103.

The Transcendent Presence in Silence

But what does one learn in the experience of suffering? In *Godric*, Buechner not only makes the Transcendent present to readers by evoking details of water and porpoise voices; he also addresses the question of suffering. Godric wonders, "Was it God who led me on the way I went? . . . Life's a list. Good tilts with ill. The [overlords] of the world grow fat. Poor folk eat earth. Even in his church, the Lord is mocked by lustful, greedy monks and priests that steal. . . . Folk lie sick with none to nurse them. Good men die before their time" (*G* 141-42). These images of human suffering are familiar and too real to ignore. Godric doesn't ignore them, but he sees beyond them. Again, water imagery makes the point as Godric thinks of all the times he has chastened his flesh by bathing in his friend the river Wear's icy waters, even though he is so old now that he must have the water brought in pails to a tub he has hollowed out in the chapel he built.

> Now that I can hardly walk, I crawl to meet him [Wear] there. He takes me in his chilly lap to wash me of my sins. Or I kneel down beside him till within his depths I see a star.
>
> . . . She is Mary's star. Within that little pool of Wear she winks at me. . . . The secret that we share I cannot tell in full. But this much I will tell. What's lost is nothing to what's found, and all the death that ever was, set next to life, would scarce fill a cup. (*G* 96)

Christ's life-giving cup overflows, and he has told Godric to enjoy him to his heart's delight. But so often God seems absent in the midst of suffering. All that Godric can say about suffering is this: Christ is stronger. Through the image of the scarcely filled cup of suffering, Buechner gives us the experience of putting suffering in its place. Again, the "ordinary" experiences of life – water, cups, stars – have shown Godric and Buechner's readers that, as Marjorie Casebier McCoy says, "the transcendent is not beyond and apart from the ordinary but some part of experience leaps out at us, calls forth faith within us at least for a moment, and, transcending other parts in significance, becomes the means for seeing some whole-ness in the tangle of events making up our life."[30]

In *Son of Laughter*, no less than in previous novels, Buechner asks, "Why is there suffering?" He makes the powerlessness and pain of Jacob's son Joseph and the apparent indifference of God to his suffering very concrete in this passage:

> a deep pit, a well dug and abandoned when it was found there was no water in it. A naked boy lies at the bottom. His hands are bound behind his back. His ankles are bound. He lies curled up with his knees to his chest as if for sleep or burial. From the nape of his neck, down his lean back and buttocks to the crook of his knees the shape of him is a single curve. He has a boy's downy beard. He is a virgin. The sand is wet with spittle where his mouth touches it. He makes no sound. The only sound is the bleating of sheep that browse above him. The pit is of no matter to them or what lies in the pit. (*SL* 215)

This fragile, naked boy whose mouth wets the ground he lies on is later hauled up by the same jealous brothers who threw him there and sold him to men traveling to Egypt. There, of course, Joseph warns the pharaoh to save grain from the seven good years to feed his people during the seven lean years, and Joseph's own brothers and father come to Egypt to buy food to save their lives. By the novel's end, Jacob finds out about the pit that Joseph was thrown into and can hardly bear to look at the eleven sons who had done such evil. Yet he must admit that "it was through their evil that the Fear [God] had worked the saving of us all" (*SL* 269). Since, in Jacob, Buechner chose a character whose story takes place before Christ's resurrection, he cannot point to the resurrection triumph in the novel's consideration of evil, but he does emphasize again that the Transcendent is present in events, even when we feel it is most absent.

As a writer who is a minister, Buechner grapples with scripture as part of his examination of the Transcendent presence in events. In a series of published lectures, he invents transcendent details for one of the most abandoned characters in the Bible: Pontius Pilate. In working with "reinvented . . . truth," which memoir writer William Zinsser calls "the only truth that the writer

---

30. Marjorie Casebier McCoy with Charles S. McCoy, 103.

of a memoir can work with,"[31] Buechner is working along the lines of literary theorist George Steiner's preferred forms of "critique" – memorizing a poem, performing a play, translating, or making allusions to previous literature in new literature one is creating.[32]

Buechner invents a scenario, saying that on the morning of the day he will face Jesus and ask "What is truth?" Pilate has quit smoking and flushed all the cigarettes in his house down the toilet. In this fragile state, he reads in his limousine the newspaper accounts of poverty, disease, crime, corruption, and ignorance and hopes he lives until he can retire from his dull government job and walk on the beach drinking martinis. When he gets to the office, his secretary makes eyes at him, but he lacks the energy for that with all his other problems. Suddenly Jesus stands before him – a country bumpkin whose bruised eye is swollen shut and whose words are obscured by his cut lip and Nazareth accent. Pilate's son's kindergarten hand-print ashtray sits on his desk, and suddenly he finds himself smoking a forbidden cigarette from the box Caesar gave him (*TT* 8-13). Pilate is in such crisis – he feels such an absence of the Transcendent in his life – that he really wants to know what truth is.

This is Buechner at his best – drawing us into a biblical story's truth by adding details and events modern readers have experienced many times. We become one with this overworked, overworldly Pilate when he asks "What is truth?" Jesus' answer, of course, was his silent presence. Buechner tells us, "before the Gospel is a word, it too like truth is silence – not an ordinary silence, silence as nothing to hear, but silence that makes itself heard if you listen to it" (*TT* 14). Words can draw us to transcendent truth, but the events of life are where truth is really revealed, and sometimes those events are silent. Buechner writes, "Truth itself cannot be stated. Truth simply is, and is what is, the good with the bad, the joy with the despair, the presence and absence of God" (*TT* 16). Those times when we seem forsaken and met with only silence are tangible events through which Buechner believes God is

---

31. William Zinsser, *Inventing the Truth: The Art and Craft of Memoir* (Boston: Houghton Mifflin, 1987), 12, 17.

32. Steiner, 7-15.

speaking – calling, even. Buechner's job, as an author, is to make the emptiness of those times real for readers – and also to make real the possibility of a still small voice.

The answers Buddhism and Christianity give to questions about suffering form the main difference Buechner sees between the beliefs of a Buddhist, which he admits he thinks he would be if he were not a Christian, and those of someone who has looked at the details of Buddha's life and the life of Christ and chosen to follow the latter. Alan Watts, who has written many books on Eastern religion, discusses evil from a Hindu perspective: "For Hindu thought there is no Problem of Evil. The conventional, relative world is necessarily a world of opposites. Light is inconceivable apart from darkness . . . and likewise . . . pleasure without pain."[33] Buechner, however, does not just examine a dispassionate theory of opposites; he looks instead to the physical presence of the Buddha and of Christ to show the transcendent truth. He writes, "Buddha sits enthroned beneath the Bo-tree in the lotus position. His lips are faintly parted in the smile of one who has passed beyond every power in earth or heaven to touch him. . . . Christ, on the other hand, stands in the garden of Gethsemane, angular, beleaguered . . . you can't even see his lips. . . . The difference seems to me this. The suffering that Buddha's eyes close out is the suffering of the world that Christ's eyes close in and hallow" (*N&T* 53-54). Looking into Christ's eyes and seeing his passion and compassion, Buechner sees the power of a God who transforms crucifixion into resurrection, but not without feeling the pain first. Both Buddha and Christ are often silent, but the texture of Christ's silence – the meaning of his actions – speaks to Buechner of a Transcendent caring.

In his writing, Buechner is willing to look hard at the suffering of Christ. He looks into the most chilling statement of God's absence in the New Testament: "By the time [Jesus had been hanging on the cross] for a while, he had no tears left to weep with and no more sweat, his tongue was so dry he could hardly wrap it around the words which are among the few he ever spoke that people remembered in the language he spoke them in, probably

---

33. Alan Watts, *The Way of Zen* (New York: Vintage Books, 1989), 35.

because having once heard them, they could never forget them no matter how hard they tried, and probably they tried hard and often: 'My God, my God, why have you – '" (*TT* 38-39). Here are harrowing details that illustrate Buechner's knowledge that God is "often more conspicuous by his absence than by his presence, and his absence is much of what we labor under and are heavy laden by" (*TT* 43).

But just as God did not answer Job in words but instead made himself present to him, God is with Jesus on the cross and in his descent into Hell and finally in his resurrection, and we learn from these events that "death and dark and despair [are] not the last reality but only the next to the last" (*N&T* 49). Buechner writes that "God himself does not give answers. He gives himself, and into the midst of the whirlwind of his absence gives himself" (*TT* 43). Buechner finally answers Jesus' haunting question this way:

> "My God, my God, why hast thou forsaken me?" . . . in a way [Christ's] words are a love song. . . . In a way, his words are the words we all of us must speak before we know what it means to love God as we are commanded to love him.
>
> "*My* God, *my* God." Though God is not there for him to see or hear, he calls on him still because he can do no other. Not even the cross, not even death, not even life, can destroy his love for God. . . .
>
> The final secret, I think, is this: that the words "You shall love the Lord your God" become in the end less a command than a promise. And the promise is that, yes, on the weary feet of faith and the fragile wings of hope, we will come to love him at last as from the first he has loved us – loved us even in the wilderness, especially in the wilderness, because he has been in the wilderness with us. (*RCR* 44-45)

Buechner is emphatic that not only in clacking branches or flowing water or tumbling children will we experience the Transcendent, but also in wilderness and forsakenness we will experience the promise that we will be helped to love God. Here again, Buechner sees God's transcendent truths being expressed in life's experiences – both the good and the painful.

Buechner does not believe, however, that God causes suffering to happen. He writes that he "does not mean that [God] makes events happen to us . . . . Instead, events happen under their own steam as random as rain" (*TS* 31). God does not cause tragedy, but God is present during it in some way and tries to tell us how we can come through a painful event with some kind of good. Like all serious Christians, Buechner sees the resurrection as a tangible event that showed that good is stronger than evil. He writes, "Christianity . . . ultimately offers no theoretical solution [to the problem of why suffering exists] at all. It merely points to the cross and says that, practically speaking, there is no evil so dark and so obscene – not even this – but that God can turn it to good" (*WT* 24). Not that Buechner denies there are times – days, moments – when it is hard to have such faith in God's power to bring good, or even to have faith in God's existence. He writes about the Christmas story and the question of whether or not it is true, "When you are standing up to your neck in darkness, how do you say Yes to that question? You say Yes, I suppose, the only way faith can ever say it if it is honest with itself. You say Yes with your fingers crossed. You say it with your heart in your mouth" (*CB* 124).

The closest Buechner comes to offering an explanation for why tragedy happens is his notion that God does not cause either bad or good actions, but leaves humans free will. He illustrates his theory with a characteristic image from real life – this time a disturbing image: "When a child is raped and murdered, the parents are not apt to take much comfort from the explanation (better than most) that since God wants man to love him, man must be free to love or not to love and thus free to rape and murder a child if he takes a notion to" (*WT* 24).[34] From the concrete evidence in his

---

34. Poet Denise Levertov came to the same conclusion about human freedom to choose as a cause of evil actions, and she came to it through the same route as Buechner: through writing about concrete images. She says, "God . . . gives to human beings the power to utter yes or no – to perceive the whole range of dualities without which there could be no freedom. . . . *for me* [this theory] was original, not only because I hadn't come across . . . expositions of it [in works of religious philosophy] but also because the concrete images which emerged in the process of writing convinced me at a more intimate level of understanding than abstract argument would have done." See Denise Levertov, "Work that Enfaiths," *Cross Currents* (Summer 1990): 153-54.

own and his characters' lives, Buechner is convinced that the Transcendent speaks in events, even when our free will allows us to ignore or misinterpret it.

Novelists send their work out into the world to be interpreted by strangers, much like the great Zen poets who were said to have written superb haiku and put them into bottles that they let go upon a river.[35] Those readers who take the bottles out of the stream may disagree on some facets of each writer's meaning. Even Steiner agrees that "No reading finally encompasses the meanings, the life-in-meaning, of the poem,"[36] but he goes on to argue that those differing interpretations are themselves evidence of a transcendent ground of truth: an original creation.

> When readers, interpreters or viewers of comparable sensibility and knowledge offer discordant responses to the same work, it is simply that their own free being has come up against differing facets of that in the aesthetic form which is itself irreducible to that form. This "otherness" seems to me to be, almost materially, like an ever-renewed vestige of the original, never wholly accessible moment of creation.[37]

Here, Steiner makes the important point that good literature delivers many meanings because the original Creator and the artist are complex and readers have free will. But the presence of many meanings in literature does not lead to the deduction that no meanings exist.

Buechner's novels, informed by his theological ideas but mainly filled with the texture of real life – the pleasures and pains of life in the flesh – offer clear glimpses of the transcendent one who redeems that life.

Author's Note:

The first time I heard Frederick Buechner's name, I was eating a bratwurst at a faculty picnic. A colleague had just been inspired by

---

35. Goldberg, 121.
36. Steiner, 210.
37. Ibid.

Godric. *Like Buechner, I was a Presbyterian searching for answers to "Why is there suffering?" so I was intrigued and remembered the name. A year later, I bought Buechner's three autobiographical volumes from a book table at the Presbyterian General Assembly. As I read of Buechner's experiences with his own recovery, motivated by his daughter's anorexia, I was moved to explore the secrets in my own life and began recovering.*

Buechner doesn't ignore suffering. He looks into its face. He has Pilate facing the beat-up Jesus, on the day Pilate has quit smoking, and asking, "What is truth?" out of a desire to know. For Buechner, the words "You shall love the Lord your God" are a comforting promise. Like Buechner, we might ask, Why is there suffering? What is truth? Have you experienced anything like the texture of water or the noise of family in which Buechner's characters find a transcendent presence?

H.S.

Works Cited

Anderson, Sherry Ruth, and Patricia Hopkins. *The Feminine Face of God: The Unfolding of the Sacred in Women.* New York: Bantam Books, 1992.

Baldwin, James. "If Black English Isn't a Language, Then Tell Me, What Is?" In *Major Modern Essayists.* Edited by Gilbert H. Muller and Alan F. Crooks, 149-52. 2d ed. Englewood Cliffs, N.J.: Blair Press, 1994.

Buechner, Frederick. *The Book of Bebb.* New York: Atheneum, 1979.

_____. *The Clown in the Belfry: Writings on Faith and Fiction.* San Francisco: HarperCollins, 1992.

_____. *The Final Beast.* New York: Atheneum, 1965.

_____. *Godric.* New York: Atheneum, 1980.

_____. *Now and Then.* San Francisco: HarperCollins, 1991.

_____. *A Room Called Remember.* San Francisco: HarperCollins, 1992.

_____. *The Sacred Journey.* San Francisco: HarperCollins, 1991.

_____. *The Son of Laughter.* San Francisco: HarperCollins, 1994.

_____. *Telling Secrets.* San Francisco: HarperCollins, 1992.

_____. *Telling the Truth: The Gospel as Tragedy, Comedy, and Fairy Tale.* New York: Harper & Row, 1977.

_____. *Wishful Thinking: A Theological ABC.* New York: Harper and Row, 1973.

_____. *The Wizard's Tide.* San Francisco: HarperCollins, 1993.

Gibble, Kenneth. "Listening to My Life: An Interview with Frederick Buechner." *The Christian Century* (16 November 1983): 1042-45.

Goldberg, Natalie. *Writing Down the Bones.* Boston: Shambhala, 1986.

Kendrick, Stephen. "On Spiritual Autobiography: An Interview with Frederick Buechner." *The Christian Century* (14 October 1992): 900-904.

Levertov, Denise. "Work That Enfaiths." *Cross Currents* (summer 1990): 150-59.

Lewis, C. S. *The Great Divorce.* New York: Macmillan, 1946.

Lynn, Steven. "A Passage into Critical Theory." *College English* (March 1990): 258-71.

McCoy, Marjorie Casebier, with Charles S. McCoy. *Frederick Buechner: Novelist/Theologian of the Lost and Found.* San Francisco: Harper and Row, 1988.

Rich, Adrienne. "Poetry for Daily Use." *Ms.* (September/October 1991): 70-75.

Steiner, George. *Real Presences.* Chicago: University of Chicago Press, 1989.

Watts, Alan. *The Way of Zen.* New York: Vintage Books, 1989.

Zinsser, William, ed. *Inventing the Truth: The Art and Craft of Memoir.* Boston: Houghton Mifflin, 1987.

Chapter Nine

It's All Telling: Narrative in *Riddley Walker*

Jane Thompson

I said, "All this what you jus ben telling be that a tel for me?"

She larft then she said, "Riddley there aint nothing what *aint* a tel for you. The wind in the night the dus on the road even the leases stoan you kick a long in front of you. Even the shadder of that leases stoan roaling on or stanning stil its all telling."

Wel I cant say for cern no mor if I had any of them things in my mynd befor she tol me but ever since then it seams like they all ways ben there. Seams like I ben all ways thinking on that thing what thinks us but it dont think like us. Our woal life is a idear we dint think of nor we dont know what it is. . . .

– Hoban, *Riddley Walker*

In the science-fiction novel *Riddley Walker* by Russell Hoban, the "idear" of "[o]ur woal life" is constantly in question. The title character and narrator, a boy of twelve in a harsh, post-nuclear-war world, sees numinous mystery in almost every object and action; from the very beginning of the book, he is preoccupied with how to solve – how even to interrogate – these mysteries. What he gradually finds out is that the narrative in which he records his search is, in itself, his confrontation with the "idear." The story as he lives and writes it *is* Riddley's search for the transcendent. And Hoban, for whom Riddley does his telling (just as, late in the novel, Riddley's puppets "tel" for him), shows in the characters' storytelling how narrative allows individuals to reach beyond themselves,

154

to maintain relationships and communities, and ultimately to perceive the social, natural, and spiritual worlds as interdependent.

Narrative is, in the novel, the most successful escape-route from the prison of isolated selfhood. Especially for Riddley himself, gestures and nonnarrative ceremonies are relatively ineffective ways to reify personal relationships or communal identities. The novel's first chapter demonstrates the advantages of narrative for Riddley by showing the stages of his initiation into adulthood, beginning with a ceremonial hunt which leaves him unmoved:

> On my naming day when I come 12 I gone front spear and kilt a wyld boar . . . . He didnt make the groun shake nor nothing like that when he come on to my spear he wernt all that big plus he lookit poorly. . . . we all yelt, "Offert!"
>
> The woal thing felt jus that litl bit stupid.[1]

But that night, the tel woman Lorna Elswint invites him into adulthood with a more compelling offer of both narrative and sex, asking him, "Whynt you be the Big Boar and Iwl be the Moon Sow" (5). She sings:

> . . . When the Moon Sow comes to season
> Ay! She wants a big 1 . . .
> Ay yee! Big Boar what makes the groun shake
> Wyld of the Woodling with the wite tusk
> Ay yee! That wyld big 1 for the Moon Sow. (5)

Her song revises the unsatisfactory hunt into a drama in which Riddley himself plays an improved (and living) boar. He no longer feels stupid – or isolated, for that matter.

Lorna can also explain his feelings of isolation; after their intercourse, she speaks to him about "some thing in us [that] don't have no name" but which looks "out thru your eye hoals" (6):

> Its all 1 girt big thing bigger nor the worl and lorn and lone and oansome. Tremmering it is and feart. It puts us on like we put on our cloes. Some times we dont fit. Some times it cant find the arm hoals and it tears us a part. . . . Now Im old I noatis it mor. It dont realy like to put me

---

1. Russell Hoban, *Riddley Walker* (New York: Pocket Books, 1980), 1; hereafter cited parenthetically in the text.

> on no mor. Every morning I can feel how its tiret of me
> and readying to throw me a way. (6)

It is this myth of mortality and of continuance of spirit which prompts Riddley to ask, "be that a tel for me?" – the question which begins his search for the "idear" of his life. Indeed, he acknowledges at the end of Chapter 1, "Thats why I finely came to writing all this down" (7): that is, his thoughts of the lonely "thing" motivate the whole narrative of the book.

Narrative, even in this first chapter, reinforces the importance of community as both a means of insuring survival and as the anchor of the most basic moral values. A folk story which Riddley baldly introduces immediately after the hunt ("Theres a story callit *Hart of the Wud* this is it" [2]) shows a family group transformed by the "Bad Time 1st and bad times after" (2) into first helpless and then savage animals:

> Ther come a man and a woman and a chyld out of a
> berning town . . . . Starveling wer what they wer doing.
> Dint have no weapons nor dint know how to make a snare
> nor nothing. . . . Freazing col they wer nor dint have
> nothing to make a fire with to get warm.
>   . . . They kilt the chyld and drunk its blood and cut
> up the meat for cooking. (2-3)

Without the support of their former society, now in ruins, even the bonds between parents and children cannot hold. The parents sacrifice the child at the suggestion of a "clevver looking bloak" (3) who makes fire for them and shares this horrific communal meal. On the one hand, this anti-Adam and anti-Eve personify an ultimate violation of the most basic moral prohibitions – do not kill your child; do not eat other people – yet, on the other hand, what saves them is their social interaction with the "clevver" stranger, who shares his skill with them and demands food from them in return. Although "Hart of the Wood" is a myth of origin insofar as it explains the conditions from which the world of the novel arose, it is a paradoxical sort of creation story, in which community is both lost and found.

"The Hart of the Wood" introduces the reader to the type of symbolic history that is transmitted among the inhabitants of

"Inland" (that is to say, the area surrounding the ruined city which was once Canterbury, now called "Cambry"). It also demonstrates the positive use made of this communal memory of the terrible past. Though the child in "Hart of the Wood" is sacrificed, the parents do survive, along with the "clevver looking bloak" (3). The Inlanders who tell such stories as "Hart of the Wood" know themselves to be living in far less comfort and security than their ancestors – as one character puts it, "*Weve come way way down from what they ben time back way back*" (124, Hoban's italics) – but this story serves as a reminder that they live in better conditions than their more immediate forebears, and that it is their communities, their shared strengths and skills, that allow them to do so. In telling himself this story, Riddley reiterates the importance of taking his place in some community group. So like Lorna's song and story, "Hart of the Wood" replaces the hunt with an experience that is more effective *because* it involves storytelling.

Riddley's hereditary job in his nomadic community of hunters, gatherers, and odd-jobbers is as a professional interpreter of narrative: he is a "connexion man" for the puppet-shows produced by Inland's government (called "The Ram" and situated on an island near what was once Ramshead). These shows are specifically designed to sustain and control the larger community of Inland. Each of the "Eusa shows" in the novel gives a symbolic account of recent events, using characters from Inland's sacred narrative, "The Eusa Story." Thus each performance combines the functions of a newscast and a religious service. The stories of conflicts between various smaller communities within Inland are retold, identifying the source of this conflict with the source of the "Bad Time." The Eusa shows are like simpler versions of "The Hart of the Wood," for the theme that unites them is ultimately that divisiveness is sin and togetherness, virtue: act together or die.

Ritual responses called "show talk" begin each performance and stress the audience's shared past and destiny:

I said, "Weare going aint we."
The crowd said, "Yes weare going."
I said, "Down that road with Eusa.
. . . They said, "He done his time wewl do our time."
I said, "Hes doing it for us."

They said, "We are doing it for him."
I said, "Keap it going . . . . New chance every time."
They said, "New chance every time." (44)

As Riddley's part in the show talk emphasizes, the shows provide a pattern by which Inlanders understand their life experiences as variations of Eusa's experience. They keep going together because Eusa's story (and, by extension, each Eusa show) shows them how.

But each Eusa show also disseminates government policies which may or may not respond to the needs of specific farming villages or nomadic groups. The unity these stories are designed to create is in some ways false, since it too simply privileges the past and its technology. The Ram seems to have forgotten the ambiguities of community that "The Hart of the Wood" symbolically portrays – its insistence that the same mutual dependence that saves one's life may also destroy one's future. Hoban, placing his main character among the relatively impoverished fents nomads, allows his story to show some of this ambiguity as well; the Eusa shows are propagandistic, but the force of their simple theme can be checked in individual communities by the connexion man, who may aggressively reinterpret shows in order to make them more useful to his own group.

Riddley gives an example of this kind of intervention in his father's work. This sample Eusa show was the government's response to a violent conflict between a nomadic fents community, much like Riddley's ov/n, and a "form" or farming village. When the fents people refused to join the form, the farmers attacked; later, the form people claimed the fents had been destroyed by pirates. In the show, a puppet carrying a pan of salt represents the fents (punning on its name, "Littl Salting"), and is approached by Eusa, who represents the form because he leads a cow. Eusa suggests that the two of them join together for protection. The "salting bloak," having been made suspicious by the insinuations of the devil-figure Mr. Clevver, refuses. Another man comes in a boat and attacks both the salting bloak and Eusa. The "Littl Shyning Man the Addom," whose dismemberment in the original "Eusa Story" symbolized the fission of the Bomb, speaks the story's moral: "Onlyes way Iwl get put to gether is when peopl pul to gether" (58). Not only does this show retell the form's account of the event and silence the fents' version, but it also deploys the characters of the Eusa story to imply that the forms *are* Inland (Eusa); the desire of the fents groups to remain independent must be destructive to Inland since it is associated with Mr. Clevver, who forced Eusa to make the bomb.

But such a version of the story is unacceptable to the fents people of the audience. They – and Brooder Walker, as their connexion man – turn the puppet-show to their own ends in the same way that the show was derived from the Eusa story, or the Eusa story was derived from its pre-war sources: by reinterpreting the show so that its account of the event reflects a more usable social message. In this case, Walker picks out the pun on "salt" with its slang connection to "assault" mentioned by Eusa in the patter at the beginning of the performance. His comment on the show is simply, "Wel you know there it is. A littl salting and no saver" (60). This interpretation succinctly commiserates with the helpless people of Littl Salting and notes that neither side has derived real "saver" – meaning savor or even salvation – from the violent event. It even contains a criticism of the tasteless quality of the show itself. The audience reacts immediately to the truth they see in this interpretation: "1/2 of them larft out and 1/2 of them syd deep" (60). Furthermore, the show and its interpretation influence the group's actions when they move their settlement away from a rapacious nearby form. Adapting these narratives to their circumstances is a cooperative endeavor, which pulls the people of the fents together and reminds them of the beliefs they share. The interplay of The Ram's revisions and the connexion man's revisions makes the "[n]ew chance every time," that the show talk promises (44).

After his father's death, Riddley is initiated into the profession of connexion man, but fails in his first interpretation. Like the role of boar-hunter, the role of literary critic is still too remote from his need to tell stories in order to extend and express his personal understanding. The show for which Riddley cannot make a "connexion" is an advertisement for a particular government project: the recovery of a pre-war computer. In the show, Eusa builds an object which he calls his new "head" and puts all his knowledge into it. But his antagonist, Mr. Clevver, steals "Eusa's head" and perverts the information it contains to create the nuclear bomb. The mutilated Littl Man the Addom appears and insists, "there wont be no Good Time til you get [the computer] back" (50).

One reason Riddley finds this show hard to interpret is that his father has just died as a result of this same project: an object excavated in a nearby form fell on the older Walker while it was being removed from its hole. Riddley, who slipped while winding the winch, begins to take the blame, but the other members of his work crew would rather blame the form for its faulty equipment. Lorna plays on this local rivalry in her funeral speech, retelling the event as a sign that the whole excavation is a bad idea:

> Widders Dump. You know what they ben doing . . . digging up that old time Bad Time black time . . . . Brooder Walker dug her up and she come down on top of him o yes.
>
> Our connexion man and what he ben connectit to? . . . Brooder Walker ben connectit to a shovel and a leaver poal and digging up Bad Time. Ben that a right connexion or a wrong 1? (24)

The show Riddley must interpret seems a government response to just this sort of complaint, but his anxiety to make a "right connexion," fueled by his personal distress and his community's controversy, blocks him.

Riddley plans his interpretation carefully and decides to conclude with a warning about the project's wisdom which seems tailored to his audience's opinion. But at the moment he begins to speak, he is overwhelmed by "a crakeling and like a roaring in the air or in my head I dint know which" (61) – a mystical experience whose insight pierces the ideology on which the puppet show was based and which glimpses again the "thing which thinks us" (7):

> Nor I werent dreaming nor I hadnt ben smoking I wernt acturely seeing Eusas head it wer jus *there* for me I cant say plainer nor that. Which it wunt stop getting bigger . . . . Not jus over us and all roun it wer coming up inside me as wel. The thot came to me: EUSAS HEAD IS DREAMING US. (61, Hoban's italics and capitalization)

This last, enigmatic statement is almost all he is able to say aloud, and his audience is not able to make much of it. "So every 1 wer lef hanging," Riddley says. "Me and all" (62).

Riddley cannot agree with the politician/puppeteers, and yet he cannot subvert the "Eusa's head" show as his father had overturned the message of the "Littl Salting" show. Though his connexion is no more enigmatic and concentrated than his father's, it is based neither on the immediate subject of the show nor on knowledge common to the whole fents audience. Everyone is "lef hanging" because the image of Riddley's brief enlightenment has been detached from the Ram narrative without being re-embedded in any new one. Only later will he learn to recreate his visions in narrative and to make social connections. Still, he continues to aspire to a storytelling beyond words, a history beyond events, a fusion of nature, spirit, and social interaction – as he says,

> Some times theres mor in the emty paper nor there is when you get the writing down on it. You try to word the big things and they tern ther backs on you. Yet youwl see stanning stoans and ther backs wil talk to you. The living stoan wil all ways have the living wood in it I know that. With the hart of the chyld in it which that hart of the chyld is that same and very thing what lives inside us and afeart of being bearthd. (161)

In this musing, Riddley combines imagery from at least three stories and from his own experience, and he reaches an understanding which he almost immediately re-embeds in narrative – developing it even further, though at this stage he is still only "walking [his] riddels . . . on this paper. . ." (8).

He speculates, "If you cud even jus only put your self right with 1 stoan youwd be moving with the girt dants of the every thing" (162); this symbol of wholeness expands in the story "Stoan" into "a stoan self of your self in the ground and walking foot to foot with you" (164). But when every man (Riddley insists [164] that only men have stone-selves) is imagined as "right with 1 stoan," his place in the great dance of everything turns out not to be one of unlimited power, as Riddley originally speculated ("What ever you done wud be right" [162]). Instead, the story's "you" does only what anyone does, walking across the earth in life and lying down on it in death. At the man's death, his stone reflection tries to "stand up" and live independently, but it cannot; it can only mirror the corpse's decay: "Vines and leaves growing out of the nose hoals and the eyes then breaking the stoan mans face a part" (164). The cycle by which individual lives rise and then fall back into other life *is* the great dance of every (living) thing.

Riddley describes "Stoan" as "[s]ome thing [that] come in to me. Some thing I lissent out of that place" in Cambry (165), and it fills his head with images foreign both to his past life and to more familiar stories. He dwells particularly on "[t]he look of that face saying so many diffrent things only no words to say them with . . . . That face in my mynd with the vines and leaves growing out of the mouf I begun to see it wer the onlyes face there wer" (165-66). He has discovered an image which synthesizes many other images, which expresses at least partly his wordless impulses. And it changes him: "I wer progammit differnt then from how I ben when I come in to Cambry," he says (166). There is no simple progression in the plot from personal development to community action, from communal identity to mystical transcendence. Instead, the book moves freely among the psychological, the social, and the mystical. Stories change the teller; stories change the audience; stories themselves change to fit differing circumstances, and those circumstances also change – perhaps as a result of the changing stories.

The complex relationships among "The Eusa Story," the Ram's Eusa shows, and the alternate puppet show that Riddley eventually develops demonstrate some of these interactive changes. At the time of the novel's opening scenes, the constant adaptations of Eusa shows to new events has gradually moved them farther and farther away from the mystical concerns and tragic outcome of the original "Eusa Story," in which all Eusa's scientific knowledge and good intentions are helpless against Mr. Clevver's machinations and his own corroding rage. Sent on a magical journey to "the wud in the hart uv the stoan" to protect Inland from its enemies (30), Eusa commits this scripture's original sin: he shoots the speaking stag called the Hart of the Wud and pulls apart the Littl Shynin Man the Addom when he refuses to answer Eusa's questions. As a result, he loses his wife and children and is driven almost to death before he has another vision of the Littl Shynin Man:

> Eusa sed, Is this a dream? The Littl Man sed, No . . . . nor yu cant wayk up owt uv it. Eusa sed, I can dy owt uv it tho cant I. The Littl Man sed, Eusa yu dy owt uv this plays & yol jus fyn me in a nuther plays. Yul fyn me in the wud yul fyn me on the water lyk yu foun me in the stoan. Yu luk enne wayr & Iwl be thayr . . . . Yu let thay Chaynjis owt & now yu got to go on thru them. (35-36)

Although Eusa is in some ways like the Inlanders reading and copying his story (the only remaining written account of the war), he is also distant from them because of his scientific knowledge and because of his guilt for the Addom's fission. Science in "The Eusa Story" is not reliable; neither is the mercy of any divine being; the world is as fluid and uncontrollable as a dream. There is no clear moral law, though evil has been done. The tradition created by "The Eusa Story" is of submission to endless and unpredictable "Chaynjis." The Eusa shows, on the other hand, do not retain the emphasis on the evils of technology that marked "The Eusa Story" – in fact, they have become advertisements for the powers and luxuries of the past, which the Pry Mincer (or Prime Minister) and his government are trying to rediscover. Riddley initially has a good deal of sympathy for the pursuit of ancient knowledge and power, but he cannot accept the human price that is continually exacted for the Pry Mincer's researches. The death of Riddley's father is only the first of these human sacrifices, which unlike the one in "Hart of the Wud" enable not survival but the distant opportunity to repeat the much vaster tragedy of nuclear war.

Both Riddley's engagement in the project of technological recovery and his revulsion from it, both his deep affiliation with the values of his society and his feelings of estrangement from specific social groups – all these, as well as his unusual approach to storytelling, make possible his development as a different kind of puppetmaster than any of the Eusa showmen. During his journeys, Riddley finds, adapts, and begins to repopularize the Punch show, a version of Punch and Judy that is evidently the pattern for the Eusa shows; however, by the end of the novel, Punch stands in thematic opposition to Eusa.

Punch first appears in *Riddley Walker* when Riddley discovers, while digging, an old and severed hand still wearing the puppet on its index finger. Riddley takes the puppet, and later has it explained to him by the Pry Mincer:

> This here figger his name is Punch which hes the oldes figger there is. He were old time back way back befor Eusa ever ben thot of. . . . Iwl show you that show . . . . Iwl pass it on to you the same thats how its meant to be you see. It aint like a Eusa show its meant to stay the same all the time. (131-32)

Like "The Eusa Story," the Punch show is supposed to be immutable, even though it has clearly been revised since the nuclear holocaust. Punch has remained constant both in name and in character, but Judy has become Pooty, a pig whom Riddley later connects to the mythic Moon Sow. She is simultaneously sex object and source of food – a point made explicit in the show when Punch attempts to eat her baby. This event harks back to the cannibalism of "Hart of the Wood," but also derives from the Punch and Judy episode involving the baby which Punch first nurtures, then beats, then throws out the window.[2] Punch, unlike the parents in "Hart of the Wood," is not starving (he has just eaten a sausage); still, he murders both the baby and Pooty, and is frying them when Jack Ketch, the "Loakel Tharty" of the law, arrives (136). Ketch demands a share of the meat, threatening to hang Punch if he does not comply. Punch kills him, and later kills "Mr. On the Levvil" (who, Riddley notes [137], looks like Eusa's Mr. Clevver) but is afterwards haunted by the ghost Drop John.

The alterations made in the original Punch pattern make it even grimmer: although the original Punch contained just as many murders, it included no cannibalism and kept its violence within the frame of slapstick comedy. The newer Punch, however, broadens its scope to dramatize the nuclear war's destruction of life, culture, and elementary morality. The difference between the newer Punch and the "Hart of the Wood" story is that, while "Hart of the Wood" portrays apocalyptic horrors, it shows them imposed

---

2. See George Speaight, *Punch and Judy: A History* (Boston: Plays, 1970), 86, 47.

by unalterable conditions; the Punch show, on the other hand, shows the same horrors motivated from within. This Punch show, though structured like a public performance, has never become part of community practice, for it serves no clear social purpose by its nihilistic portrayal of motiveless malignity.

A step in Riddley's journey from critic to artist takes place in the ruins of Canterbury, when he creates a private, stageless Punch show with "old black Punch on my right hand and Greanvine on my lef" (172). Greanvine is a wooden carving of a head with vines growing from its mouth which Riddley discovered shortly after he "lissent" his story "Stoan." The image of self-surrender that Grean-vine presents is a perfect contrast to Punch's active exploitation of those around him. In the dialog that Riddley imagines for them, Greanvine asks most of the questions while Punch gives decisive answers:

> Greanvine said, "Wel then is there hoap of a tree?"
> Punch said, "Theres hoap of the wud in the hart of the stoan."
> Greanvine said, "What stoan is that then?"
> Punch said, "Balls. Which thems the stoans what never dys."
> Wel of coarse Punch wud say that. Thats how hes that way myndit. Me I dint have Punchs balls nor I wernt all that sure them wer the stoans what never dys. (172)

Though Riddley ends this show feeling Punch's materialism and solipsistic individualism acutely, the Punch he has created is now speaking within Greanvine's – and Inland's – conceptual and theological framework. The references to sexual organs in the dialogue are not merely jokes with a vicious edge, as they are in the Pry Mincer's Punch show, but have a symbolic dimension. When Punch claims to be "the balls of the worl" (172), he is moving beyond being a character whose actions are directed by sadistic impulses and begins to represent some essential factor in the human spirit. He stands, like a Jungian shadow figure, at the intersection of the individual and the collective.

Riddley eventually develops a version of the Punch show to perform in public, but its first and only performance in the novel is disrupted; therefore, it is difficult to predict exactly how his version of the story would differ from the Pry Mincer's, or whether this most recent adaptation would satisfy an audience. Probably Punch will never be easy for Inland's communities to accept, since he represents those very impulses that no one wants to acknowledge in himself or herself. Riddley does not feel that reluctance because he intuitively recognizes Punch: when he first hears Punch's voice, he comments that "some how it wernt no stranger to me" (133). This recognition allows him to internalize the symbolism of the show, allowing all that he shares with other Inlanders to shape his presentation. To these influences and models, he adds an attitude toward the practice of his art that is best described as worshipful. He says of the job of puppeteering:

> Ready to cry ready to dy ready for anything is how I come to it now. In fear and tremmering only not running a way. In emtyness and ready to be fult. . . .
>
> . . . [A] figger show its got its own chemistery and fizzics. What it is its all ways trying to fynd out what it is jus now this same and very minim going thru its chaynjis. . . . them same and very Chaynjis what the Littl Shyning Man tol Eusa of.
>
> . . . If youre a show man then what ever happens is . . . took in to your show. If you dont know whats happent sooner youwl hear of it later youwl hear your figgers tel of it 1 way or a nother. (204-6)

Riddley frames his conception of his role as artist in mystical terms. He seems to give up conscious individual thought while working the puppets and in return becomes more fully part of external events, since the puppets explain them to him as well as to the audience in terms of the eternal Chaynjis.

A heckler in the audience of the first performance says that Punch is "crookit" (215) like the deformed "Eusa folk" who show the genetic effects of the nuclear war. Punch looks like an outcast and belongs to the post-war world of the audience – while Eusa, since he is both pre-war scientist and post-war victim, has a transcendence of character which makes him more a symbol of Inland than a representation of the inner person. The Big Man of this fents identifies just this conflict when he replies to the heckler that there are two kinds of crookedness, outer and inner, "Which

Im beginning to think may be this here humpy figger is some kynd of a nindicator" (215). When the heckler later upsets the puppet theater and stops the show, it is not a misunderstanding of Punch which motivates him, but his unwillingness to see what Punch does indicate. And even though the show is never completed, it has lasting effects on the community, for both the Big Man and the connexion man join the show group with their families, reclaiming the nomadic lifestyle that the Eusa show about Littl Salting was meant to combat.

The Punch show challenges the Eusa show at just the point where it has become weakest: its explanation of the nature and source of evil. While the Eusa show, like any other fiction, has both a sociological and a metaphysical dimension,[3] its performances seem to be emphasizing the former at the expense of the latter. Both of the Eusa shows described in the novel show a preference for centralized authority and an interest in pulling together the Littl Shyning Man – that is, recapturing the knowledge of the past. They ignore the moral questions raised by a science that has already destroyed a whole culture, and they positively deny the guilt of the scientist. In one of the shows Eusa says, "The Hart of the Wud and the Littl Shyning Man the Addom they cant live without you get the knowing of them nor you cant get the knowing of them til you kil the one and open up the other" (53). Eusa in this show is not guilty of the war, not motivated by desires for power or even knowledge. The war is caused by the atom itself, which needs to be split.

The Punch show reacts against such evasions by emphasizing the opposite idea: that human beings carry evil within themselves. This is unwelcome but necessary knowledge, especially since the reinvention of gunpowder, which takes place late in the book, will appeal to just those impulses which the Eusa show ignores. Punch demonstrates that to seek such power is to seek both physical and spiritual death, that as Riddley's puppeteering partner Orfing says, neither a community nor an individual can "move the out side of things frontways and leave the in side to take care of its self. Which

---

3. See Brian Wicker, *The Story-Shaped World: Fiction and Metaphysics: Some Variations on a Theme* (London: Athlone, 1975), 45.

I think its the in side has got to do the moving its got to move every thing and its got to move us as well" (203). Inland requires a narrative which tells its community members about "the in side," although individuals may continue to find such a reminder of human limitations abrasive. Still, it is these multifarious "Chaynjis" of narrative which provide that "[n]ew chance every time" (44), and Inlanders as a group know it.

Nevertheless, Thomas Morrissey's assumption that Riddley's Punch show will inevitably replace the old Eusa show, and that such a replacement will be a gain for the society,[4] seems too simple in the context of the novel's constant interplay among stories, its frequent acknowledgement of the multiple and ambiguous nature of truth. Certainly, to read the novel as Morrissey does makes of it a strongly conventional science fiction text, for it already contains such familiar elements as a post-nuclear-war setting, a society modelled after anthropological descriptions of "primitive" cultures, a language full of created slang, and an adolescent male hero.

But Hoban does not treat any of these elements routinely. No reliable records of the war survive in the world of the novel, and the legends characters tell contain no explicit mention of what country or political group may be considered at fault; thus Hoban's novel does not comment in any obvious way on today's politics. The "primitive" society is not homogeneous, rigid, or static; it does not directly punish those who vary from cultural norms, nor are those norms encoded in restrictive rules. Conflict is negotiated in several more or less successful ways. Hoban's created dialect is much more elaborate and consistent with linguistic science than other science-fiction slangs. Riddley, though he questions the practices of the society around him, cares deeply for its values; he neither remakes his world nor resigns himself to conformity. He is not like the third son of the fairy tale – and like many heroes in less thoughtful science fiction – whose victory in the end is individual and material; instead, as the novel ends he is still trying to establish a place in community practice in which he may,

---

4. Thomas J. Morrissey, "Armageddon from Huxley to Hoban," *Extrapolation* 25 (fall 1984): 212.

through his art, integrate and share his moments of personal enlightenment.

Against the context of other stories of the world in catastrophe, Hoban's novel stands out for its revisionary approach not only to the tropes of its genre, but to the ideological stances underlying such tropes. The literary dialect of *Riddley Walker* illustrates this point. Hoban's use of spellings which recall real-world mistakes, as well as the book's constant flow of fragments and run-ons, at first seems to show a degeneration of language. David Dowling, in his study of *Fictions of Nuclear Disaster*, compares Hoban's linguistic world to that described in Jack London's prototypical disaster novel *The Red Plague*. London describes his characters as speaking

> in monosyllables and short jerky sentences that were more a gibberish than a language. And yet, through it ran hints of grammatical construction, and appeared vestiges of the conjugation of some superior culture. Even the speech of Granser was so corrupt that were it put down literally it would be almost so much nonsense to the reader.[5]

Clearly, as Dowling notes, "Hoban's novel owes much to London's,"[6] but the fact that Riddley's dialect is *not* "so much nonsense to the reader" prompts that reader to reevaluate his or her first perception of "gibberish." As the narrative progresses, cross-references within the novel – such as images from "The Hart of the Wood," "The Eusa Story," or "Stoan" – become more important, deemphasizing the reader's discovery of "vestiges . . . of some superior culture" in Riddley's world. Hoban's readers do not feel the simple condescension on which London's narrator insists.

Like *The Red Plague*, many science fiction texts create an essentially false dualism between the "primitive" characters and the enlightened reader. Many also treat spiritual experience, especially organized religion, as a mere opiate, and the overthrow of established religions as only a political struggle – the most famous example being Frank Herbert's *Dune*, in which the Bene Gesserit

---

5. Jack London, quoted in David Dowling, *Fictions of Nuclear Disaster* (Iowa City: University of Iowa Press, 1987), 150.

6. Dowling, *Fictions of Nuclear Disaster*, 150.

order dresses its genetic experiments in the trappings of religious directives, a policy which in the end is shown to be poor science as well as hypocritical religion. Other science fiction stories address spiritual issues by implying that science is in the wrong, as Arthur C. Clarke does in "The Nine Billion Names of God," when his Tibetan monks correctly predict the end of the world.

Hoban does not uphold this basic opposition. Although *Riddley Walker's* structure depends heavily on paired characters, events, social roles, performances, and so forth, in most cases the relationship between the parallel elements is not a simple contrast. (Notice, for instance, the complementarity of the tel woman and the connexion man, or of the Eusa show and the Punch show.) Similarly, the concepts of science and religion are inextricably commingled. As characters seek enlightenment, they play the languages, disciplines, and impulses of technical and spiritual development against each other, vibrating from one to the other as if that movement were itself the journey to the truth – and for some characters, at some times in the plot, it is.

The model for many of the characters' endeavors, as for many of their narratives, is "The Eusa Story," whose main figure is both a focus for devotion and a prototype of intellectual attainment: "a noing man vere qwik he cud tern his hand tu enne thing" (30). The Pry Mincer describes his scientific goals in the very language of "The Eusa Story," as "looking for that Littl Shyning Man . . . to put him to gether" (40). The Ardship of Cambry rants in ecstacy, "WE PROGAMMIT THE GIRT DANS OF THE EVERY THING. . . . WE RUN THE MANY COOLS OF ADDOM AND THE PARTY COOLS OF STOAN" (95, Hoban's capitalization) – and in fact part of the Pry Mincer's research involves ritually torturing the Ardship in the hope of deducing practical knowledge from his mystical speeches. Characters in the novel frequently reenact, as well as allude to, community stories and songs, and gain scientific knowledge from moments of mystic revelation and from comparing and interpreting various versions of Eusa's story.

Riddley, for instance, has a vision of something apparently akin to radar while traveling with the Ardship of Cambry:

> . . . I had like a mynd flash of colourt lites with clicking and bleaping . . . I could like feel the woal circel of the

dead towns in me and see a line of grean lite sweeping
around that circel from the senter.

    Lissener [the Ardship] said, "What is it?"

    . . . I said, "I don't know its jus a line of grean lite
sweaping and ther come up blips." Which Id usit that word
times a nuff but never til then did I ever think of putting
the word *blip* to a blob of grean lite. (89)

(In the world of the novel, "blip" is normally the word for an omen.)
By going to Fork Stoan, as Riddley's interior radar suggests, the
two evade their pursuers and find a dead trader from whose body
they take a bag of sulphur, therefore making possible the rediscovery of gunpowder later in the book, as well as continuing a trip
patterned after the children's rhyme "Fools Circel 9wys":

Horny Boy rung Widders Bel
Stoal his fathers Ham as wel
Bernt his Arse and Forkt a Stoan
Done It Over broak a boan . . .
When the Ardship of Cambry comes out of the hoal. (5)

    The Pry Mincer realizes that the sulphur is important to his
research because he finds Riddley's situation analogous to that of
Eusa's sons. He explains to Riddley:

"2 littl sons . . . . Each littl son with 1/2 the Littl Shyning
Man." He pickt up a bag of yellerboy stoan [sulphur] and
shook it. "1/2 the Littl Shyning Man," he said agen. . . .
"May be its time to put that Eusa family to gether. 4 souls
in the brazing boal." (144)

Putting Eusa's family together is a chemical process to the Pry
Mincer; he derives his formula for combining four "salts" in a
brazier from "The Eusa Story," from his misinterpretation of words
in a twentieth-century description of a painting of the St. Eustace
legend, and from the "reveal" by Riddley's father, "A littl salting
and no saver" (60).

    Later, Riddley and the Pry Mincer find out that the actual
formula for gunpowder has been preserved in the secret songs that
dyers and charcoal burners share. An old charcoal burner called
Granser consents to make what he calls the "1 Littl 1" for them, but
will not let anyone watch him, or hear the ritual words he says.

The powder ignites (perhaps this, too, is part of the ritual), and Granser's head is blown off; it lands on top of a gate-pole. This bizarre death mimics Eusa's, as related in a story Riddley has heard from both the Ardship and the Pry Mincer.

This particular story becomes more and more important as the novel progresses. For one thing, it is the only story which is presented in directly competing versions. Other stories have gradually mutated or have been radically changed at some time in the novel's past. The Eusa shows, by means of the connexion men's interpretations, can presumably have widely differing meanings in different locations, but a given show's dialog would probably not change much from one performance to another. But these two stories of Eusa's death are of particular importance to their tellers and to the communities with which they are affiliated precisely because they are significantly different. Moreover, both the Ardship and the Pry Mincer tell their stories to justify the enmity between the Ardship's "Eusa folk" and the Pry Mincer's government, as well as to win Riddley over to an alliance with one of these communities. Two different ethical systems are expressed by these variations of a single basic plot.

The Ardship tells his story while he and Riddley are in hiding from the Pry Mincer's men. Riddley rescued the Ardship before knowing who he was or realizing the torture from which he was escaping. The Ardship explains,

> Time back way back who ben the Puter Leat who ben the Power Leat in Cambry? Eusa folk is who it ben. Who . . . gone Badstock crookit and seed of the crookit? Us the same Eusa folk. . . . Who ben the first ardship of Cambry? Eusa. . . . They kilt Eusa but they didnt kil all the Eusa folk . . . . And the knowing whats in them the Ardship wil know. (80-81)

It is for this inheritance of knowledge that each successive Ardship is tortured to death by the current Pry Mincer. In the Ardship's story, "Eusa gone crookit from Bad Time" (81) as the rest of the power elite also did. Escaping from bombed-out Cambry, Eusa makes his way to the Ram, where he is refused shelter unless he will tell the Ram people how to make their own bombs. When he refuses, they beat him to death "with col iron" (81) and put his head on a pole. The head speaks: "You had a chance to do a right thing but you done a wrong thing. Youve took my head youve took it on yourself itwl be with you from now on" (82). A tidal wave cuts off the Ram, making it an island. The Ram people, out of remorse, create the Eusa puppet shows, in which Eusa's wooden head may still speak to and for them.

The Pry Mincer naturally tells this story in quite a different way. He has less reason to believe that Riddley wants to hear his explanations, for he guesses that the Ardship has already told his version. But the Pry Mincer's commitment to storytelling as a means of gaining knowledge is stronger than the Ardship's – in fact, he points out how similarly he and Riddley feel about narrative:

> O Riddley . . . you know the same as I do. What ben makes tracks for what wil be. Words in the air pirnt foot steps on the groun for us to put our feet in to. . . . Dint Lissener tel you who ben the 1st Ardship then? . . . Dint he tel you how the Eusa folk stoand Eusa out of Cambry for what he done? (121)

The very nature of the rhetorical questions with which the Pry Mincer begins his narration reveal an acute sense that his is a supplemental story; while acknowledging the Ardship's prior claim on Riddley's loyalty, the Pry Mincer seeks to undermine that claim. In this official story, then, it is the Eusa folk who take Eusa from town to town, torturing him in each and at last killing him in Cambry: "They beat him to death then with col iron becaws it ben col iron he done Inland to death with. Mynd you this wer his oan folk done it to him" (121). When Eusa's head is placed on a pole, it declares, "Onles part of Inland kep ther hans clean of this ben the Ram" (121). The head swims out to tell the Ram people to begin their Eusa shows and the cycle by which, every twelve years, a Pry Mincer tortures an Ardship in the nine dead towns. Eusa concludes, "When the right head of Inland fynds the right head of Eusa, the anser wil come and Inland wil rise up out of what she ben brung down to" (122). Then the head swims out to sea and disappears.

Each version describes the creation of the storyteller's community and shows Eusa endorsing present beliefs and practices. Each blames the other's community for Eusa's death. But the two versions are more deeply complementary. For instance, though the

Pry Mincer stresses the idea that Eusa's *own* people tortured him, it's not clear in his story what relationship exists between Eusa and his people. The Ardship, however, does define how Eusa is connected to the Eusa folk. Both stories note that Eusa was beaten with "col iron," but only the Pry Mincer explains why. The Ardship's story stresses guilt – both Eusa's own, which makes him ask to be displayed as "a lessing and a lerning" (81), and the feeling his head induces in the people on the Ram. The Pry Mincer's story, on the other hand, stresses actions over motivations, especially actions meant to solve problems or expiate wrongdoing.

When Granser dies, the stories' meanings shift again, for this grisly literalization of the stories' central metaphor also literalizes the interdependence between a sense of sin and an impulse toward expiation, both necessary to Riddley's own moral development. Looking at Granser's head on the pole, Riddley asks, "wil you tel?" (194) and imagines that it does speak to him. At first it accuses: "What if its you whats making all this happen? What if every thing you think of happens?" (194). But when Riddley tries to retreat from both action and guilt, by suggesting, "I wont think no mor" (195), the head will not let him:

> Words come: That dont make no diffrents. If you dont think then some thing else wil think your thots theywl get thunk any how.
> I said, "What can I do then aswl be my oan doing?"
> Words come: Whats the diffrents whos doing it? (195)

Riddley's interior play-script combines the concerns of both versions of Eusa's death, and thus bridges the ethical systems of the two communities which constitute Inland's spiritual and temporal authority. Riddley is living a truer "connexion" than any his father made.

But this moment is no final epiphany – in fact, Riddley never reaches the end of his journey, concludes his puppet show, or figures out what kind of an idea "[o]ur woal life is" (7). By the end of the novel, he has found stories more effective than "real" action and has patterned his own actions on stories; he has seen stories influence others' beliefs and actions, and has seen the strength of other beliefs remaking the stories that would threaten them; he has seen stories in opposition and he has woven stories together; and he has wrapped all these narratives, at the last, in the narrative that is the novel. He is still puzzling over possible connections on the last page: "Why is Punch crookit? Why wil he all ways kill the babby if he can? Parbly I wunt ever know its just on me to think on it" (220); yet he commits himself at the very last to continue his quest: "Stil I wunt have no other track" (220).

As the various narratives Riddley encounters have shaped his experience, Riddley's own story may transcend the boundaries of the novel form to reach into the reader's life. The very "ending" of the novel, so strikingly without resolution, is like the interrupted or unresolved narratives which Riddley has heard and told, and like the necessarily unfinished lives of the readers. As Hoban says in one of his essays, "We make fiction because we *are* fiction. . . . because there was a time when something said, 'What if there are people?'"[7] Narratives play between the desire to record and keep experience in an explanatory frame (as the Eusa shows explain events to the Inlanders) and the desire to move onward, to apprehend and to take part in change (as the Eusa shows urge Inlanders to change). Ultimately, the use of narrative is to reach beyond reason to something that Hoban has specifically identified in another context as religious:

> Reason is not sufficient; I know what I cannot explain. . . .
> We must find in ourselves the shapes of letting go because
> we're not free to become what we're going to be next until
> we let go of what we are now. . . . We need to stop putting
> our retention above the thing to be retained which cannot
> be retained, which must be let go of so that we can move
> with the sound and Ether that spreads in circles from
> Shiva's drum in the continuance of creation.[8]

Riddley's "track" runs in these circles, and *Riddley Walker* invites its readers to move in them as well.

---

7. Hoban, "Household Tales by the Brothers Grimm," in *The Moment Under the Moment* (London: Pan Books Limited, 1993), 146.

8. Hoban, "Mnemosyne, Teen Taals, and Tottenham Court Road," in *The Moment Under the Moment,* 235.

Author's Note:

When I first saw Hoban's novel in a bookstore, I picked it up to browse and was instantly hooked. Riddley's voice spoke in my ears for days. Hoban is also the author of children's books: there is a series involving a badger named Frances, of which my favorite as a child was Bedtime for Frances. *He also wrote* The Mouse and His Child. *These books, while naturally less complicated than* Riddley Walker, *actually have many of the same themes. Frances and the clockwork mice are also storytellers.*

Riddley Walker *raises a number of questions: Can narrative really serve the many, varied, and vital purposes Hoban seems to assign it? If so, how is narrative in* Riddley Walker *more of a transcendent experience than narrative in any other novel or short story or children's book? Or is it? Is the interdependence of social, natural, and spiritual built into every narrative? And if they are, why don't we seem to recognize those elements more often?*

J.T.

Works Cited

Clarke, Arthur C. "The Nine Billion Names of God." In *From the Ocean, from the Stars*, 169-87. New York: Harcourt, Brace and World, 1958.

Dowling, David. *Fictions of Nuclear Disaster*. Iowa City: University of Iowa Press, 1987.

Herbert, Frank. *Dune*. Radnor, Pa.: Chilton Book Co., 1965.

Hoban, Russell. "Household Tales by the Brothers Grimm." *The Moment Under the Moment*. London: Pan Books Limited, 1993. 141-55.

_____. "Mnemosyne, Teen Taals, and Tottenham Court Road." *The Moment Under the Moment*. London: Pan Books, Limited, 1993. 217-36.

_____. *Riddley Walker*. New York: Pocket Books, 1980.

Morrissey, Thomas J. "Armageddon from Huxley to Hoban." *Extrapolation* 25 (fall 1984): 197-213.

Speaight, George. *Punch and Judy: A History*. Boston: Plays, 1970.

Wicker, Brian. *The Story-Shaped World: Fiction and Metaphysics: Some Variations on a Theme.* London: Athlone, 1975.

Chapter Ten

Silone's *Bread and Wine:* It's Still the Same Old Story

Paul J. McGuire, S.C.J.

In the ongoing debate between religion and a thoroughly secular point of view, a great deal hinges on religion's claim that the ultimate meaning and value of human life is derived from a transhuman source. In many other matters, such as the dignity of the human person, the need for a just society, responsible stewardship for the environment, the religionist and the secularist often find themselves in agreement, though not always for the same reasons. Contrary to Camus' contention that the priest must be resigned to the fate of the plague victims because of his belief in a transcendent reality, for the believer the transcendent actually functions as the model for human action. The religious believer claims to know a power that comes from beyond the reach of human potential, but whose presence can be known within the scope of human life.

One of the characteristics of modern Western culture, distinguishing it from almost all other times and places, is its denial of transcendence. The usual explanation for this is the ascendancy of scientific rationality, which counts as real only what is quantifiable and verifiable by human reason, and an equally rational technology that increasingly exercises control over material reality for the physical comfort of human society. In the words of sociologist Peter Berger, the former has rendered transcendence unthinkable; the latter has made it unnecessary.[1] The result of this modern outlook

---

1. Peter L. Berger, *A Far Glory. The Quest for Faith in an Age of Credulity* (New York: Doubleday, 1992), 26.

has been the loss of any sense of inherent meaning in life (the universe has no purpose or "end") and the emancipation of human freedom to choose its own destiny (without the guidance of a higher authority, as Immanuel Kant said in his essay "What Is Enlightenment?").

In other cultures (premodern or non-Western), humanity is rescued from the pointlessness of profane existence by meaningful contact with a greater-than-human wisdom and power. The myths of these people relate the mighty deeds of the god(s), and those deeds, in turn, reveal the truth about reality and become the model for meaningful human behavior. Mircea Eliade has written extensively on the function of myth to reveal the mystery of the sacred sphere of reality. Once human beings know the myth of what the god(s) did, they also know what they should do. Religion is an imitation of the god(s) whose deeds are revealed in the myth.

Consider, for example, the myths of the earliest agricultural people. Typically, in the beginning, a divine being "allowed himself to be immolated in order that tubers or fruit trees should grow from his body."[2] The primordial act was the self-sacrifice of a god who died to become the food that gives life to the people. When a farmer in that culture plants or tills or harvests, he is not just toiling at physical labor, he is participating in the divine act whereby the god brings life to the people. He is doing the most meaningful thing possible, and the pattern for his behavior is modeled in the action of the god.

Contrast that, Eliade writes, with "agricultural work in a desacralized society. Here it has become a profane act, justified by the economic profit that it brings. The ground is tilled to be exploited; the end pursued is profit and food."[3] No god reveals the meaning or offers guidance to the farmers; the point of reference and sole justification lie within the material world. It is farming for food and profit. It is only a temporal activity that is governed by transitory concerns. It does not open out into a more meaningful experience or connect with a larger sense of life.

---

2. Mircea Eliade, *The Sacred and the Profane. The Nature of Religion*, trans. Willard R. Trask (New York: Harcourt Brace Jovanovich, 1959), 101.

3. Ibid., 96.

From a religious perspective any life designed by mere human initiative and governed by the standards of material values is cut off from the world of sacred stories that reveals what is real and explains what is to be done. The myths alone contain the principles and paradigms for human conduct. The divine deeds recounted there become an invitation to human beings to transcend their finite limits by imitating the behavior of the god(s). The concept of the divine paradigm is found not only among so-called primitive religions; it is also a major feature of the Christian scriptures. A recurring theme of the New Testament is the disciple's obligation to imitate the Master. To cite but a few examples of Jesus' teaching: "You must be made perfect as your heavenly Father is perfect" (Matt. 5:48). "Be compassionate, as your Father is compassionate" (Luke 6:36). "What I just did was to give you an example: as I have done, so you must do" (John 13:15). And St. Paul wrote to the Christians at Corinth: "Imitate me as I imitate Christ" (1 Cor. 11:1).

In the novel *Bread and Wine*, Ignazio Silone has created a character who is an artistic embodiment of the modern attempt to find the sacred within the sphere of the secular. The main character, Pietro Spina, was an Italian communist who returned from exile to his native district Abruzzi on the eve of the Ethiopian War (1935-36). He disguises himself as Don Paolo Spada, a priest who is convalescing away from his home diocese and therefore is without canonical faculties to carry out any official priestly ministry. This ruse cloaks him in the respectability of the cassock, as it provided the cover story for his own need to regain his physical health. But Spina quickly discovers that assuming the role of Don Paolo "is not a harmless bit of play-acting."[4] In a series of episodes with the local peasants, and through a rediscovery of the sacred stories of his youth, Spina achieves a breakthrough that regrounds his commitment to social justice as it retrieves his original motivation.

---

4. Ignazio Silone, *Bread and Wine*, trans. Eric Mosbacher (New York: Signet Classic, 1986), 75; hereafter cited parenthetically in the text. The novel was originally published in Switzerland in 1936 under the title *Brot und Wein*. The original text was completely revised by the author in 1955 and was published in Italy for the first time as *Vino e Pane*. The 1986 Signet Classic edition is a translation of the revised text and contains a reprint of a 1962 "Author's Note" in which Silone explains his reasons for the revision.

The novel tells the story of a transformation, the gradual conversion to a new vision and new way of life. Spina's project did not grow out of any of the then-current world views (which he considered failed experiments); rather it arose out of a return to the source from which they, and he, drew their original inspiration. The society that Pietro Spina came home to was a patchwork of competing and collaborating forces, dominated by one totalitarian party (Fascism), sanctioned by a Church that blessed the status quo in exchange for institutional privilege, but threatened by another totalitarian party (Communism) that acted surreptitiously in the name of the people, the *cafoni*, whose peasant code sustained them in a precarious state of subsistence under a long succession of masters. In the end Spina has to make a choice. He agrees with Cristina Colamartini, his young, confident and feminine alter-ego, that the solution is "to give oneself, to lose oneself in order to find oneself." He adds, however, that the question still remains, "But to whom and how is one to give?" (259). The story reaches its culmination when Spina realizes his what and how. The choice he makes can be appreciated better in the context of the choices he does not make.

Fascism. Of the four alternatives confronting Pietro Spina, the one which was never a real option was the choice for the Fascist party. His rejection of Fascism was complete; his motives were both political and, in the first place, spiritual. From his youth he possessed, or was possessed by, a restless spirit that was not satisfied with the way things were. With no thought for caution or expediency, he protested at the punishments his elders unjustly imposed on his fellow students, often at the cost of his own severe punishment. In his final essay written at school he had declared, "I don't want to live in accordance with circumstances, conventions and material expediency, but I want to live and struggle for what seems to me to be just and right without regard to the consequences" (20).

Although he joined the Communist party a year after graduation, for him it was never purely and simply a question of politics. Both his mentor, Don Benedetto (221), and his protégé, Luigi Murica (254), recognized that. For Spina the issue was always deeper, at the level of spiritual freedom where human dignity and meaning hung in the balance. The essential question was never as much about political theories as it was "the use to be made of our lives" (151). He believed that human beings discovered their humanity in their struggle against "everything that prevents millions of people from becoming human" (259). In a conversation with a former classmate, he said: "Freedom is not a thing you can receive as a gift. . . . One can be free even under a dictatorship on one simple condition, that is, if one struggles against it. A man who thinks with his own mind and remains uncorrupted is a free man. A man who struggles for what he believes to be right is a free man" (33).

He regarded the current Fascist government as the latest embodiment in a long line of false messiahs who enslaved the people through taxation and expropriation of land, deified the leader, raised an army of mercenaries to keep the peace at home while waging foreign wars of aggression to maintain the prestige of the dictator and satisfy the greed of his cronies. The Fascists had come to power on the promise to overthrow "the Church, the dynasty and capitalism" (145), but once in power they betrayed the people by joining in league with the bankers. In conversations with Brother Gioacchine (110), an itinerant monk, and later with several student activists, he called for a "second revolution" to overthrow the Fascists and free the country from imprisonment by the banks (152).

The Church. Pietro Spina's rejection of the Church was different. Raised a Catholic, of course, in his youth he exhibited signs of intense religious devotion, at one time expressing the desire to become a saint (20). His teacher, Don Benedetto, thought he would end up in a monastery (222). Instead, Spina left the Church, "not because he doubted the correctness of its dogmas or the efficacy of the sacraments, but because it seemed to him to identify itself with a corrupt, petty, and cruel society that it should have combated" (87).

He came to see the Church alternately as morally compromised by its complicity with the state and practically ineffective in its ministry. With Don Benedetto he compared the pope to Pontius Pilate and, alluding to the 1929 Concordat between the Vatican and the Fascists, asked whether John the Baptist or Jesus would have offered to sign a concordat to avoid execution (217-18). This was the Church acting as it had done so often in the past, blessing the victors for a share in the spoils. The resultant loss of moral authority reduced the Church to an ornamental role whose irrelevance was symbolized by its concern for immodesty in dress, "the scourge of our time," according to one socially prominent cleric (17). Even when the Church did not completely abandon the people, it functioned merely as a bureaucratic office whose principle task was to tally up the number of recipients of its administrative services (18, 226).

Communism. When Spina joined the Young Socialists and later became a Marxist, his primary motivation grew out of his disillusionment with the Church and the need to channel his idealism in a constructive way. This need to translate ideals into practical action was a trait of his that remained constant throughout life. It was not something he learned from the Marxist doctrine of praxis. Before and after his time in the party, he remained consistently committed to practical action as the way to realize one's ideals.

His activities on behalf of the party led to his extended exile from his homeland. Though little is said of those years, when he returned he was a man deeply troubled and confused about his loyalties. The International Party, directed from Moscow, was becoming more bureaucratic and remote from the people. As he assumed the disguise of Don Paolo, he debated within himself, "Have I, then, escaped from the opportunism of a decadent Church only to end up in the Machiavellianism of a political sect?" (88). He concluded that if this was heresy, nevertheless he could not in good faith avoid these questions for the sake of the truth. He came to see his convalescence among the people as an opportunity "to escape that professionalism, to return to the ranks, to go back and find the clue to the complicated issue" (88).

His conflicted loyalties became apparent when he interrupted his convalescence to travel to Rome for meetings with his party contacts. His conversations with two of them, Battipaglia and Uliva, reveal his ambivalence. Battipaglia, a functionary acting on orders from headquarters, pressured Spina to endorse the decisions of the majority of the party and to approve the reports which he had been sent. Spina rejected both demands. In the name of his conscience and for the sake of the practical work that needed to be done he could no longer give the party the kind of allegiance it demanded. He vowed not to "form opinions on matters outside my experience" (164). Their meeting ended on a note of bitter recrimination, foreshadowing Spina's ultimate break with the party.

In contrast, when he met with Uliva, Spina attempted to rekindle his friend's zeal. Uliva had been a former party operative who subsequently became disillusioned with politics and embittered by life. "We must remain united with the workers' cells," Spina urged him (169). Uliva had spent ten months in prison for his antigovernment activities, but after his release he found himself rejected by his relatives and unable to gain work in the city. He watched as former activists accommodated themselves to the power of the state, while the true believers in the revolution were eliminated by imprisonment or death. The party itself, he said, had become "a bureaucracy in embryo" (169), aspiring to totalitarian power in the name of different ideals. If the Communists overthrow the Fascists, it would mean merely the exchange of one tyranny for another. Uliva's despair was complete. In a final nihilistic act, he chose "anti-life" and committed himself to terrorist destruction. He accidently blew himself up when a bomb he intended to detonate at a church service attended by the whole government exploded prematurely in his apartment.

Although Spina shared his friend's disaffection with the party, he remained devoted to its ideals. To this end he continued to make contacts with potential conspirators who would be willing to work directly with the *cafoni*, or as they are called in official government documents, "the rural population" (125). In this way he stood apart from the complicity of a party hack like Battipaglia without falling into the inertia or self-destruction of Uliva's despair. He told a party loyalist in Rome, "I can't sacrifice for the party's sake the reasons for which I joined" (176). He refused to identify the party with its ideals; that, he said, "would be like putting the Church before Christ." He returned from Rome no longer an agent of the party but still determined to carry on the struggle among the people.

The Peasants. When he had first arrived at his village retreat, Spina wistfully hoped to go back to the "ordinary, real life" (75) of those who still obeyed the ancient law that says: "Thou shalt earn thy daily bread in the sweat of thy brow." But for him that was no longer a possibility. Like the others who had gone off to the cities, his life in the cafes and libraries made it impossible to return to the soil. He had become "an outcast," neither a politician nor a peasant, unable to continue as he had and unable to go back to his ancestral ways. From this outsider's perspective he began to grasp the toll that conformism and fatalism exacted from the peasants in exchange for an ordinary life free from all theories and abstractions.

He was frustrated by their resignation to fate. Government taxation and intimidation had reduced them to lives of servile poverty and fear. They grumbled, as they had always done, but they also obeyed, as always. They accepted the good and the bad as inevitable (99), and they accommodated themselves to a world in which "God put the grass where there are no sheep and sheep where there's no grass" (120). Spina could never comfortably settle among those who refused to take part in the struggle for human freedom and dignity. As much as he admired and loved the *cafoni*, he could never simply become one of them.

The world offered him the choice to submit or rebel. He could submit by going over to the party or the state, or by giving in like the Church or the peasants. He could rebel by assuming the role of the outsider, the outlaw who put his life at risk for ideals. Only after he assumed the role of Don Paolo and began to live with the people did the possibility of a new way of living become apparent. This new alternative emerged as he reread the stories of his youth and discovered in their symbols and narrative the means to retrieve his past and reappropriate his original vision.

The Transformation. Spina's return to Italy is described in terms of rebirth and regeneration: he sleeps in a manger, he bathes in a fresh stream, and he is fed a double portion of bread and wine. With the help of an erstwhile friend, Pietro Spina is reborn as Don Paolo Spada. But assuming the guise of a priest has consequences that he had not anticipated.

Living in solidarity with the people changes Spina's point of view about them. Although he could never completely identify with them, nevertheless he experiences life as it happens among them. He can no longer play the role of the armchair reformer or the expert-in-exile. He learns firsthand that the political theories of the party and the state are nothing but abstractions that will never inspire the peasants. In a scene that is symbolic of his futile efforts to convert the people to the gospel of Marx, Spina delivers an impassioned sermon on the glories of Soviet Communism to a man who is apparently interested and receptive, only to discover that he is a deaf-mute who understands only a few signs (118). Spina has no more success in trying to convert the other peasants. Yet despite the failure of his rhetoric, he forges a genuine bond of friendship with them. He understands their frustrations and sees the potential in their traditional folkways.

The quality of his care is most apparent in the "priestly ministry" Spina dispenses to the peasants. Although his cover story makes it known that as a priest convalescing outside of his diocese he is not authorized to administer the sacraments, nevertheless the abandoned, priestless people of the region spontaneously seek him out. The first day after he has assumed his priestly disguise, the landlady at his hotel pleads with him to hear the confession of her daughter, who lies dying as the result of a self-induced abortion. Spina is moved to tears at the sight of her and, without dissimulating the sacrament, he assures her that she has already done sufficient penance. He enacts a "natural sacrament" of reconciliation, comforting her with the same words that Jesus used in the gospel: "Courage . . . Do not be afraid . . . Your sins are forgiven" (55–56).

Several other people confess their sins to him, and he treats them with the same compassionate understanding. He gains a reputation as a wonder-worker when a woman attributes the health of her child to his miraculous touch. At one point, as he walks in a garden arguing with himself about the value of party loyalty, some women observe him and conclude that he is talking to the birds, "just like St. Francis" (88). They stop short of declaring him to be the Christ, however, because they cannot discern the stigmata in his hands, and so content themselves with the conclusion that their priest is "a saint, a real saint." Often, like Jesus, Spina practiced an indiscriminate table-fellowship with the people and was their guest at simple meals of bread and wine.

More important than anything else, however, Spina rediscovers the stories of his youth, and these give both shape and direction to his new life. As a student he had devoured the lives of the saints, though his teacher, Don Benedetto, did not suspect the extent he might be carried away by them (20). Later in life, Spina acknowledges that he remained "more or less a Christian" because of the gospel stories he had learned from his mother (252). He is reintroduced to these stories by the packet of books that has been provided for him to complete his priestly disguise: the breviary, the *Eternal Maxims* of St. Alfonso, the *Introduction to the Devout Life* by St. Francis de Sales, and the lives of various Italian saints (64). As Don Paolo, and out of a hunger for something to do, he begins rereading these sacred books. This activity has a strange and haunting impact on him as he senses he is picking up on a thread of his earlier life.

Spina also begins to retell his own life story, being careful to conceal his real identity. He confides to Cristina the stories of "his youth, his village, his first studies, his early religious experiences and his first steps in real life" (89) and as he does so, "without realizing it, he ended by infusing life into his fictitious role, nourishing it with the still-vivid memories of his youth." Unlike his former schoolmates, he remains convinced of the necessity of being committed to the ideals that had first inspired his life. His contemporaries found it necessary to abandon the poetry of youth and the dreams of schoolboys as they adapted to political realities and the requirements of domestic life. Neither as Spina the revolutionary nor as Spada the convalescent priest is he ever able to make that accommodation. Cristina is astonished at the account that he gives of himself, and remarks that he sounds like an eighteen-year-old boy (90). When Bianchina, the young girl he had consoled after her abortion, later tells him that he is different from other priests, he agrees with her and adds, "Perhaps the biggest difference is that they believe in a very old God who lives above the clouds sitting on a golden throne, while I believe He's a youth in full possession of His faculties and continually going about the world" (154). In the end this is what Spina will do, in imitation of God.

The reawakening of his youthful idealism leads Spina to seek out like-minded companions among the young people of the district. From his meetings with Pompeo and Alberto and other idealistic students, he gradually begins to discover a meaning in the circumstances forced upon him by his illness (153). He now has the opportunity to hand on the message and arouse the conscience of the next generation. Although he does not attempt to form cells along party lines, he calls for a second revolution that will topple the exploitative capitalist banking system. His inspiration is no longer the ideal of the workers' paradise, but a vision of a new humanity living out its true dignity in freedom. He aims to forge bonds across generational lines among those committed to take seriously "the principles proclaimed by our fathers or schoolmasters or priests" (153).

In an emotional meeting with Luigi Murica, another student activist, the elements of Don Paolo's renewed way of seeing things crystallize into a new attitude and a new way of acting. In Rome, Murica had been arrested for his anti-Fascist activities. With a mixture of threats and persuasion, the police prevail upon him to become a collaborator and inform on his comrades. Eventually, guilt-ridden and dispirited, he secretly makes his way back home, convinced that his transgressions are irremediable and his fate, hopeless. In despair he goes to Don Benedetto, who convinces him that nothing is irreparable as long as life lasts, and that good is born out of evil that is repented. When a "reborn" Luigi Murica repeats his confession to Don Paolo, he, too, refuses to judge the young man. No longer a party leader compelled to follow the party's rules, he is now able to act as an ordinary man, respecting the conscience and integrity of another ordinary man (240).

He finds the models for this new style of living and relating in lives of the saints, in the stories of the martyrs across the centuries who were united by a bond that recognized "no god other than the god that was alive in their souls" (258). They are the bolder spirits who always "refused to burn incense to the state idols." They form a communion of saints that keeps the presence of Christ alive in the world. They are the people who declare their solidarity with all other human beings, accepting no artificial barriers or distinctions. They ratify their ideals by their opposition to the evils that oppress or exploit people and diminish their opportunity to live out their lives with full human dignity. They act out their story in every generation, and for generations to come they will live on as their story is retold and becomes the inspiration for future prophets and martyrs. Cristina sums it up: "In all times and in all societies the supreme act is to give oneself, to lose oneself in order to find oneself. One has only what one gives" (259).

When this story is reenacted in the arrest and killing of Luigi Murica, the event becomes the catalyst that propels Spina on a renewed mission of solidarity and service. When Murica is found with papers extolling truth, brotherhood, and labor, he is arrested and tortured in a cruel parody of Christ's passion. A chamber pot for a crown, a broom for his scepter, he is blindfolded and robed with an old carpet as the soldiers punch and kick him and finally trample the life out of him with their nailed boots. But that is not the end of him. When an old friend remembers the quality of his character and his message, Spina remarks: "If we live like him, it will be as if he were not dead" (263).

The wake held at Murica's home becomes a Eucharistic banquet for family and friends, for strangers and beggars, who gather at table to share a meal of bread and wine in memory of him. The unity he has preached is symbolized by the one bread made from many grains and the wine made from many grapes. When these are crushed and trampled upon, they become the food and drink that brings people together and gives them strength. Murica has poured his life into making this bread and wine, and now those who share his food also share his life. His vision of the human community united in solidarity and without fear is realized in the meal that symbolizes the gift of his life.

The tranquility of the wake is interrupted when Bianchina brings word to Spina that he has been betrayed to the militia, who are on their way to arrest him. He hastily returns to his room, where he gives Cristina his diary and, without further word of farewell, he sets out on foot over the snow-covered mountains with a renewed dedication to carry on his mission in other towns and villages of the region. He leaves, wearing an ordinary felt hat that "could equally well be adapted to ecclesiastical or lay purposes, depending on how it was shaped or worn" (262), indicating that his new role will combine the priestly ministry of Don Paolo Spada with the social activism of Pietro Spina.

Although the novel ends on a note of suspense (Does he survive? If so, what is his fate?), nevertheless the major moral and religious conflict is resolved. It is not so much that Spina rejects the Church and the party; rather he finds the source of inspiration that grounds them in truth but transcends them in authority. He could not commit himself to a closed system whose ultimate point of reference is within the system itself, whether in the person of *Il Duce, Der Führer,* the commissar, or the pope. Instead, by committing himself to the inviolability of his own human dignity and freedom, he discovers a way of living that opens beyond itself to a point of reference that transcends human potential while at the same time validating it.

In the end Spina discovered this truth in stories, the gospel stories of his youth and the lives of the saints who imitated Christ. In them he found God where God has always been found: in the shadows, along the margins, in the least likely places among the people who are esteemed the least. The night before Luigi Murica's murder and his own escape, Don Paolo sat by a hearth with the *cafoni* who asked him to tell them some stories. He consulted the index to the lives of the saints and

> then he started telling in his own way the story of the martyrdoms. . . . The story was always different but always the same. There was a time of trials and tribulations. A dictatorship with a deified leader. A musty old Church, living on alms. An army of mercenaries that guaranteed the peaceful digestion of the rich. A population of slaves. Incessant preparation of new wars of rapine to maintain the prestige of the dictatorship. Meanwhile mysterious travelers arrived from abroad. They whispered of miracles in the East and announced the good tidings that liberation was at hand. The bolder spirits, the poor, the hungry, met in cellars to listen to them. The news spread. Some abandoned the old temples and embraced the new faith. Nobles left their palaces, centurions deserted. The police raided clandestine meetings and made arrests. Prisoners were tortured and handed over to a special tribunal. There were some who refused to burn incense to the state idols.

They recognized no god other than the god that was alive in their souls. They faced torture with a smile on their lips. The young were thrown to wild beasts. The survivors remained loyal to the dead, to whom they devoted their secret cult. Times changed, ways of dressing, eating, working changed, languages changed, but at bottom it was always the same old story. (258-59)

The stories of the martyrs disclosed a communion of saints stretching back to the original exemplar, who had "not come to be served but to serve – to give his life in ransom for many" (Mark 10:45). Spina rediscovers the truth of this story in two ways: As a priest he acts as "another Christ," healing, forgiving, uniting, reconciling, inspiring others. Forced by circumstances to carry out the duties of a priest, he finds the elements of his own life project in the priestly reenactment of the Christ-role. Then, after a lapse of almost twenty years, he retrieves the stories of his youth and appropriates them as his own story. The lives of Christ and the martyrs give shape and direction to his life, they give him a language that helps make sense of the events that threaten to overwhelm him, and they convincingly portray a life committed to integrity and self-sacrifice as the only kind of human life worth living.

At the conclusion of the novel, Spina comes to exemplify a modern type of Eliade's premodern "religious man." Unable to find a cause worthy of his commitment, he rediscovers the sacred stories that inspired his youthful ideals. Not only do they rekindle the fire of his zeal, but they also reveal the patterns of behavior which will allow for the fullest achievement of his human dignity. He becomes what he needs to be and acts as a fully responsible human being by imitating the deeds of God contained in the gospel story of Jesus. As Eliade has written: "It is in the myth that the principles and paradigms for all conduct must be sought and recovered."[5] For Spina the stories of the gospel and the lives of the saints become privileged points of contact that reveal the presence of the transcendent in the ordinary rhythms and circumstances of human life.

In a 1949 essay on *The God That Failed*, Silone wrote:

---

5. Eliade, 102.

The day I left the Communist Party was a very sad one for me, it was like a day of deep mourning, the mourning for my lost youth. . . . But my faith in Socialism (to which I think I can say my entire life bears testimony) has remained more alive than ever in me. In its essence, it has gone back to what it was when I first revolted against the old social order: a refusal to admit the existence of destiny, an extension of the ethical impulse from the restricted individual and family sphere to the whole domain of human activity, a need for effective brotherhood, an affirmation of the superiority of the human person over all the economic and social mechanisms which oppress him. As the years have gone by, there has been added to this an intuition of man's dignity and a feeling of reverence for that which in man is always trying to outdistance itself, and lies at the root of his eternal disquiet.[6]

In both this autobiographical essay and his autobiographical novel, Silone gives expression to the Christian affirmation that the transcendent which humanity requires for its fulfillment is to be found by way of a method of immanence. The restlessness of the human heart, its inner dynamism and insatiable longing, cannot be satisfied by the attainments of scientific rationality or rational technology or the failed gods of Party, Tribe or Nation. Nothing that is man-made or is imposed by an external authority can meet the requirements of this underlying human need. Rather, in the words of Silone's contemporary, German Lutheran theologian Dietrich Bonhoeffer, the "beyond" is "within." "The transcendence consists not in tasks beyond our scope and power, but in the nearest thing to hand. God in human form . . . [is] . . . man existing for others, and hence the Crucified. A life based on the transcendent."[7] This is the story that Pietro Spina rediscovers in the lives of the saints and the gospels, and which he sees played out anew in the lives of the peasants. It is the same story that gives shape and meaning and purpose to his own life as it puts him into contact

---

6. Ignazio Silone, *The God That Failed*, ed. Richard Crossman (New York: Colophon Books, 1963), 113-14.

7. Dietrich Bonhoeffer, *Letters and Papers from Prison*, ed. Eberhard Bethge, trans. Reginald H. Fuller (New York: Macmillan, 1962), 238.

with that Power which transcends human achievement while, at the same time, it fulfills human aspirations.

Author's Note:

Dorothy Day would not lend her copy of Silone's Bread and Wine *to Robert Coles, the story goes, because it was one of those books she kept coming back to. There are obvious similarities between Silone's Italian peasants and the street people Day clothed and fed in her "hospitality house" on the Lower East Side. But more significantly for Day, Silone's story was a story about telling stories, making sense of what has happened.*

Good stories are not just entertainment. They enlighten and they baffle; they clarify and they puzzle; and they challenge. That's the way Jesus told stories. When asked a question, he usually responded either with another question or with a story.

Stories also await the response of the reader. The stories that Silone's protagonist heard and read and told needed to be completed by his action.

What stories are awaiting our response? How does one enter into the story, come into contact with the power that makes the story a moving, ennobling, heartening tale? How do stories serve as a mirror enabling us to find our own reflection, see our own warts, discover our own distinctive features? What common stories offer a path to transcendence?

P.J.M.

Works Cited

Berger, Peter L. *A Far Glory. The Quest for Faith in an Age of Credulity.* New York: Doubleday, 1992.

Bonhoeffer, Dietrich. *Letters and Papers from Prison.* Edited by Eberhard Bethge. Translated by Reginald H. Fuller. New York: Macmillan, 1962.

Eliade, Mircea. *The Sacred and the Profane. The Nature of Religion.* Translated by Willard R. Trask. New York: Harcourt Brace Jovanovich, 1959.

Silone, Ignazio. *Bread and Wine.* Translated by Eric Mosbacher. New York: Signet Classic 1986.

_____. *The God That Failed.* Edited by Richard Crossman. New York: Harper Colophon Books, 1963, 76-114.

V.

Self and Society

Chapter Eleven

"Something Deep Within the Grain" in the Moral Ambiguities of Joan Didion

Ann Angel

What universal truths can be found deep within individual experiences in the America of the past thirty years? If we study dropping out and turning on, flower children or hippies, New York gangs on "wilding" sprees, natural disasters and political upheaval, can we learn anything about ourselves? Can we discover something deep within our grain if we compare urban decay to the peaceful green of the Berkeley campus? Can we find that something of transcendent value is really there, deep within the individual?

Joan Didion thinks so. In the preface to her collection of essays, *Slouching Toward Bethlehem*, she admits that she writes to find out about herself. She says, ". . . whatever I do write reflects, sometimes gratuitously, how I feel."[1] Didion believes that examining general American cultural themes, discovered in her personal experience, can relay a larger message: The message in the collected essays found in *Slouching Toward Bethlehem* is that moral ambiguity is strongly evident when things fall apart. But things seem to come together again with infinite possibility in *After Henry*, Didion's collection of essays from the late 1980s and early 1990s. According to Didion's theory, things fall apart when the actions of many are a direct contradiction of what they hold valuable. Didion's experience seems to have taught her that when things fall apart,

---

1. Joan Didion, *Slouching Toward Bethlehem* (New York: Washington Square Press, 1981), 13; hereafter cited parenthetically in the text as *StB*.

individuals can discover what they hold dear if they look deep within the grain of their personal experience.

Didion readily admits that values are personal: that she has always written from this framework is clear. As early as 1964, Didion described herself as "A relatively articulate member of the most inarticulate segment of the middle class, the kind of woman who sets store by her great grandmother's orange spoons, by well-mannered children, by the avoidance of chic and by a sense of sin."[2]

A careful reading of Didion's early work reveals that when individuals try to make sense of general events – be they the middle class exodus by America's youth to Haight Ashbury, or the collective consciousness of California scholars in the Center for the Study of Democratic Institutions – they discover the moral ambiguities in contemporary society. Although it is the social disorder of the 1960s that Didion describes in this collection, it could as easily be examples of the social disorder of the 1990s. In fact, in *After Henry*, in order to establish the portrait of American youth who create their own social order, Didion describes a gang as it stands accused of brutalizing and raping a young jogger. In *Slouching Toward Bethlehem*, she chronicles American flower children creating a distinct social order thirty years earlier. By analyzing popular myth surrounding this wilding scene or the earlier popular myth of the American drug scene, Didion illustrates the ambiguous moral nature of a social order that contradicts personal moral codes. Later essays reveal a heightened awareness that most of us need to create some meaning from this ambiguity.

With a reporter's ability to record observations, Didion pares away the popular myth that hippies and drugs are America's downfall or that gang violence is America's ruin. She replaces this myth with the singular truth that unless we respond as moral individuals to events, we will accept the bad, even become part of the problem.

No matter what cultural group she depicts in her essays, Didion's message is that our collective uncertainty about right and wrong leads to cultural decay. While each of us searches for

---

2. Joan Didion, "The Way We Live Now," *National Review* (March 24, 1964): 267.

something to believe in, our hope that the individual understanding of the good and evil inherent in these events can be universally accepted keeps us from falling apart completely. Sometimes our understanding of good and evil, however, clashes with our own or others' behavior.

As evidence that society is falling apart because we are a morally ambiguous culture, Didion's essays rely on the portrayal of a socially-disillusioned group's flawed efforts to find a more workable social order. Didion's style is to juxtapose significant details with understated irony in order to guide her readers to understand the ambiguities at play in each scene. Sometimes she interjects her own perceptions to ensure that we understand the moral ambiguity of each situation. For instance, in the essay "Slouching Toward Bethlehem," Didion exposes the irony of the hippie movement. She contrasts the values this group held dear – free love and dropping out – with the drugs and poverty that characterized the movement and finally destroyed it.

Didion shows us a moment of perceived "freedom" in the image of a young man rocking on the kitchen floor of a "Hippie shelter." On bad acid, he is oblivious to his surroundings. The young man, who stares at his toes in wonder, is too out of it to notice that he is being cared for by Arthur Lisch, a "Digger," a member of a "group of anonymous good guys with no thought in their collective head but to lend a helping hand" (*StB* 107), who is on the phone attempting to set up a VISTA volunteer shelter to house the youth who have fled the Midwest to find themselves in Haight Ashbury. Lisch insists VISTA is needed because people are starving and sleeping in the streets. But Lisch's request for help for the hippies is rejected on the grounds that "they're doing it by choice." Didion comments, "By the time he hangs up he has limned what strikes me as a pretty Dickensian picture of life in the edge of Golden Gate Park. . ." (*StB* 107).

Another Digger named Deadeye "has a clear evangelistic gaze and the reasonable rhetoric of a car salesman. He is society's model product. I try to meet his gaze directly because he once told me he could read character in people's eyes, particularly if he has just dropped acid, which he did, about nine o'clock this morning" (*StB* 114). He has found a solution to keeping the Haight's hippies off the streets. Deadeye has a pocketful of one hundred LSD tablets that he intends to sell in order to pay the rent on the apartment the Diggers use. Didion's readers cannot help but make the connection that this apartment shelters the homeless and starving teens who have sought and failed to find their salvation or even a hot meal amidst the rhetoric of peace and love that is the soul of Haight Ashbury.

We can discern the singular truth found in the center of the ambiguous nature of moral codes as Didion views them – that good and bad, right and wrong are one – as it unfolds through another Haight Ashbury character. "Max mutters that heaven and hell are both in one's karma" (*StB* 105). As Didion once explained, this particular essay "dealt directly and flatly with the evidence of atomization, the proof that things fall apart. . ." (*StB* 11).

In "Pacific Distances," an essay that Didion began in 1977 and completed in 1991, this theme resurfaces with a subtle difference. Didion recalls that as a child she had waited, even practiced, for things to fall apart. As a child, she imagined that this would occur in her grade school hallway with an atomic blast to the back of her exposed head. It never came. As an adult, Didion uses transcendent symbolism to describe the event she feared:

> I realized that I was no longer anticipating the blinding flash, and that expectation had probably been one of those ways in which children deal with morality, learn to juggle the idea that life will end as surely as it began, to perform in the face of definite annihilation. And yet I know that for me, and I suspect for many of us, this single image – this blinding white light that meant death, this seductive reversal of the usual associations around "light" and "white" and "radiance" – became a metaphor that to some extent determined what I later thought and did.[3]

Although as a child Didion waited for the end, as an adult Didion glimpses the infinity found in life's moral lessons.

Often, Didion allows her characters to illustrate her personal morality with only minimal commentary on their actions. She relies

---

3. Joan Didion, "Pacific Distances," in *After Henry* (New York: Vintage, 1992), 123.

most often on juxtaposing contemporary social codes against the immoral.

When Didion does use her own voice, it is subtle in its irony, but strong in its point. "I think a lot about . . . how it is possible for people to be the unconscious instruments of values they would strenuously reject on a conscious level. . ." she writes in the essay "Slouching Toward Bethlehem" (*StB* 107).

In later essays Didion explores the realization that popular culture may contribute to moral ambiguity because it distorts the truth or moral message of specific events. This is most clear in her "wilding" essay, "Sentimental Journeys," which analyzes the public response to the New York jogger rape. The public attempts to identify isolated events as universally accepted examples of moral decay. If the "wilding" incident becomes the symbol of social moral decay, the "wilding" victim must become the symbol of all that is good. Didion describes the jogger's evolution from a young banking executive to "New York's ideal sister, daughter, Bacharach bride: a young woman of conventional middle-class privilege and promise whose situation was such that many people tended to overlook the fact that the state's case against the accused was not invulnerable."[4]

Didion's theory that we attribute universal meaning to incidents relies on the underlying assumption that we each carry our own moral code, our individual sense of sin, a sense as personal as a fingerprint. This could mean that our need to find universal meaning in incidents reflects humanity's need to glimpse transcendent possibility in daily events.

The personal qualities in Didion's writing then are strong evidence of transcendence because she unravels in each essay her own moral distinctions – that something deep within – that helps us to define our own morality. We attribute our own meaning to Didion's words. This meaning becomes part of our own moral code. The very act of Didion's writing about events then helps to create universal meaning and a realization that if there is moral ambiguity, there is transcendence.

---

4. "Sentimental Journey," in *After Henry,* 258.

With each writing, Didion discovers universal understanding. The process, however, is not easy. Didion admits to uncovering troubling thoughts and feelings, as well as fear. While writing "Slouching Toward Bethlehem," she was so overwhelmed by the disorder she found that she became physically and emotionally ill. Yet she is able to see that despite chaos and disorder, we search for a seed of morality or truth, a common good at the core of our own lives, if not in human nature.

To support her arguments that we hold together because, even as we are a morally ambiguous culture, we search for truth, Didion often writes about her personal search for truth. Her understanding of this truth becomes clearest in her essay, "On Morality." ". . . [W]e have no way of knowing – beyond that fundamental loyalty to the social code – what is 'right' and what is 'wrong,' what is 'good' and what 'evil'" (*StB* 165). She writes that to understand the human condition or perhaps to find some meaning in our existence, we continue to search for a universal moral code. "Of course," she writes, "we would all like to 'believe' in something, like to assuage our private guilts in public causes, like to lose our tiresome selves, like perhaps, to transform the white flag of defeat at home into the brave white banner of battle away from home" (*StB* 165). But Didion laments, "it is difficult to believe that 'the good' is a knowable quantity" (*StB* 162).

Didion, nevertheless, finds some good or truth captured in the symbolism we unearth in our individual experience. We are allowed an allotment of dreams and wishes and beliefs, she asserts. "For better or worse, we are what we learned as children: My own childhood was illuminated by graphic litanies of the grief awaiting those who failed in their loyalties to each other" (*StB* 161). But she admits that her early life was also touched by magic. And this may be where she gained the dedication to search for truth. For Didion, as a child and even into adulthood, this magic was captured in the cowboy image of John Wayne. She dreamt of the day her prince in cowboy boots would promise to build her a house "at the bend in the river where the cottonwoods grow." And although Didion grew up and married and found out that life simply doesn't evolve like a cinema love story, she admits, "Deep in my heart where the artificial rain forever falls, that is still the line I wait to hear" (*StB* 44).

Didion explains why childhood dreams are so important when she writes, "Our favorite people and our favorite stories become so not by any inherent virtue, but because they illustrate something deep in the grain, something unadmitted. Shoeless Joe Jackson, Warren Gamaliel Harding, the *Titanic: how the mighty are fallen.* Charles Lindbergh, Scott and Zelda Fitzgerald, Marilyn Monroe: *the beautiful and damned"* (*StB* 81).

Didion's essay, "On Self-Respect," clarifies what she means when she talks about "something deep in the grain." Didion believes that each of us must find human good or truth on a personal level. It isn't so much doing what is expected or considered right as it is doing what we believe to be right for us. It is self-respect. She explains, "There is a common superstition that 'self-respect' is a kind of charm against snakes, something that keeps those who have it locked in some unblighted Eden, out of strange beds, ambivalent conversations, and trouble in general. It does not at all. It has nothing to do with the face of things, but concerns instead a separate peace, a private reconciliation" (*StB* 147).

Didion says she writes to come "to grips with the disorder of the times we inhabit," and much of her work in this collection centers on disorder. Essays such as "Slouching Toward Bethlehem" and "Sentimental Journey" describe disorder with a hint of insight. But "On Morality" and "On Self-Respect" offer us a solid glimpse of social order, or something deep within the grain, at least from Didion's personal eye view, and we discover that Didion comes to terms with social chaos and moral ambiguity only when she can find a personal truth, or as she asserts, the "private reconciliation" of self-respect.

Didion's essays never reflect complete despair. Even in the chaos of Haight Ashbury, she can find self-respect in such people as the Diggers. She says "people with self-respect exhibit a certain toughness, a kind of moral nerve; they display what once was thought of as *character*, a quality which although approved in the abstract, sometimes loses ground to other, more instantly negotiable virtues" (*StB* 148). We know that, in Didion's eyes, John Wayne had character, and so did Arthur Lisch.

We can know if we have character or if we are part of the social disorder by measuring our response to events. In responding, we aspire to the transcendence of moral good. In not responding, we will encounter the morass that occurs when ". . . one runs away to find oneself, and finds no one at home" (*StB* 151).

Author's Note:

The way the story goes, Joan Didion worked as a reporter in California during the '60s without much thought about her journalistic role. Like most reporters, she strove to be fair and objective. Then one day, she was sent to cover a suicide in progress. She stood before a five-story building and stared up at a woman standing on a ledge. Didion waited for her to jump so she could write her report and go home. According to the story, Didion never wrote that article. Instead she experienced an epiphany. As she waited, she realized she was more concerned about the way the woman's toes curled tightly onto the ledge. Didion wondered how much terror comingled with despair in the woman's mind. She was intrigued by the question why. It was important to make sense of everything at play here in order to understand human nature. From then on, the story goes, Didion sought the answer to why events play out as they do.

Why do the individual events of our own lives make us realize the need for moral meaning? How do these events reflect human nature? our community values? How does one navigate the moral ambiguity of our own culture and daily existence?

A.A.

Works Cited

Atwain, Robert. *Ten on Ten: Major Essayists on Recurring Themes.* New York: St. Martin's Press, 1992.

Didion, Joan. *After Henry.* New York: Vintage, 1992.

_____. *Slouching Toward Bethlehem.* New York: Washington Square Press, 1981.

_____. "The Way We Live Now." *National Review* (24 March 1964): 267.

Chapter Twelve

Transforming Violence in O'Connor's *The Violent Bear It Away*

Kathleen Scullin

If you ask most readers of Flannery O'Connor to describe her fiction, almost certainly "violent" would come to mind. Principally, they might refer to physical violence: to various murders (by gunshot, stoning, deliberate drowning) and to other acts such as self-blinding or being gored by a bull. But grotesque actions also inflict a kind of emotional violence on both characters and reader: in one story, a husband abandons his retarded wife at a roadside restaurant; in another, a man steals a woman's wooden leg while supposedly seducing her. In O'Connor's novel *The Violent Bear It Away*, not only do the characters inflict various forms of violence on each other; even the epigraph and title seem to suggest the disturbing inference that violence is somehow necessary to "bear away" heaven.

Why does O'Connor seem drawn to violence, particularly in this novel? The question, of course, is partly unanswerable. As she often protests in her letters, she chose neither her subjects nor her *métier*, but wrote according to her own particular way of seeing. Moreover, violence in her fiction functions in complex and often ambivalent ways, challenging readers to ask not only why O'Connor uses so much violence but why the characters incur so much suffering, especially since violence often opens a character to a religious epiphany. Is this violence then to be seen as a divine weapon against human resistance?

Although there can be no simple answer to the problem of evil – of which violence is a part – the reader needs to recognize that while the violence in O'Connor's fiction may serve divine ends, it usually proceeds not from God but from human beings. In *The Violent Bear It Away* – as in the rest of her fiction – given who the characters are, how strongly they are drawn to the transcendent, and how fiercely they resist, there is no avoiding some form of violence. Each of the major characters – old Mason Tarwater, his nephew George Rayber, and his great-nephew Francis Marion Tarwater – experiences grace as a form of violence. True, they are all extremists by temperament; they cannot live by half measures, even if they tried – and Rayber does try to impose upon himself a kind of psychological *via media*. They have powerful wills and feelings, and they are powerfully drawn by the mysterious force of grace. O'Connor images this inborn force as "blood"; each feels the call to religious commitment deep in his blood.[1] But although they are perhaps extraordinary in their radical experience of that call, they struggle for selfhood like many of us, mistaking autonomy for freedom and self-will for selfhood; and their willfulness un-leashes much of the novel's violence.

That Flannery O'Connor saw a profound difference between self-will and authentic selfhood is evident in a number of passages in her letters. To her friend "A," she wrote,

> You confuse self-abandonment in the Christian sense with self-torture. . . . Self-torture is abnormal; asceticism is not . . . . Writing is a good example of self-abandon-ment. I never completely forget myself except when I am writing and I am never more completely myself than when I am writing. It is the same with Christian self-abandon-ment.[2]

O'Connor did not try to explain the paradox that only when she lost herself in her art did she find her truest self; but it is significant that she equated this experience with the Christian self-abandon-

---

1. See Flannery O'Connor, *Three by Flannery O'Connor* (New York: New American Library, 1983), 192.

2. Flannery O'Connor, *The Habit of Being: Letters of Flannery O'Connor*, ed. Sally Fitzgerald (New York: Farrar, Straus & Giroux, 1979), 457-58; hereafter cited in text as *HB*.

ment expressed in the Gospel imperative that one must lose one's life in order to find it (Matt. 16:25). And although her concerns are theological rather than psychological – that is, her fiction is centered in the drama of conversion rather than in the drama of coming to selfhood – she recognized that surrender to God does not fundamentally diminish a person's freedom and integrity. Rather, she saw "God as the ground of [a person's] essential self."[3] In her incarnate view of human existence, submission to the authentic forces in one's own psyche and submission to the mysterious ways of God are all part of the same act of coming to selfhood.

O'Connor underscores this essential connection in a letter to Dr. T. J. Spivey:

> To my way of thinking, Goldbrunner has used Jung in the only way that I think he can be used, which is in helping the person face his own psychic realities, or those realities that the great mystics have always faced and that the Church teaches . . . we must face. Goldbrunner can do this because he believes in the objective reality of God. St. Catherine of Genoa said, "God is my best self," by which she realized probably what Jung means but a great deal more. (*HB* 382)

O'Connor does not expand upon this remarkable sentence of St. Catherine's,[4] but the understanding that God is the source of each person's true identity grounds O'Connor's fiction. Her characters, however, typically cannot believe that by surrendering to grace they will find themselves. They fight to hang on to what Thomas Merton calls the "false self": "an illusory person . . . who wants to exist outside God's will and God's love" and is therefore "outside

---

3. David Eggenschwiler, *The Christian Humanism of Flannery O'Connor* (Detroit: Wayne State University Press, 1972), 139.

4. Thomas Keating, in a chapter titled "Guidelines for Christian Life, Growth, and Transformation," articulates several principles that, together, gloss St. Catherine's "God is my best self":

    Our basic core of goodness is our true Self. Its center of gravity is God. . . .

    God and our true Self are not separate. Though we are not God, God and our true Self are the same thing.

    See Thomas Keating, *Open Mind, Open Heart: The Contemplative Dimension of the Gospel* (Rockport, Maine: Element, 1991), 127.

of reality."[5] Thus, caught in a fundamental misrelation to their true being, they experience grace as a threat, a violence to the self, and they resist.

Distinguishing between the false self, which human beings typically *experience* as "myself," and the true self, hidden from consciousness except in rare moments of wholeness, helps to clarify why readers often misunderstand the nature of Tarwater's struggle for freedom and conclude that he submits to his vocation at the expense of a full life.[6] The problem is not only that, as O'Connor lamented, readers lack her spiritual vision, but that they naturally identify with Tarwater, caught up in the false self, resisting whatever curtails the exercise of self-will.[7]

For Rayber and young Tarwater, being oneself means being in control; Rayber controls with his brain, his refusal to accept what he cannot understand, and Tarwater with his will, his refusal to belong to anyone else and his resolve to "act out a no." But each one fights a tide within, an ineluctable pull toward the transcendent. He cannot resist this force without doing violence to himself and others.[8]

---

5. Thomas Merton, *New Seeds of Contemplation* (New York: New Directions, 1972), 34.

6. The distinction I make between self-will and true freedom is essential to understanding some passages in O'Connor's letters that are, in the fashion of personal letters, somewhat cryptic. To Alfred Corn, for instance, she wrote,

    Rayber and Tarwater are really fighting the same current in themselves. Rayber wins out against it and Tarwater loses; Rayber achieves his own will, and Tarwater submits to his vocation. (*HB* 485)

    Rayber "wins" and Tarwater "loses" only by the criteria of the false self; in submitting to his "vocation," Tarwater accepts the life he is called to live.

7. In "The Fiction Writer and His Country," O'Connor comments that the reader whose vision is distorted poses a challenge for the Christian writer: "The novelist's problem will be to make . . . [distortions] appear as distortions for an audience which is used to seeing them as natural; and [the writer] may well be forced to take ever more violent means to get [this] vision across to this hostile audience." See Flannery O'Connor, *Mystery and Manners* (New York: Farrar, Straus & Giroux, 1969), 33-34.

8. David Eggenschwiler makes this point in demonstrating that O'Connor is an anagogical writer whose work must be read on multiple levels. Thus, "It would be a basic distortion not to realize that in [O'Connor's] work to be estranged from God is necessarily to be estranged from one's essential self. . . . This

This complex interrelationship between resistance to God – a resistance, ultimately, to the true self – and violence is expressed simply in the warning issued by a child-preacher, which is heard by both Tarwater and Rayber: "Be saved in the Lord's fire or perish in your own!"[9] Grace, then, principally operates by violence in this novel, not, perhaps, because God would have it so but because the characters cannot see that the personal cost of surrender to God is slight, compared with the cost of resistance.[10]

---

spiritual and psychic estrangement also causes an estrangement from other[s], thus [engendering] some form of anti-social, or more precisely, 'anticommunal,' behavior." See Eggenschwiller, 13.

O'Connor keenly felt the dangers of internal division, stating that she needed to see with both human eyes and the eyes of faith in order to write with integrity: "To try to disconnect faith from vision is to do violence to the whole personality, and the whole personality participates in the act of writing." See *Mystery and Manners*, 181.

9. *The Violent Bear It Away*, in *Three by Flannery O'Connor*, 205; hereafter cited parenthetically in the text.

10. Critics have examined the role violence plays in O'Connor's fiction from widely varying perspectives. (1) Some critics link this violence with the action of the divine or some other force that represents ultimate Reality: P. Albert Duhamel associates the religious, prophetic view of reality with violence and states that Tarwater's drowning of Bishop arises "from an intuitive, committed view of reality." See P. Albert Duhamel, "Flannery O'Connor's Violent View of Reality," *Catholic World* 190 (February 1960): 284. Kathleen Feeley and Richard Giannone agree that violence returns characters to reality but see love as the ultimate power in the fiction. See Kathleen Feeley, S.S.N.D., *Flannery O'Connor: Voice of the Peacock* (New York: Fordham University Press, 1982), 162, and Richard Giannone, *Flannery O'Connor and the Mystery of Love* (Urbana: University of Illinois Press, 1989). (Giannone's entire book examines this thesis.) André Bleikasten takes an essentially Manichaean view, seeing violence as the weapon of both Satan and God in the war for control of the world. See André Bleikasten, "The Heresy of Flannery O'Connor," *Critical Essays on Flannery O'Connor*, eds. Melvin Friedman and Beverly Lynn Clark (Boston: G. K. Hall, 1985), 153. Ruthann Knechel Johansen takes the mythic perspective that opposites exist "in a sacred unity," (e.g., good/evil, God/Satan), and thus "O'Connor unmasks the violence that exists at the heart of the sacred, illustrating how violence used sacrificially restores order to a community or society." See Ruthann Knechel Johansen, *The Narrative Secret of Flannery O'Connor: The Trickster as Interpreter* (Tuscaloosa: The University of Alabama Press, 1994), 8. (2) Other critics argue that unresolved tensions within O'Connor find expression in her fiction: Josephine Hendin speculates that the radical tension between O'Connor's public conformity to Southern niceties and her inward resistance generated a rage that erupts in her fiction. See Josephine Hendin, *The World of Flannery O'Connor*

Although *The Violent Bear It Away* is a densely textured novel, its plot line is relatively simple. The central characters comprise a three-generation family: Old Mason Tarwater, a religious prophet without a sect, is uncle to George Rayber and great-uncle to Francis Marion Tarwater, the fourteen-year-old protagonist. Rayber, having rejected his uncle's faith to embrace rationalism, lives in a city some distance from Powderhead, a clearing in the woods where the old man has raised young Tarwater from infancy, preparing him to take his place as a prophet to preach the word of God. The old man's death initiates the action. Young Tarwater, resolved to reject his calling and set his own course, burns down the house, intent on destroying the body, and goes to Rayber (his uncle). Intending to

---

(Bloomington: University of Indiana Press, 1970), 12-16. Inez Martinez believes that O'Connor's characters are caught in a conflict between libidinal and antilibidinal forces, as was O'Connor herself. See Inez Martinez, "Flannery O'Connor and the Hidden Struggle of the Self," *Flannery O'Connor Bulletin* 16 (autumn 1987): 53-54. Frederick Asals explores the spiritual tension of "seeing" with two sets of eyes (i.e., those of personal experience vs. those of the Church) that O'Connor herself recognized (see *Mystery and Manners* 180), a conflict that in Asals' view is connected with both the violence and the sense of mystery in O'Connor's fiction. See Frederick Asals, "Flannery Row," *Novel* 4 (fall 1970): 95-96. (3) Still other critics see violence as essential to the aesthetic of O'Connor's visionary art: John R. May reads O'Connor as a prophetic writer who uses violence to get her readers to see distortions as she sees them. Joyce Carol Oates sees O'Connor working out Chardin's vision of forces that break down egotism and rationalism, opening people to a transforming higher consciousness. See Joyce Carol Oates, "The Visionary Art of Flannery O'Connor," in *Flannery O'Connor*, ed. Harold Bloom (New York: Chelsea House Publishers, 1986), 49, 52. Jefferson Humphries regards O'Connor as an aesthetic guerilla, using demonic forces to practice "violent dissidence" on behalf of the Church against modern positivistic forces. See Jefferson Humphries, "Proust, Flannery O'Connor, and the Aesthetic of Violence," in *Flannery O'Connor*, ed. Harold Bloom, 114. (4) The most complex and illuminating discussion of violence in O'Connor's fiction is by Gilbert H. Muller. See especially Gilbert Muller, "Violence and the Grotesque," in *Nightmares and Visions* (Athens, Ga.: University of Georgia Press, 1972), 76-98. Muller explores O'Connor's use of violence to reflect the distorted world without God, confront characters with their own complicity in the problem of evil, and open them to transformation.

Several of the above critics, and others whom I have not cited, note that O'Connor's characters suffer violence in proportion to their alienation from God and/or themselves, but none has explored the thesis of this essay, linking violence to the characters' estrangement from their true being, which is inextricably transcendent and human.

resist both Rayber's influence and his own inner urge to begin his mission by baptizing Bishop, Rayber's retarded son, Tarwater drowns (but simultaneously baptizes) Bishop. Heading back to Powderhead, he is raped by a stranger, a trauma that opens him to radical conversion and acceptance of his call to be a prophet.

Although the old man dies before the novel opens, he is the theological center of the novel, having accepted his call to be a prophet and sown the seeds of faith in his two nephews. But he, too, has experienced grace as violence to the false self, especially through a purification narrated early in the novel. In the pride of his youth, he had envisioned himself as the arm of God, sent to proclaim and preside over "the destruction awaiting a world that had abandoned its Savior" (126). He indulged himself in righteous fury while he "raged and waited" for the Almighty to heed his call that the sinners suffer judgment. Having waited so long that he feared the "Lord Himself had failed to hear the prophet's message" (126), he at last saw the "finger of fire" he had been expecting:

> [But] before he could turn, before he could shout, the finger had touched him and the destruction he had been waiting for had fallen in his own brain and his own body. His blood had been burned dry and not the blood of the world. (126)

In this richly symbolic passage, O'Connor evokes the prophet's cleansing of pride and self-will. Chastened by his mistakes, he bears Rayber no malice when he abducts the infant Tarwater from his house, having "learned enough to hate the destruction that had to come and not all that was going to be destroyed" (126).[11]

Old Tarwater remains a powerful presence in his nephews' lives, having communicated to them the force of truth and life when they were children. Inevitably, then, when they begin to resist God's call, he becomes the human object of that rebellion.

Rayber, who has severed all ties from the old man, believes that he has rescued himself from his uncle's influence and cured

---

11. I do not mean to suggest that Mason Tarwater, having undergone a conversion experience, is without flaws. For him, as for anyone, conversion implies an ongoing struggle between self-will and selflessness. For an excellent discussion of old Tarwater's struggle, see David Eggenschwiler, 118-24. Later in this essay, I will examine O'Connor's complex portrait of the old man.

himself of the effects of the old man's baptism by becoming a thoroughgoing rationalist. But the seeds of faith, and also of love for the old man, have taken root in him. Following his nephew to a revival meeting one night, Rayber suffers a religious experience in which he violently rejects a child-preacher's message precisely because he is so vulnerable to it. Standing outside the window and seeing the child, Lucette Carmody, introduced, he immediately feels a rush of indignation. He sees her, like himself, as "[a]nother child exploited" (199), who has fallen under the "spell" of some adult's religious zeal. But the memories of the signal event of his childhood that return to him, triggered by hearing her story, betray his rational analysis. When Rayber was seven, the old man stole him away to Powderhead, baptized him, and instructed him in the fundamentals of Christian faith. When the boy's atheist father came to claim him, cynically approving of the baptism because "One bath more or less won't hurt the bugger" (201), the boy longed to escape, to race back to "the stream . . . where he had been born again, where his head had been thrust by his uncle into the water and brought up again into a new life" (200). The memory testifies to the truth that he cannot face: He feels akin to Lucette not because she is exploited but because she is a child enthralled by the mystery of God. Deceived about the "mysterious connection" (203) between them and feeling that she *knows* him, has "looked directly into his heart," he imagines himself her rescuer, silently pleading, "Come away with me . . . and I'll teach you the truth, I'll save you, beautiful child!" (204). Thus when she looks directly at him and shouts, "I see a damned soul before my eye! I see a dead man Jesus hasn't raised. His head is in the window but his ear is deaf to the Holy Word!" (205),[12] her words so shock him that he must silence the voice coming through his hearing aid:

---

12. The scope of this paper does not permit me to develop the rich thematic connections between violence in the novel and Lucette Carmody's preaching about how Jesus' birth and life on earth provoked disbelief, hostility, and finally violence. Significant links include Lucette's emphasis on how God's will can feel like death rather than life ("Love cuts like the cold wind and the will of God is plain as the winter"); her contrast between people's expectations of the Messiah ("[A] golden fleece will do for his bed. . . . His mother will ride on a four-horned white beast") and the ordinariness and sheer poverty of his birth – a "blue-cold child" born to a "plain winter woman"; and Lucette's

He was groping fiercely about him, slapping at his coat
pockets, his head, his chest, not able to find the switch
that would cut off the voice. Then his hand touched the
button and he snapped it. A silent dark relief enclosed him
like shelter after a tormenting wind. For a while he sat
limp beneath the bush. (205)

In attacking Lucette's words, Rayber also attacks himself; fiercely
slapping himself about the head and chest, he symbolically assaults
the child within his mind and heart who is mysteriously connected
to Lucette. Retreating to his deafness exacerbates the spiritual
deafness Lucette warns him against but also deafens him to his
own being.

However, it is Bishop, his retarded son, who poses the
greatest danger to Rayber's rational control and through whom he
experiences a persistent call to his authentic self. As a rationalist,
he views Bishop as an offense to human dignity, "an *x* signifying
the general hideousness of fate" (192). But however unwillingly,
he loves the child; moreover, Bishop, who has the fish-colored
eyes of old Tarwater, reminds Rayber of "the old man grown
backwards to the lowest form of innocence" (191). Serenely innocent, Bishop evokes irrational forces in Rayber that come "rushing
from some inexplicable part of himself" (192), a place impervious
to reason and will:

Anything he looked at too long would bring it on. Bishop
did not have to be around. It could be a stick or a stone,
the line of a shadow, the absurd old man's walk of a
starling crossing the sidewalk. If, without thinking, he lent
himself to it, he would feel suddenly a morbid surge of
the love that terrified him – powerful enough to throw him
to the ground in an act of idiot praise. It was completely
irrational and abnormal. (192)

Thus, Rayber's inexplicable feelings for Bishop issue from a deep
capacity for reverence and love. Ordinarily, he staves off his
feelings for his son by keeping a safe physical distance. But one

---

recognition of the terrible truth about rationality laid bare by the crucifixion
– that the desire for a reasonable Messiah who doesn't interfere with peace
of mind cloaks the desire to kill the unreasonable one (202-4).

day, when he allows the child to clamber onto his lap and settle back against him, he relaxes just enough to be nearly overcome by his "hated love" and realizes that "He should have known better than to let the child onto his lap" (208).

Rayber recognizes the polarity within him in a moment of "chilling clarity of mind in which he [sees] himself divided in two – a rational and a violent self" (207). At this moment, he is simply cautioning himself to handle Tarwater with the "rational" part of himself. To yield to the "violent self" would mean succumbing to an anger verging on madness. But this "violent self," wider and deeper by far than that, is the buried current of his own life's mystery; from it comes love of his idiot son and of the old man, his religious impulse, and his primal feeling for Powderhead, the old man's clearing in the wilderness that Rayber inherits. When he visits the place and suddenly realizes that it is now his, he can still the wild beating of his heart only by quickly calculating the value of the wood (232). Reason is the weapon he offers his nephew Francis Marion Tarwater to counter the old man's mad vision of salvation.

Stubbornly independent, the boy wants no part of either Mason Tarwater's nor Rayber's salvation, although he is haunted by the conviction that he is called to commit himself to life as a prophet. He is not entirely opposed to the idea when it fires his imagination, as when the old man would emerge from a struggle with God in the woods, looking

> the way the boy thought a prophet ought to look. . . . as
> if he had been wrestling with a wildcat, as if his head were
> still full of the visions he had seen in its eyes, wheels of
> light and strange beasts with giant wings of fire and four
> heads turned to the four points in the universe. (127-28)

Tarwater's recollection of such times suggests not only the child's natural attraction for the extraordinary but also his willfulness; *he* has decided "how a prophet ought to look." He has also decided that a prophet ought to be elevated above common humanity. Thus when the old man tells him that his ministry must begin by baptizing Bishop, "The boy doubted very much that his first mission would be to baptize a dim-witted child" (128).

Wanting freedom on his own terms, the boy is impressed with the old man's freedom to be himself, a spirit so palpable that the boy "even felt he could smell his [great-uncle's] freedom, pine-scented, coming out of the woods" (135). But when the old man would speak to him of "spending eternity eating the bread of life," or of the "sweat and stink of the cross" (128), or of being "born into bondage and baptized into freedom, into the death of the Lord" (135),

> [t]hen the child would feel a sullenness creeping over him, a slow warm rising resentment that this freedom had to be connected with Jesus and that Jesus had to be the Lord. (135)[13]

Young Tarwater cannot bear the idea that freedom requires subjection. And so, just as Rayber exploits reason to be free, Tarwater exerts his will, refusing to be governed by or belong to anyone but himself.[14] But he conceives his freedom in negative terms: the ability to say no and act on that no, and so to define himself by what he is not.

It is important to recognize, however, that Tarwater quite naturally needs to declare independence from both of his uncles. At fourteen, he stands on the threshold of adulthood, and for the first time, alone in the world. He must choose whether to accept or reject the life for which old Tarwater has prepared him and discern for himself what the old man meant by saying, "I saved you to be free, your own self!" (132). If he simply puts on the identity fashioned for him by either of his uncles, he does not make a free personal response to his vocation. He is instinctively right,

---

13. Here, the narrator refers to Tarwater at an earlier age. However, sometimes, as on p. 151, the narrator refers to him as a child. Richard Giannone interprets this reference "as a sign of [Tarwater's] spiritual regression set off by the menace of Buford's compassion." See Giannone, 125.

14. In an earlier draft of the scene at the Cherokee Lodge, O'Connor more pointedly emphasized Tarwater's fierce need for autonomy. In this draft, Tarwater crosses out "Frank Rayber" – the name Rayber has entered into the guest register – and prints instead, "Francis Marion Tarwater. Powderhead, Tennessee. BELONGS TO HIS SELF." In the published version, however, Tarwater concludes with the phrase "NOT HIS SON" (217). O'Connor revised the earlier draft after Sally Fitzgerald suggested that "BELONGS TO HIS SELF" was too self-conscious for Tarwater. See *HB* 345.

then, in refusing to submerge his personality and in wanting to receive a mission unique to himself.[15] But as becomes increasingly clear, he is too immature, prideful, and balky to recognize that true freedom could consist of anything other than unfettered will.

Intending to act out his freedom not to be a prophet, he sets out for Rayber's house in the city.[16] There, the more he resists his call to be a prophet, the more violently he suffers from a "peculiar hunger" and a weakness brought on by "city food" (219). Drawn toward a Pentecostal church that Tarwater claims he just wants "to spit on," he halts at a bakery window and stares hungrily at a loaf of bread with "the face of someone starving who sees a meal he can't reach laid out before him" (197). Although the food Rayber provides is indeed poor by comparison with the ample home-cooked meals the boy is used to, Tarwater's hunger, like Rayber's deafness, suggests the inseparability of the spiritual and the physical; refusing to eat the "bread of life," he cannot satisfy himself with Rayber's food. By the time Rayber takes him and Bishop on an outing to the Cherokee Lodge, Tarwater is so hungry that he gorges himself on barbecues and beer, then throws up into the lake. After drowning Bishop in that lake, he can't eat at all. In O'Connor's fiction, where the divine works in and through the physical, the unconscious self communicates one's spiritual condition through the body. As Joyce Carol Oates astutely notes, O'Connor's understanding of the unconscious differs from Freud's in that she was committed "to the divine origin of the unconscious."[17]

Rayber and Tarwater each resists his own inner truth with a force that damages not only himself; it erupts into violence toward others and renders each of them vulnerable to violence from others.

---

15. See John F. Desmond, *Risen Sons: Flannery O'Connor's Vision of History* (Athens, GA: University of Georgia Press, 1987), 112-13.

16. One indication that Tarwater is deluding himself by trying to flee to the city to find himself is that, on an earlier visit to the city with his great-uncle, the child instinctively felt "that this place was evil – the ducked heads, the muttered words, the hastening away. He saw in a burst of light that these people were hastening away from the Lord God Almighty" (138-39). In a clearer, less divided state of mind, he would hardly have sought himself in a place where he perceived that so many are lost to themselves.

17. Joyce Carol Oates, *New Heaven, New Earth: The Visionary Experience in Literature* (New York: The Vanguard Press, 1974), 151.

Years before Tarwater's birth, Rayber invited old Tarwater to live with him and violated the old man's personhood by using his freely shared stories as data to publish a case study on religious obsession. When young Tarwater comes to live with him, Rayber tries to force him to become *his* son, renaming him "Frank," exchanging his Powderhead clothes for new ones, indoctrinating him according to his views.

Tarwater not only resists Rayber's control but inflicts a far greater violence by drowning Bishop. Hearing the sounds of struggle on the lake where Tarwater and Bishop are out in a rowboat, and realizing that a "cataclysm" is about to occur, Rayber grabs for "the metal box of the hearing aid as if he were clawing his heart" (242). Through this device, he hears the bellows and other sounds of his son's final struggle: "The machine made the sounds seem to come from inside him as if something in him were tearing itself free" (242). As the final bellows of his son fall silent,

> He stood waiting for the raging pain, the intolerable hurt that was his due, to begin, so that he could ignore it, but he continued to feel nothing. He stood light-headed at the window and it was not until he realized there would be no pain that he collapsed. (243)

He is the victim both of his own refusal to love and of Tarwater's refusal – abetted by Rayber – to accept his mission.

Tarwater's resolute assertion of self-will increasingly subjects him to forces he cannot control. Sitting in the cab of a truck after the drowning, he relives the event in a vivid dream, throughout which he is unable to close an "inner eye" that keeps "watching, piercing out the truth" (251) from the distorted images of his dream. This "eye," the metaphysical equivalent of Tarwater's stomach, *sees* the truth that he refuses to see. He is not "in charge" but is caught between two forces: Bishop and the shadowy evil "stranger" who, having engendered a spirit of rebellion in Tarwater, has accompanied him from Powderhead. Tarwater is caught between Bishop's "fish-colored" eyes, "fixed" on him "serenely" like the old man's, and the stranger's violet-colored eyes, "fixed on him with a peculiar look of hunger and attraction," daring him to "act" out his "NO" (251). The boy is so torn that, in the act of drowning Bishop, he involuntarily blurts out the words of baptism. These two acts come from two "wills" at war within him, and "it is the boy's deeper and truer will that, in performing the baptism, triumphs over his superficial (but still murderous) self-will."[18] Tarwater, body flailing in the truck's cab, "might have been Jonah clinging wildly to the whale's tongue. . . . as he struggled to extricate himself from a monstrous enclosing darkness" (252). He has become a Jonah, having fled a divine mission and been swept powerless into an abyss.

The Jonah allusion also suggests a theological context for what Tarwater suffers in being raped by a stranger after the drowning of Bishop. While it may be tempting to see this terrible violation in moral terms – Tarwater as the victimizer now become victim – this novel is about conversion rather than retribution. Being violated reveals to Tarwater the disastrous spiritual course he is on and radically calls him to conversion. He is drawn onto a dangerous path at the beginning of the novel by listening to a voice that sounds like his own, which questions the need to obey the old man's wishes now that he is dead. The voice, taking shape in his mind's eye as a "stranger," slyly modulates to "friend," then "mentor." Tarwater begins to heed the reasonable-sounding voice, now recognizable to the reader as the devil's, which sets about loosening the boy's grip on reality, on the truth of his own perceptions. Using sophistry and half-truths, the stranger discredits the old man, calling him a "crazy man even when he wasn't in the asylum" (145), and a hypocrite, "the only prophet I ever heard of making liquor for a living" (149). He undermines and distorts the boy's faith: "How do you know if there was an Adam or if Jesus eased your situation any when He redeemed you?" (150). In this dialogue, he is especially artful:

> [the stranger's voice:] The way I see it. . . . [y]ou can do
> one thing or you can do the opposite.
>
> Jesus or the devil, the boy said.

---

18. Ralph C. Wood, *The Comedy of Redemption: Christian Faith and Comic Vision in Four American Novelists* (Notre Dame: University of Notre Dame Press, 1988), 91.

> No, no, no, the stranger said, there ain't no such thing
> as a devil. . . . It ain't Jesus or the devil. It's Jesus or *you*.
> (146)

Although Tarwater at this point remains unconvinced of the
stranger's new paradigm, it works its way into his mind, so that
soon he begins to see himself as threatened by the call to follow
Jesus.[19] He is thus locked into what Marion Montgomery calls the
"excruciating dramatic paradox" of much contemporary writing:

> In electing the self – in declaring "I will not serve" or (in
> its softer modern formulation) "I will be myself, of myself" –
> one destroys the self.[20]

Heading back toward Powderhead after he has drowned
Bishop but before he is raped, Tarwater is blind to his true state
of being, still seeing himself "tried in the fire of his refusal, with
all the old man's fancies burnt out of him," and resolving that now
he will never have to trudge "off into the distance in the bleeding
stinking mad shadow of Jesus, lost forever to his own inclinations"
(254-55). He intends to take possession of his old home, but he
does not even inhabit his own being; walking beside him is a "gaunt
stranger" who is *himself:* "the ghost who had been born in the
wreck and who had fancied himself destined at that moment to the
torture of prophecy" (255). Resolved to "answer for his freedom"
to the storekeeper who confronts him with what he has done to
his great-uncle, he turns inward to his "mentor" for the right words
and, to his horror, out of his mouth spews an obscenity "like the
shriek of a bat" (257). He is dispossessed.

He pays a terrible price to discover what he has surrendered
by enlisting the "stranger" to help him remain "inviolate" from any
invasion of his freedom (219). Through linking imagery, O'Connor
suggests that Tarwater's seduction by the voice of the stranger at

---

19. Joyce Carol Oates' analysis of the choices in O'Connor's fiction illuminates
this passage: "She [O'Connor] sees [the human being] as dualistic: torn between
the conventional polarities of God and the devil, but further confused because
the choice must be made in human terms, and the divine might share
superficial similarities with the diabolical." See Oates, *New Heaven, New Earth*,
150.

20. Marion Montgomery, *Why Flannery O'Connor Stayed Home* (La Salle, Ill.:
Sherwood Sugden & Company, 1981), 244.

the beginning ultimately exposes him to the power of the actual stranger/rapist at the end. Both the "stranger" that takes shape in Tarwater's mind and the stranger at the end wear a panama hat; both lure him into intoxication; and the liquor that the "stranger" urges him to drink in the early scene, as it penetrates the boy's throat, foreshadows the rape at the end: "A burning arm slid down Tarwater's throat as if the devil were already reaching inside him to finger his soul" (149-50). Only after he has been violated, however, does Tarwater see such a connection.[21] In a state of estrangement from anything that could safeguard him, he accepts the ride from the stranger with the panama hat and the violet eyes, failing to note that the man offers him a ride without his having signalled for one. He accepts a cigarette whose smoke has "a peculiar odor" (259), and then the flask, to defy "all his great-uncle's warnings about poisonous liquor" (260). As he loses consciousness and thus loses the control he so prizes, the man can do everything that Tarwater has resisted: strip him of his clothing, force an intimacy upon him, violate his person.

When Tarwater returns to consciousness and discovers what he has suffered, his mouth, opened in a horror beyond sound, signifies his being, so emptied that it is "beyond rage or pain":

> The boy's mouth twisted open and to the side as if it were going to displace itself permanently. In a second it appeared to be a gap that would never be a mouth again. . . .
> Then a loud dry cry tore out of him and his mouth fell back into place. (261)

At this climactic point, he begins to return to himself. He reclothes himself and begins to set fire to cleanse the area where he lay and to destroy any place that the stranger might have touched. Then Tarwater, hearing the "stranger" nearby and *seeing* now that the two "strangers" – the voice and the rapist – are spiritually one, dramatically sets fires to wall off and to destroy him. The cycle is

---

21. In a letter that was not included in *The Habit of Being*, O'Connor specifically connects Tarwater's "stranger" and the rapist: "The man who gives him [Tarwater] a lift is the personification of the voice, the stranger that has been counseling him all along; in other words, he is the devil, and it takes the action of the devil to make Tarwater see for the first time what evil is." See Giannone, 255.

complete: At the beginning, he sets fire to the house which, he believes, holds the body of the old prophet who had warned, "even the mercy of the Lord burns" (134); at the end, he sets fire to the voice that seduced him to rebellion. In "being true," he is now also "seeing truly."[22]

In this novel and much of O'Connor's other fiction, violence plays a prominent role in the drama of redemption: characters resist violently, work violence upon themselves and each other, and suffer grace through violent means. But equating grace with violence greatly oversimplifies and diminishes O'Connor's complex vision of the action of grace. Throughout *The Violent Bear It Away*, she weaves a subtle but significant network of images to suggest what a world open to grace might look like, in moments when human beings operate in harmony with divine love and mercy, and therefore in harmony with themselves and others. Thus, while violent redemption may represent what often happens in the world of O'Connor's fiction, it in no way represents the inevitable or the ideal.

In the first sentence of the novel, the reader learns something that Tarwater does not learn until the end: that Buford Munson, a neighbor, has worked all day to bury old Tarwater's body in a Christian manner, the boy being too drunk to fulfill his promise to bury the old man. This act of charity not only honors the dead; it spares the boy from committing an intended act of desecration when he burns the house, thinking to destroy the body – and with it, the tangible reminder of his call to serve God as a prophet. From the beginning, then, even as Tarwater, in violent rebellion, is subject to violence, he is also subject to a gracious mercy, though at this point he neither wants nor recognizes mercy. Buford Munson's simple act of service, a tangible sign of divine love and mercy, frames this novel. The acts of self-will, intransigence, and pride that follow – which invite and beget violence – are themselves subject to the larger design of mercy, outside the characters' control.

Even Rayber and Tarwater, who so vehemently resist the urge to surrender to the mysterious inner force of grace, at times relax

---

22. Feeley, 19.

their guard enough to let the goodness of a moment touch them: to yield to the "intimacy of creation" (136). In these moments, they are most themselves and most apt to perform a simple act of service. Each of them at one point ties Bishop's shoes. In each scene, this homely gesture is linked to a moment of intimacy with this child: Rayber experiences a moment of pure paternal love as he holds the child on his lap (208); Tarwater free-falls for a moment into the "silent country" of his true being as he gazes intently into the child's eyes (216; 218).

Glimpses into old Tarwater's life offer another kind of perspective on the effects of living attuned to God and oneself. Having abandoned himself to God's will, the old man does not lose himself; he becomes wholly himself. Although faithful to his calling, true in vision, and humble before God, he is realistically flawed; conversion does not obliterate personality.[23] He can be contentious, judgmental, and vindictive, relishing victory over the enemies of the Almighty – as when he shoots at Rayber, who comes to Powderhead to reclaim the infant Tarwater. As O'Connor insisted to a critical reader, "A character has to be true to his own nature and I think the old man is that. He was a prophet, not a church member" (*HB* 407).[24] However, sprinkled throughout the novel is evidence of his healthy appetite for the pleasures of ordinary life: his large girth testified to a love of food; he had a still and, presumably, enjoyed the liquor; he "liked to linger and discourse" with a local storekeeper, finding her "as pleasant as a shade tree" (257); and he radiated to Tarwater a sense of "glee" in his own freedom (135). By contrast, his nephews deny themselves physical and emotional pleasures in order to guard against any human weakness that might make them susceptible to surrender. Rayber

---

23. Thomas Keating's distinction between what is and what is not lost in Baptism applies to the conversion experience in O'Connor: "In Baptism the false self is ritually put to death, the new self is born. . . . Not our uniqueness as persons, but our sense of separation from God and from others is destroyed in the death-dealing and life-giving waters." See Keating, 128.

24. In one of her essays, O'Connor unsentimentally compares a religious convert to the wolf of Gubbio – which St. Francis allegedly converted in response to the urgent plea of Gubbio's citizens to rid them of this attacker: "The moral of the story, for me at least, is that the wolf, in spite of his improved character, always remained a wolf." See *Mystery and Manners,* 169.

even realizes that he has imposed a bleak asceticism upon himself "at the cost of a full life" (193).

At the end of the novel, after young Tarwater's cathartic burning of the woods to banish the last traces of the evil that has possessed him, a cluster of peaceful, life-giving images signal and accompany Tarwater's conversion. They begin with Tarwater's return to the clearing above the burnt house, where he expects to face the gaping grave that testifies to his "broken covenant" (264). This is a key moment; before he can receive mercy, he must know and feel that he has broken faith with his great-uncle and with God. What he sees first is the corn the old man planted, a foot high, growing in newly plowed ground. "A deep-filled quiet" and a sense of mystery fill the air (265). As his hunger returns, he sees Buford Munson and runs toward him, hoping to go home and eat with him. At this point, his stomach contracts with the old nausea; his body is still tortured by the spirit's refusal to enter that mystical "country where he had vowed never to set foot" (265). But when he forces himself to look at the half-dug grave and sees instead the wooden cross and the freshly mounded earth, evidence of a reverent burial and not a desecration, his body begins to manifest the spirit's healing: "The boy's hands opened stiffly as if he were dropping something he had been clutching all his life" (266).

Released from his guilt, he sees a vision in which multitudes are being fed, the old man among them. It is a moment of reconciliation with the old man and of accepting their mutual hunger for the transcendent, the "bread of life," a hunger that, before the old man's death, Tarwater had scorned:

> Had the bush flamed for Moses, the sun stood still for Joshua, the lions turned aside before Daniel only to prophesy the bread of life? (135)

Although he no longer looks for an extraordinary sign, he now has eyes to see literal reality transformed into a marvelous vision:

> He whirled toward the treeline [where he has set the fire to immolate the stranger]. There, rising and spreading in the night, a red-gold tree of fire ascended as if it would consume the darkness in one tremendous burst of flame. . . . He knew that this was the fire that had encircled Daniel, that had raised Elijah from the earth, that had

spoken to Moses and would in the instant speak to him. (267)

This vision arises from Tarwater's new consciousness and new way of exercising freedom. In accepting his spiritual call, he has grown more human: more open to new ways of seeing and reflecting on experience. As David Eggenschwiler notes,

> Such a change of consciousness, like the epiphanies throughout Miss O'Connor's works, is not simply received but also attained as an act of free will. It is a creative, volitional act of perception that is appropriate to the character, his experiences, and his circumstances but that is not determined by them. The commentators who have claimed that Tarwater lacks freedom in accepting his calling have seen him as a fairly static character who finally stops fighting and gives in to his fate. They neglect to see that a series of revelations, made possible by the boy's experiences, makes him able to accept that calling.[25]

Seeing the vision, Tarwater throws himself to the ground and receives a message that is his own, born of his experience, and different from the old man's, who preached "the terrible speed of justice" (159). The young man hears the command to "GO WARN THE CHILDREN OF GOD OF THE TERRIBLE SPEED OF MERCY" (267). That Tarwater will preach his own message is one sign that, in submitting to his vocation, he loses neither his freedom nor his uniqueness. A second sign is that as the novel ends, he heads "toward the dark city, where the children of God lay sleeping" (267) to exercise his call, in contrast with the old man's preaching in the wilderness.[26]

Tarwater's message is as mysterious, as paradoxical, as the verse from Matthew's Gospel that O'Connor chose for her epigraph:

---

25. Eggenschwiler, 132.

26. The contrast between the two Tarwaters' sense of prophecy is briefly glimpsed early in the novel, on the trip to the city, when the boy, believing that "It was to the city that prophets came and he was here in the midst of it," rebukes his uncle for not prophesying. The old man, unmoved, calmly replies, "I'm here on bidnis [i.e., legal business]" (139).

FROM THE DAYS OF JOHN THE BAPTIST UNTIL NOW,
THE KINGDOM OF HEAVEN SUFFERETH VIOLENCE,
AND THE VIOLENT BEAR IT AWAY. (Matt. 11:12)

An important clue to the significance of this verse for O'Connor
was left in her library. In Emmanuel Mounier's *Personalism*, she
marked this passage, noting in the margin alongside it, "the violent
bear it away":

> It is difficult, even in philosophizing, to manage the
> language of love with discretion, especially in the presence
> of sensitive souls who feel an invincible repugnance
> against allowing any place or any value to use of force.
> What do they understand of Gandhi's cry, "I would run
> the risk of violence a thousand times rather than permit
> the emasculation of a whole race."
>
> Love is a struggle; life is a struggle against death;
> spiritual life is a struggle against the inertia of matter and
> the sloth of the body. The person attains self-conscious-
> ness, not through some ecstacy, but by force of mortal
> combat; and force is one of its principal attributes. Not the
> brute force of mere power and aggression, in which man
> forsakes his own action and imitates the behavior of
> matter; but human force, which is at once internal and
> efficacious, spiritual and manifest.[27]

O'Connor's linking this passage with her novel underscores several
points relevant to this essay: that the force required in soul-making
is not the same as aggressive "brute force"; that the struggle toward
self-consciousness is also a spiritual struggle; and that this violence
is required of those who "bear heaven away." Thus she communicates an insight into the wager on transcendence with which she
is usually not credited. Her characters (and readers) are asked to
wager that they will find themselves, rather than lose themselves,
by allowing themselves to be drawn into God's design for them.

---

27. Feeley, 160-61.

Author's Note:

This essay originated in a teacher's desperate attempt to salvage The Violent Bear It Away *for students who had rejected its "messages" without having understood them. For them, the novel promoted a "sick" religion, in which the end (Tarwater's submission to God) justifies the immoral and violent means (a drowning, a rape); in which a boy commendably tries to escape the effects of fundamentalist brainwashing but succumbs at the end, much to the author's approval; and in which religion manifests itself as violence, not as love.*

My response, which was to suggest that the violence in the novel largely arises from human beings estranged from and at war with themselves, does not, however, necessarily resolve the many issues this novel raises. Is O'Connor promoting a religion of obsession and violence, as many readers seem to think? When a work contains perversion, by what criteria do we decide whether the author is actually critiquing rather than supporting it? In O'Connor's fiction, can one submit to God rationally? Is it possible that God can and does act violently?

K.S.

Works Cited

Asals, Frederick. "Flannery Row." *Novel* 4, 1 (fall 1970): 92-96.

Bleikasten, André. "The Heresy of Flannery O'Connor." In *Critical Essays on Flannery O'Connor*, edited by Melvin J. Friedman and Beverly Lynn Clark, 138-58. Boston: G. K. Hall, 1985.

Desmond, John F. *Risen Sons: Flannery O'Connor's Vision of History*. Athens, Ga.: University of Georgia Press, 1987.

Duhamel, P. Albert. "Flannery O'Connor's Violent View of Reality." *Catholic World* 190 (February 1960): 280-85.

Eggenschwiler, David. *The Christian Humanism of Flannery O'Connor*. Detroit: Wayne State University Press, 1972.

Feeley, Kathleen, S.S.N.D. *Flannery O'Connor: Voice of the Peacock*. New York: Fordham University Press, 1982.

Giannone, Richard. *Flannery O'Connor and the Mystery of Love*. Urbana: University of Illinois Press, 1989.

Hendin, Josephine. *The World of Flannery O'Connor*. Bloomington: University of Indiana Press, 1970.

Humphries, Jefferson. "Proust, Flannery O'Connor, and the Aesthetic of Violence." In *Flannery O'Connor*, edited by Harold Bloom, 111-24. New York: Chelsea House Publishers, 1986.

Johansen, Ruthann Knechel. *The Narrative Secret of Flannery O'Connor: The Trickster as Interpreter*. Tuscaloosa: The University of Alabama Press, 1994.

Keating, Thomas. *Open Mind, Open Heart: The Contemplative Dimension of the Gospel*. Rockport, Maine: Element, 1991.

Martinez, Inez. "Flannery O'Connor and the Hidden Struggle of the Self." *Flannery O'Connor Bulletin* 16 (autumn 1987): 52-59.

May, John R. *The Pruning Word: The Parables of Flannery O'Connor*. Notre Dame: University of Notre Dame Press, 1976.

Merton, Thomas. *New Seeds of Contemplation*. New York: New Directions, 1972.

Montgomery, Marion. *Why Flannery O'Connor Stayed Home*. La Salle, Ill.: Sherwood Sugden & Company, 1981.

Muller, Gilbert H. *Nightmares and Visions: Flannery O'Connor and the Catholic Grotesque*. Athens, Ga.: University of Georgia Press, 1972.

Oates, Joyce Carol. *New Heaven, New Earth: The Visionary Experience in Literature*. New York: The Vanguard Press, Inc., 1974.

_____. "The Visionary Art of Flannery O'Connor." In *Flannery O'Connor*, edited by Harold Bloom, 43-53. New York: Chelsea House Publishers, 1986.

O'Connor, Flannery. *The Habit of Being: Letters of Flannery O'Connor*. Edited by Sally Fitzgerald. New York: Farrar, Straus & Giroux, 1979.

_____. *Mystery and Manners*. New York: Farrar, Straus & Giroux, 1969.

_____. *Three by Flannery O'Connor*. New York: New American Library, 1983.

Wood, Ralph C. *The Comedy of Redemption: Christian Faith and Comic Vision in Four American Novelists.* Notre Dame: University of Notre Dame Press, 1988.

Chapter Thirteen

The Archetypal Task of Forgiveness in T. S. Eliot's *The Family Reunion*

Mary Beth Duffey

In a rarely performed and much misunderstood play, *The Family Reunion*, T. S. Eliot addresses the need for forgiveness in family life. What makes this play so remarkable is not the external plot of domestic discord but the internal path Eliot takes to confront it. Eliot relies on myth and even archetype to ground his characters in a narrative that transcends their own time and place. He allows us to experience the mythic dimension of family life and so transcend the limits of our own family concerns. He leads us through the labyrinth of the unconscious, where another layer of the narrative unfolds. In *The Family Reunion* we meet ourselves, our families, and our archetypal roots.

In a play that touches the mythic dimension of family, we respond to something deeper than our individual experience as family members, though surely those identifications are important. We are in touch with reality that resonates with the very fibers of our humanity. C. G. Jung calls this reality an "archetype." He affirms its vitality as a "living psychic force" that manifests itself from age to age in myths, legends, poetry, dreams, just as surely as in drama. "Archetypes were and still are living psychic forces that demand to be taken seriously, and they have a strange way of making sure of their effect. . . ."[1] When we are in the presence of an archetypal situation, we are in touch with something beyond ourselves, and

---

1. C. G. Jung, *Psyche and Symbol* (Garden City, N.Y.: Doubleday), 119.

yet at the same time, we are in touch with the deepest parts of ourselves. Jung has described this experience beautifully:

> It is as though chords in us were struck that had never resounded before, or as though forces whose existence we had never suspected were unleashed. . . . At such moments we are no longer individuals, but the race: the voice of all mankind resounds in us. . . . The impact of an archetype . . . stirs us because it summons up a voice stronger than our own.[2]

To listen to "a voice stronger than our own" is to be attentive to the archetypal dimension of life. It is to transcend the "here and now," while still being grounded in "the here and now." To recognize the presence of myth wherever and whenever it emerges in the modern world seems imperative. Friedrich Nietzsche's image of the modern person "stripped of myth" is a stark warning:

> Man stripped of myth stands famished among all his pasts and must dig frantically for roots, be it among the most remote antiquities. What does our great historical hunger signify, our clutching about us of countless other cultures, our consuming desire for knowledge, if not the loss of myth, of a mythic home, the mythic womb?[3]

In an age when the modern person stands "stripped of myth," drama offers not only an encounter with those myths but a communal celebration of their power. Drama that taps the archetypal allows us to transcend a demythologized world and step into a richly symbolic one, even for a few brief hours in the theatre.

Our visual image of transcendence often suggests a reality above us, superior to our earthly existence, hovering somehow over our temporal reality. But transcendence might also be imaged within us, at the core, deep in the unconscious parts of ourselves and of our species. It is this sense of transcendent reality that pervades T. S. Eliot's *The Family Reunion.*

---

2. C. G. Jung, "On the Relation of Analytical Psychology and Poetry," *The Spirit in Man, Art and Literature* (New York: Pantheon Books, 1966), 101.

3. Friedrich Nietzsche, *The Birth of Tragedy* (Garden City, N.Y.: Doubleday, 1956), 137.

The two major motifs of the play – coming home and being reconciled – are themes that have their roots in myth and archetype. In *The Family Reunion* T. S. Eliot taps the ancient themes of homecoming and reconciliation by grounding his tale in the Christian redemption myth, as well as in the Greek tragedy of Orestes. Harry's forgiveness is achieved by following the rubrics of the Christian penitential rite: communal confession, reconciliation with the communion of saints and the benediction. Like his Greek analogue Orestes, Harry is pursued by the Eumenides. His reconciliation occurs only when he can face what he has done and the haunting knowledge of why he has done it.

As the play opens, the Monchensey family is gathering to celebrate the birthday of the matriarch, Amy. But the rising energy of the play points to another event – the arrival of Harry, who has been away for eight years. His homecoming to Wishwood, after the sudden death of his wife, constitutes the external "family reunion" of the Monchenseys, their reason for coming together. When Harry arrives, he is highly agitated and almost paranoid in his behavior – closing curtains, looking over his shoulder, speaking of "spectres" that he had sensed before, but now that he is home actually sees. He tells the gathered clan to stop pretending that nothing has changed because something irrevocable has happened. Within moments of his arrival, he feels compelled to announce that his wife's death was not accidental, that in fact, he has killed her. The reaction of each family member is disbelief. They rationalize that her drowning was such a shock to Harry that he is now manifesting delusional thinking.

But his Aunt Agatha, who serves as a kind of spiritual guide to Harry, listens to his confession and tells him:

> . . . you only hold a fragment of the explanation.
> It is only because of what you do not understand
> That you feel the need to declare what you do.
> There is more to understand; hold fast to that
> As the way to freedom.[4]

Throughout the drama, Harry's anxiety is manifested in his talk of pursuit by forces he cannot escape. The "spectres" are

---

4. T. S. Eliot, *The Family Reunion* (New York: Harcourt Bruce & World, 1939), 31; hereafter cited parenthetically in the text.

identified in the stage directions as "the Eumenides" – an explicit connection with the Orestian myth. But in *The Family Reunion* the Eumenides are also an embodiment of guilt. As long as Harry evades the Eumenides (and his guilt), he is pursued by them. But once he understands the origin of his guilt (indeed his own origin), he is released, reconciled, and even redeemed.

Agatha will ultimately help Harry to discover the truth about his past, a truth that connects him with his dead father. This connection with his father (the spiritual "family reunion" of the play) sets him free. He is freed from "that awful privacy" (103) of personal guilt, but bound to the common suffering of all human kind.

In his climactic scene with Agatha, Harry confirms the connection between his homecoming quest and the need to recover a lost self:

At the beginning, eight years ago,
I felt, at first, that sense of separation,
Of isolation unredeemable, irrevocable –
It's eternal, or gives a knowledge of eternity,
Because it feels eternal while it lasts. That is one hell.
Then the numbness came to cover it – that is another –
That was the second hell of not being there,
The degradation of being parted from myself,
From the self which persisted only as eye, seeing.
All this last year, I could not fit myself together:
When I was inside the old dream, I felt all the same
    emotion
Or lack of emotion, as before: the same loathing
Diffused, I not a person, in a world not of persons
But only of contaminating presences.
And then I had no horror of my action,
I only felt the repetition of it
Over and over, when I was outside,
I could associate nothing of it with myself,
Though nothing else was real. I thought foolishly
That when I got back to Wishwood, as I had left it,
Everything would fall into place. But *they* prevent it. (96)

The Eumenides pursue Harry throughout the drama, preventing Wishwood from being a facile solution to his problem of

234 \ *Self and Society*

self-discovery. Harry finally realizes that he has been fleeing the Eumenides. The flight leads him home to "the last apparent refuge, the safe shelter" of Wishwood:

> This last year, I have been in flight
> But always in ignorance of invisible pursuers.
> Now I know that all my life has been a flight
> And phantoms fed upon me while I fled. Now I know
> The last apparent refuge, the safe shelter
> That is where I meet them. That is the way of spectres. . .
> (110)

Wishwood cannot, however, shield Harry from the Eumenides. He is, in fact, even more intensely aware of their presence. At home they are made visible. Harry's homecoming reinforces the "sense of latent evil" that he feels. Northrop Frye explains:

> Harry is, like the women of Canterbury, haunted by a sense of latent evil hiding behind his life. If nothing changed in time . . . Harry might find his other self in boyhood at home, his counterpart in the rose garden. But as his aunt Agatha foresees, his self-recognition is of the ironic kind, as in Henry James' *The Jolly Corner* to which she refers. What happens is the opposite: Harry's haunting sense of evil is objectified at Wishwood in the form of the Furies.[5]

In his essay "The Father in the Destiny of the Individual," Jung uses the epigram: "The Fates lead the willing, but drag the unwilling."[6] These words aptly describe the relationship between Harry and the Eumenides. As long as Harry remains "unwilling" and unconscious, the Fates (the Eumenides) "drag" him. Once he becomes "willing" and conscious, he is led by them; only then can he say: "I must follow the bright angels" (111).

Amy, Harry's mother, dismisses the existence of the Eumenides and, without realizing it, she indicts the family as the pursuers: "There is no one here / No one but your family" (110). Familial demands can pursue a person all the days of his life,

---

5. Northrop Frye, *T. S. Eliot* (New York: Grove Press, 1963), 92.

6. C. G. Jung, "The Father in the Destiny of the Individual," *Freud and Psychoanalysis* (Princeton: Princeton University Press, 1961), 303.

impeding self-realization. Harry's homecoming had begun as both an escape from the pursuing Eumenides and a search for himself. His experience of homecoming *angst* is a result of these ambivalent drives. There is a stark psychological realism in the longing to recapture a lost self, a longing that the literal homecoming simply cannot fulfill. It seems then that an interior homecoming is required for the lost self to be recovered and wholeness achieved.

Among the needs that prompt homecoming is the need for a sense of belonging. This need is first articulated by Mary in her remembrance of childhood days at Wishwood:

> . . . I was only a cousin
> Kept here because there was nothing else to do with me.
> I didn't belong here. It was different for you. (52)

As a child, Harry *did* belong at Wishwood. Now he returns seeking that sense of belonging, but like the hollow tree, which belonged to them and they to it, this sense of belonging is missing.

Harry's "lost self" is ultimately connected with a father whom he has scarcely known. The search for a father is prompted by a need to clearly know himself. The return to Wishwood is the outward, concrete act that points to an interior search for origins. The person who comes home meets both innocence and guilt at Wishwood – the innocence of lost childhood and the guilt of parents scarcely known. Harry learns of his father's frustrated desire to kill his mother. This knowledge connects Harry with his father in a bond that he has never before known. Early in the play, when Harry confesses openly to his family that he has killed his wife, there is controversy about the credibility of his confession. Although the confession is not accepted by his family, Harry has made it in a straightforward and direct manner. Still the confession does not release Harry from his guilt.

Harry's reconciliation comes only when he begins to see the connection between his father's frustrated desire and his own act. Harry has done the very thing his father intended to do. Together with the communal forgiveness of his family, the bond with his dead father seems to release Harry from the "private misery of guilt." In this, Eliot appears to be collapsing two essential doctrines of his newly acquired Catholic Creed: the forgiveness of sins and the communion of saints. It is not enough for Harry merely to confess. He must forgive and be forgiven by his family. As part of the "communion of saints," the family includes both living and dead members. If it is the communal nature of his confession that releases Harry from guilt, the community includes both living and dead members of the Monchensey family. For Eliot, reconciliation requires a reach backwards to the past and a connection with those who people the present.

If Harry *belongs* in any sense to his family, he belongs by the very fact of his guilt. Just as original sin is the symbol of the shared guilt that connects the human family, individual family members belong to one another through guilt as well. Whenever "the sins of the fathers are visited upon the sons" in individual families, guilt becomes a credential for belonging. It is this sense of belonging that will finally allow Harry to leave Wishwood freely and consciously, no longer pursued by the Eumenides, or possessed by his family. This conscious and willing leave-taking fulfills the most urgent need that prompts the homecoming – the task of individuation. The homecoming becomes the process of coming home to oneself.

Harry intuits "some origin of wretchedness" (97) in his own background. The return to Wishwood awakens in Harry a sense of shame that is somehow associated with his father:

Here I have been finding
A misery long forgotten, and a new torture
The shadow of something behind our meagre childhood
Some origin of wretchedness. Is that what they would
     show me?
And now I want you to tell me about my father. (97)

In response, Agatha begins by describing Harry's father objectively as "an exceptionally cultivated country gentleman . . . something of an oddity to his neighbors . . . a solitary man" (98). But Harry pushes for a more subjective response. His questioning is a quest for his true origins: "Tell me, now, who were my parents?" (98). Agatha's answer is the personal and poignant story of her involvement with Harry's father. At the time of Harry's conception, Agatha and Harry's father were involved in an affair that seems to have been both a sexual and a loving relationship. Although it was

Amy who conceived Harry, Agatha feels that Harry was in some sense her child, or at least the child who might have been hers.

The animosity between Harry's parents, even at the time of his conception, had prompted Harry's father to plot Amy's death. It was Agatha who intervened to stop the murder. Her motive was a simple and pure love for the unborn child she felt was, in some mysterious way, her own child:

> I found him thinking
> How to get rid of your mother. What simple plots!
> . . . a dozen foolish ways, each one abandoned
> For something more ingenious. You were due in three
>   months time;
> You would not have been born in that event: I stopped
>   him. . . .
> I did not want to kill *you*!
> You to be killed! What were you then? Only a thing called
>   'life' –
> Something that should have been mine, as I felt then
> Most people would not have felt that compunction
> If they felt no other. But I wanted you!
> If that had happened, I knew I should have carried death
>   in my womb.
> I felt that you were in some way mine!
> And that in any case, I should have no other child.
> (100-101)

The revelation of the murder plot functions in two ways: (1) It establishes an essential link between Harry and his father; (2) It suggests the spiritual motherhood of Agatha, who serves as a "guardian" figure for Harry. Once he is cognizant of his father's desire to kill his mother, Harry is simultaneously aware of the bond that unites him to his father. That bond is guilt. Harry believes he has done the very thing his father had wanted to do. He has lived out the unconscious desire of his father.

Harry's realization of his father's desire reveals the power of transgenerational unconsciousness. C. G. Jung sees the unconscious contents of parents as the most powerful inheritance a child receives from them. He states: "The things which have the most powerful effect upon children do not come from the conscious state of the parents but from their unconscious background."[7] The "unlived life" of the parent is often lived out in succeeding generations. Jung observes how dangerous this inheritance can be to the child:

> What usually has the strongest psychic effect on the child is the life which the parents . . . have not lived . . . . To put it bluntly, it is usually that part of life which they have always shirked, probably by means of a pious lie. That sows the most virulent germs.[8]

The Jungian analyst Irene Claremont De Castillejo finds this psychological phenomenon dramatized in *The Family Reunion*:

> . . . the son Harry pushes his wife overboard without really meaning to do so, and only later discovers that he had unwittingly carried out his father's unadmitted desire to get rid of his own wife. All but Harry thought it was an accident.
>
> In actual life one is constantly coming across such things, and it is brought home to me again and again that "the sins of the fathers are visited upon the children to the fourth generation." The real sin is the failure to be conscious when one is capable of being conscious. For it is unconsciousness that gives libido to the repressed talent or desire so that succeeding generations are forced to enact it. Harry would not have had to push his wife into the sea had his own father been fully aware of his own desire and then consciously refrained from carrying it out.[9]

In the climactic scene with Agatha, Harry's search for a lost self and his search for a father come together. Both quests draw him homeward; both questions are resolved by Agatha's story. The acknowledgement of shared guilt does not oppress Harry. Rather, it seems to release him. Harry receives the information about his father, shameful as it is, with a strange joy and a sense of relief.

---

7. C. G. Jung, introduction to *The Inner World of Childhood,* by Frances Wickes (New York: D. Appleton, 1927), xvii.

8. Ibid., xviii-xix.

9. Irene Claremont De Castillejo, *Knowing Woman* (New York: Harper & Row, 1973), 120.

Agatha's story furthers Harry's search for a father. It not only gives Harry the grim facts of his father's life, but it also makes an implicit connection between Harry's life and his father's life, between his father's guilt and his own. This connection at the deepest psychic level between father and son establishes a spiritual bond. At the same time, Agatha's story helps Harry make the necessary break from his mother. The search for a father is typically impeded by a strong mother-complex; in myth, legend, and fairy tale the mother often stands between father and son.

Amy's death seems to be a direct consequence of her separation from Harry. Her death alerts us to an end as well as a beginning. On a symbolic level, Harry has begun a new life. The death of his mother appears to be the necessary price for that rebirth, or at least the unavoidable consequence of his independence. The death-in-birth/birth-in-death paradox, a familiar theme in Eliot's work, helps to establish the synchronic nature of time wherein past, present, and future are one.

In *The Family Reunion* the synchronic nature of time embraces a larger theme – that of reconciliation. To what end is time synchronic? What difference does the synchronicity of time make in human relationships? In *The Family Reunion* those characters who transcend the time-space continuum, who come to see past, present, and future as "eternally present," are capable of reconciliation. If the past is contained in the present, the opportunities for reconciliation of a past event remain available. Forgiveness, even of a deceased or distant person, is immediately accessible at any present moment. Forgiveness is imperative, in fact, if the future is to be anything more than a treadmill on which the past occurs over and over again.

Reconciliation is communal in the broadest sense. It includes not only the community of the living but the community of the dead as well. Harry's reconciliation comes through communion with his dead father. It transcends the time-space continuum to release him from "that awful privacy" of personal guilt. Shared guilt, which is familial in origin, suggests the mythic notion of "original sin."

In his introduction to Frances Wickes' *The Inner World of Childhood*, Jung uses the term "original sin" to refer to the inherited guilt passed on through the unconscious from one generation to another.[10] Jung emphasized the grave moral responsibility of parents to become conscious lest they pass on their own unconscious desires to their offspring. To become conscious is to come to personal knowledge. And that knowledge is vital. Jung warns: "Nature has no use for the plea that one 'did not know.' Not knowing acts like guilt."[11]

In *The Family Reunion,* if "not knowing acts like guilt," knowing acts like forgiveness. Once Harry knows the truth about his father, he comes to know himself more fully. Once his father's unconscious is brought to light, Harry is freed of its tyranny.

Agatha, who "has only watched and waited," recognizes that Harry's reconciliation has required the painful process of becoming conscious. She believes that the "knowledge must precede the expiation." Expiation comes primarily through knowing, through becoming conscious:

> What we have written is not a story of detection,
> Of crime and punishment, but of sin and expiation. . . .
> It is possible that you have not known what sin
> You shall expiate, or whose, or why. It is certain
> That the knowledge of it must precede the expiation.
> It is possible that sin may strain and struggle
> In its dark instinctive birth, to come to consciousness
> And so find expurgation. It is possible
> You are the consciousness of your unhappy family
> Its bird sent flying through the purgatorial flame.
> Indeed it is possible . . .
> The burden's now yours
> The burden of all the family. (101-2)

Harry accepts the burden of his family's guilt. Because he is conscious of it, he can say: "Everything tends toward reconciliation" (101).

As the play ends, Agatha summarizes the tragedy of the Monchensey family. They are a family "cursed" by unconsciousness. The curse has pursued Harry from his earliest days. When he

---

10. C. G. Jung, introduction to *The Inner World of Childhood*, xix.

11. Ibid., xx.

becomes conscious of it, however, he is freed from it. The curse is compared to a child in Agatha's final speech. Both are "formed in a moment of unconsciousness"; both grow and are fulfilled in time:

> A curse comes to being
> As a child is formed.
> In both, the incredible
> Becomes actual.
> Without our intention
> Knowing what is intended
> A curse is like a child, formed
> In a moment of unconsciousness. (106)

The curse is ended in its own time; it is not subject to the ordinary temporal laws of immanence. The curse points to a temporal (transcendent) reality:

> It cannot be hurried
> And it cannot be delayed. (120)

Consciousness is required:

> So the knot be unknotted,
> The crossed be uncrossed.
> The crooked be made straight
> And the curse be ended. (131)

Agatha's final lines affirm the transgenerational effects not only of the curse but of its completion. The curse is ended in three consciously undertaken ways:

> By intercession
> By pilgrimage
> By those who depart
> In several directions
> For their own redemption
> And that of the departed. (131)

Not only is Harry redeemed as his pilgrim journey begins, but his pilgrimage simultaneously accomplishes the redemption "of the departed." The curse begun at his conception is ended at Amy's death. It is, of course, not Amy's death alone which brings the curse to its completion, but Harry's new life. Harry's reconciliation with his departed parents is life-giving. It is no mere coincidence that

Amy's death and Harry's new life come about at the same dramatic moment.

There is a kind of birth in death and a kind of death in birth. This paradox of the circularity of life and death is the play's final truth. The closing line of the play is a requiem benediction: "May they rest in peace" (131). For the departed, as well as the living, that peace depends on the ending of the curse. As long as the curse prevails, there can be no rest, no peace for living or dead. As long as the unconscious contents remain unconscious, a curse follows a family for generations. But once the curse is lifted through consciousness, the living are freed from the bondage of the past, and the departed may finally "rest in peace."

The Family Reunion is not only the story of a family reunited after many years. It is more aptly the story of an individual's interior reunion, set in the context of his family. Harry comes home to himself in that interior sense that is the true homecoming. The search for origins is similarly an internal process. The guilt that drives him homeward at the play's opening is experienced by Harry as "the cancer that eats away the *self*" (30). Healing comes when the guilt is reconciled and the self is restored. Individuation in this play becomes no mean selfish pursuit of individuality, but a struggle for soul survival.

Individuation, the movement toward self-knowledge, involves not only the individual, but the family, and the world at large. To lift the burden of one's own unconscious contents from the collective store becomes a moral mandate:

> The more we become conscious of ourselves through self-knowledge, and act accordingly, the more the layer of the personal unconscious that is imposed on the collective unconscious will be diminished. . . . This widened consciousness is no longer that touchy, egotistical bundle of personal wishes, hopes, fears, and ambitions . . . instead, it is a function of relationship to the *world* of objects, bringing the individual into absolute, binding, and indissoluble communion with the world at large.[12]

---

12. C. G. Jung, *The Basic Writings of C. G. Jung* (New York: Random House, 1959), 148.

The universal quality of the unconscious requires that its contents are never entirely personal or individual: "We can now see that the unconscious produces contents that are valid not only for the person concerned, but for others as well, in fact, for a great many and possibly for all."[13] The unconscious points to potential relatedness not simply with one's family, but with the world in general. The relationship between the individual and society, the responsibility to the world outside the family, and the broadest concept of "belonging" are all addressed by the unconscious. "The processes of the collective unconscious are concerned not only with the more or less personal relations of the individual to his family or to a wider social group, but with his relations with society and to the human community in general."[14]

In *The Family Reunion* the relationship between the Monchensey family and the outside world is characterized by conflict. The conflict is outward enough to concretize domestic turmoil as the play's chief dramatic action. But in this very interior play, the sources of tension are always internal; the roots of conflict are subliminal.

Wishwood is an insular family home and the home of an insular family. The Monchenseys do not often welcome outsiders into their family circle. Amy describes Harry's wife as an outsider, who never really belonged. "She never would have been one of the family / She never wished to be one of the family" (20). Mary, who is Harry's cousin, is the most distant relative at Wishwood. She tells Harry about her feeling of estrangement as a child:

> . . . I was only a cousin
> Kept here because there was nothing else to do with me.
> I didn't belong here. (52)

Dr. Warburton, the family physician, is also an outsider; he is welcomed only because he is useful. Mary expresses relief that another outsider is joining them for dinner. The exclusiveness at Wishwood has become oppressive to Mary:

> Well, there's something to be said for having an outsider;
> For what is more formal than a family dinner? (46)

---

13. Ibid.
14. Ibid., 149.

Downing, Harry's servant, is acutely conscious of being an outsider. He keeps a respectful distance from family affairs. The Monchenseys are careful not to discuss Harry's problems in Downing's presence. Yet Downing tells the family quite openly: "After all these years that I've been with him? I think I know his Lordship better than anybody" (124). Downing's kinship with Harry comes from a psychic bond. The affinity allows Downing to understand Harry so well that he, too, is capable of seeing the "ghosts," as he calls the Eumenides. Downing calmly remarks: "I wondered when his Lordship would get / round to seeing them" (25). Downing's perception of them reveals his intuitive understanding of his master's psyche. Downing is an outsider in every sense of the word: blood line, social class, education. Yet he knows Harry better than anyone in the family. The relationship between Harry and his servant Downing is a paradigm for the relationship an individual may have with the outside world.

For a family like the Monchenseys, estranged from the outside world and insulated at Wishwood, there are no opportunities for new life and creativity. When outsiders are denied entry into the family circle, the life line stops and the vitality of that family is aborted.

Harry gradually begins to see an essential connection between himself and society. He rejects the insularity of his upbringing as a member of the Monchensey family and accepts the common pain that connects him with the human family. He no longer sees his life as an "isolated ruin," but rather as "part of some huge disaster":

> . . . What you call the normal
> Is merely the unreal and the unimportant
> I was like that in a way, so long as I could think
> Even of my own life as an isolated ruin,
> A casual bit of waste in an orderly universe
> But it begins to seem just part of some huge disaster
> Some monstrous mistake and aberration
> Of all men, of the world, which I cannot put in order. (88)

The essential connection between the individual and society is affirmed by the Chorus in Part I and repeated in Part II. Early in the play, the Chorus includes the audience with the use of the pronoun "We," a traditional choric device. The universality of the theme is suggested in the Chorus' observation:

> We all of us make the pretension
> To be the uncommon exception
> To the universal bondage. (43)

This "pretension" is belied, however, by "certain inflexible laws" that connect the individual to a reality beyond himself, beyond narrow family identification. In Part II the Chorus continues the theme:

> And whether in Argos or in England
> There are certain inflexible laws
> Unalterable, in the nature of music.
> There is nothing at all to be done about it.
> There is nothing to be done about anything.
> And now it is time for the news
> We must listen to the weather report
> And the international catastrophes. (94)

Once these "inflexible laws" that connect the individual to society through the human condition are recognized, "there is nothing to do" but "listen to the news." Eliot's sense that "there is nothing at all to be done about it . . . nothing to be done about anything" is not to be taken in the absurdist tradition. It is not a statement of nihilism. Quite the contrary! In the realization that "there is nothing to be done" about individual suffering, pain, and guilt, the individual turns to society. He "listens to the news" and "the international catastrophes" that connect him with the sufferings of all humanity. Those sufferings are part of the universal lot of all people of all time, "whether in Argos or in England."

In every age and culture, it seems to be the task of the artist to call the society back to the essential truth that we are all part of one another. We become aware of our interrelationship when we experience the commonality of our suffering. Jung saw the artist's responsibility to society in terms of this unique ability to "restore the psychic balance" in the culture. That balance is threatened whenever the archetypal dimension of life is ignored. Jung states:

> Whenever conscious life becomes one-sided or adopts a
> false attitude, these images instinctively rise to the surface

in dreams and in the visions of artists and seers to restore the psychic balance, whether of the individual or the epoch. In this way, the work of the artist meets the psychic needs of the society in which he lives, and therefore means more than his personal fate, whether he is aware of it or not.[15]

In his important discussion of the relationship between psychology and literature, Jung describes the voice of the artist as the voice of humankind. The true poet is always expressing more than his personal voice. Jung goes so far as to suggest that the transpersonal quality of the work is its claim to artistry:

The essence of a work of art is not to be found in the personal idiosyncrasies that creep into it – indeed, the more there are of them, the less it is a work of art – but in its rising above the personal and speaking from the mind and heart of the artist to the mind and heart of mankind.[16]

In *The Family Reunion*, as in all of his work, T. S. Eliot faithfully accepts this mandate. Eliot speaks from his own mind and heart to "the mind and heart of mankind" in the way he allows his work to address the archetypal. Eliot's principle that a work of art relies on its tradition for its power and worth is strikingly similar to Jung's theory of the transpersonal quality of art.

T. S. Eliot's insistence that a work of art relies on tradition has important implications for a play whose tradition is more than culturally traditional. *The Family Reunion* relies on the central myth of Western culture, the Christian redemption myth or Paschal mystery. Harry's redemption occurs through a cycle of death and rebirth. His reconciliation follows the rubrics of an ancient Christian penitential rite: communal confession, reconciliation with the communion of saints, and the benediction. But the Christian tradition is only part of the heritage Eliot taps in this play. The Greek myth of *Orestes* supplies the play's plot structure, and the use of the Chorus and verse dialogue connect the play with the most ancient forms of theatre art. Probing the play's sources even deeper, we

---

15. Jung, "On the Relation of Analytical Psychology and Poetry," 104.
16. Ibid., 101.

discover what Jung refers to as the "deepest springs of life."[17] The archetypal images that we have seen in *The Family Reunion* suggest that Eliot has tapped the most important tradition available to him – the contents of the collective unconscious, that dimension of human consciousness where we are all family.

In her insightful handbook on the spiritual direction of children, Polly Berrien Berends compares human consciousness to a flower whose petals are families, generations of families opening to fuller consciousness:

> I think each family is a petal opening, each generation is part of the petal. It is one petal in the great opening flower of human consciousness. Our problems are not our shame; they are our work. Each of us has certain work to do to grow beyond the generation before us. Not only for ourselves and our children but for the whole flower. Beyond us, below, are deep roots into truth. Beyond us, above, is the light of love. We are trying so hard, and we can't do it; it is all happening by grace, and we can't stop it.[18]

Berend's observation: "Beyond us, above, is the light of love" reflects a traditional image of transcendence. But it is her stunning statement that precedes it – "Beyond us, below, are deep roots into truth" – that locates the healing core of family life. These "deep roots of truth" (the unconscious) are where Eliot's *The Family Reunion* takes place and where perhaps all true family reunions occur. Like Harry who discovers that "everything tends toward reconciliation" (101), we too may experience the healing truth for our own families, a truth that would embrace the whole human family:

"It is all happening by grace, and we can't stop it."[19]

17. Ibid., 82.

18. Polly Berrien Berends, *Gently Lead* (New York: HarperCollins, 1991), 172.

19. Ibid., 172.

Author's Note:

Modern drama, from the time of Ibsen to the present, has been consistently concerned with family relationships. Ibsen's audiences may have been tempted to predict the collapse of the family as an institution. Clearly, the apocalyptic vision of the demise of the family haunts our own time. But as the century and the millennium come to a close, the family remains a concern of contemporary dramatists.

Why? What prompts the modern playwright to continue to people our stages with families? And why are they so "dysfunctional"? Are there archetypal experiences at work in these plays – something deeper than our individual experiences as family members?

Do dream and drama archetypes tell us who we are and where we come from? If the familial archetypes suggest that we are all born into families, into relationship, into connection, do we also die into relationship, into connection, or (as Eliot's play suggests) into reunion?

M.B.D.

Works Cited

Berends, Polly Berrien. *Gently Lead.* New York: HarperCollins, 1991.

De Castillego, Irene Claremont. *Knowing Woman.* New York: Harper & Row, 1973.

Eliot, T. S. *The Family Reunion.* New York: Harcourt, Brace & World, 1939.

Frye, Northrop. *T. S. Eliot.* New York: Grove Press, 1963.

Jung, C. G. *The Basic Writings of C. G. Jung.* Ed. Violet Staub de Laszlo. New York: Random House, 1959.

_____. "The Father in the Destiny of the Individual." In *Freud and Psychoanalysis. The Collected Works of C. G. Jung.* Eds. Herbert Read, Michael Fordham, Gerhard Adler. Princeton: Princeton University Press, 1961.

_____. Introduction to *The Inner World of Childhood*, by Frances Wickes. New York: D. Appleton, 1927.

_____. "On the Relation of Analytical Psychology & Poetry." *The Spirit in Man, Art and Literature.* New York: Pantheon Books, 1966.

_____. *Psyche and Symbol.* Garden City, N.Y.: Doubleday, 1958.

_____. *Symbols of Transformation.* Princeton: Princeton University Press, 1956.

Kelsey, Morton. *Myth, History and Faith.* New York: Paulist Press, 1974.

Nietzsche, Friedrich. *The Birth of Tragedy.* Translated by Francis Golffing. Garden City, N.Y.: Doubleday, 1956.

VI.

The Wager

Chapter Fourteen

Camus: Wagering on Immanence

James Conlon

We ordinarily make a sharp distinction between belief and non-belief, perhaps allowing for gray territories in between. Maybe the division should be done differently, between those who are easy in their belief or non-belief, and those who see agony in either place. In this sense, Madalyn Murray O'Hair and Jerry Falwell have a lot in common: so do Pascal and Camus.

    – John Garvey, "The Gnostics among Us"

Pascal was one of the first moderns to see with sharp poignancy that modernity's hopes for the power of reason were definitely exaggerated. Unfortunately, regarding the ultimate nature of reality – the existence of God and the destiny of the human spirit – theoretical reason was and ever would be silent. The kind of evidence the modern mind expected for its mathematical and physical convictions could never be mustered for its metaphysical ones. Even for the foundational question of God, the evidence is ineradicably inconclusive. "Reason can decide nothing here."[1]

    But Pascal realizes that, unlike most theoretical issues, the questions of God and immortality do not admit the luxury of suspended judgment. Given the practical import of these questions,

---

This essay was originally published in the May 1995 issue of *The Modern Schoolman* (Volume 72). It is reprinted here by permission.

1. Blaise Pascal, *Pensées and the Provincial Letters*, trans. W. F. Trotter and Thomas M'Crie (New York: The Modern Library, 1941), 81 (233).

not to decide itself becomes a decision. Thus, human beings are faced with an agonizing dilemma: They must form ultimate convictions, but theoretical reason provides no direction about which convictions to form.

In response to this dilemma, Pascal adopts a truly original strategy. He asks not whether God's existence is a reasonable conclusion but whether the choice to believe in God's existence is a reasonable choice. What this does is refocus the question from whether the belief is true to whether it is valuable, that is, whether it is in our interest. And although reason cannot help us at all with the first question, Pascal finds it very effective in helping us with the second.

Once this change of focus occurs, Pascal argues that the problem of belief can be formulated as an either/or wager and the choice determined by the standard calculations of probabilistic decision theory. If God exists, complete and eternal happiness is possible for human beings; if not, they have only the fleeting joys and inevitable miseries of this life. Thus, wagering that God exists means infinite gain if one wins and relatively minimal loss if one loses. Given this situation, Pascal argues, God is the incontestably reasonable choice. "Let us weigh the gain and the loss in wagering that God is. Let us estimate these two chances. If you win, you win all; if you lose, you lose nothing. Wager, then, without hesitation that He is."[2]

Since the problem of God's existence, of the existence of metaphysical purpose and intrinsic meaning, cannot be effectively solved by pure reason, it comes down in the end to something of a gamble. However, this does not reduce our most fundamental convictions to mere whims, to arbitrary conventions or flips of a coin. Though inextricably intertwined with human interests, gambling (as well as the heart)[3] has its own reasons, and it is on them that our metaphysical convictions will stand or fall.

Modern thinkers as diverse as Kant and Kierkegaard have accepted the inevitability of some form of Pascal's strategy. Even contemporary efforts to deal afresh with the issue, from the

---

2. Ibid.
3. Ibid., 91 (277).

painstaking historical analysis of Hans Küng's *Does God Exist?*[4] to the metaphorical brilliance of George Steiner's *Real Presences*,[5] seem unable to find a fundamentally different strategy from that proposed by Pascal.

Albert Camus, a contemporary thinker, was profoundly immersed in the dilemma of belief that Pascal describes. Likewise, he wholeheartedly embraced Pascal's fundamental strategy for practical resolution. What makes him unique, however, is that while he accepts the terms of Pascal's wager, he argues for the opposite conclusion.

Two novels by Camus, *The Stranger* (1942) and *The Plague* (1947), can be read as efforts to answer the questions posed by Pascal's wager. Camus' literary method is, of course, quite different from Pascal's. Rather than a logical computation between two abstract ideas, Camus carries out his analysis in the form of a confrontation between fictional characters. In each of the novels, the narrator/protagonist is carefully contrasted with a priest (representing transcendence). Using this more concretized method, Camus argues that the finite world is a much better bet than the transcendent God. Drawing on an analysis of the character contrasts in the two novels, this paper will present Camus' refutation of Pascal, his reasons for wagering on immanence rather than transcendence.

What makes Meursault, the main character of *The Stranger,* "strange," is not that, as has often been claimed, he is devoid of feelings, but that his feelings are so contrary to the expectations of others – including the readers of the novel. Even in the novel's notorious opening sentence, it is clear that Meursault's relationship to his mother is not that of cold indifference. His term for her, "Mamam," is tender and almost endearing in its straightforward childlikeness. He definitely *does* feel emotions toward his "*Mamam,*" but decidedly not the emotions about her death that a

---

4. Hans Küng, *Does God Exist?* trans. Edward Quinn (Garden City, N.Y.: Doubleday, 1980), 535ff.

5. George Steiner, *Real Presences* (Chicago: University of Chicago Press, 1989), 214.

son is expected to feel. The unconventional nature of his emotional life, however, should not be mistaken as the lack of one altogether.

What characterizes Meursault's emotional life, what distinguishes it so radically from the one that we are accustomed to, is its immediacy. His emotions happen with an almost pristine spontaneity. They are totally oblivious to cultural expectations and unaffected by personal ambition. Changes in the climate and the day's colors captivate and fascinate him far more than any civic event. Meursault lives in the plenitude of the sensuous moment, a moment ordinarily obscured by societal mores and by one's own personal goals. His emotions are so unconventional precisely because they happen beyond or before convention.

Nowhere is this characteristic of his emotional life clearer than in this relationship with Marie. Marie had worked for a short time in Meursault's office. Significantly, they did not connect at that time, even though there seemed to be a mutual attraction. The day after his mother's funeral, Meursault meets Marie while swimming. Shorn of society's trappings, immersed in the primordial fluidity of the water, they form a sensuous connection mediated only by the barest minimum of language. Sunning themselves on a float, he rests his head on her stomach "for a long time," and feels her heart beating softly on the back of his neck.[6] There is a natural and direct innocence to their sexual communion that night, one which Meursault tries to recapture the next morning (Sunday) by finding "the salty smell Marie's hair had left in the pillow" (*S* 21).

Unlike Meursault, Marie needs something more than the immediate values of their union; she seeks some verbal and societal validation:

> That evening Marie came by to see me and asked me if I wanted to marry her. I said it didn't make any difference to me and that we could if she wanted to. Then she wanted to know if I loved her. I answered the same way I had the last time, that it didn't mean anything but that I probably didn't love her. (*S* 41)

---

6. Albert Camus, *The Stranger*, trans. Matthew Ward (New York: Vintage, 1988), 20; hereafter cited parenthetically in the text as *S*.

Meursault's response to her questions has been offered as a prime example of his callous and unfeeling indifference. This does not seem accurate to me. There is a genuine – if unconventional – spirit of sacrifice in his willingness to marry Marie *if* it would please her. He feels an undeniable closeness to her, but the words "I love you" and all the romantic baggage they imply "[don't] mean anything," don't add anything essential to the reality of that closeness. "Marie and I swam out a ways, and we felt a closeness as we moved in unison and were happy" (*S* 50). Meursault is not unfeeling toward Marie or indifferent about his relationship with her, but he sees no need to bless it with socially sanctioned words or ceremonies. Swimming is all the baptism their union needs.

Properly understood then, Meursault is not a callous and indifferent monster, but someone with an acute sensitivity to the immediacy of an experience and a radical indifference to the conventional proprieties surrounding that experience. It is this combination, and not some masochistic tendency on her part, that makes him lovable, valuable, in Marie's eyes (*S* 42).

But if Meursault is not some immoral monster, is he really a moral hero? It has become almost mandatory in answering this question to quote Camus' own reference to Meursault as "the only Christ we deserve."[7] But what exactly does this mean? In what sense, if any, is Meursault a serious alternative to Christ?

Obviously, both Christ and Meursault embody values that are radically opposed to the conventional pieties of their societies, and both are willing to affirm these values in the face of death. Meursault is condemned not so much for killing an Arab as being the kind of person that he is: not crying at his mother's funeral, not expressing the requisite regrets, and not parroting the standard religious convictions to the magistrate. Granted, Meursault's values are not professed with the same self-conscious assurance as are Christ's, but both steadfastly refuse to lie, to feign feeling, to play the expected, submissive game.

But while integrity in the face of death is true of many heroes, the link with Christ seems a crucial one, and Camus takes great

---

7.   Albert Camus, *Lyrical and Critical Essays*, ed. Philip Thody, trans. Ellen Conroy Kennedy (New York: Alfred A. Knopf, 1968), 337.

pains to make the similarities between the lives of the two specific and numerous. For example, the father of each is a questionable presence, and Christ's relationship with his mother, like Meursault's, appears distant and unaffectionate.[8] Also, both seem to attract disreputable characters as their primary companions; both have a disreputable Mary/Marie as a friend. In addition, both men are basically silent before their accusers. ("The presiding judge asked me if I had anything to say. I thought about it. I said, 'No.' That's when they took me away" [*S* 107].) Finally, Meursault imagines his execution as being accompanied by the same "cries of hate" as was Christ's. He even describes his own execution with Christ's spirit of accomplished closure: "For everything to be consummated, . . ." (*S* 123). Such parallels leave no doubt that Camus intends Meursault to be understood as a Christ-like figure.

But if Meursault's life and death are similar to Christ's, his values certainly are not. Meursault is Christ-like in that he challenges the conventional values of his society, but the values that he would convert society to are quite different. The magistrate calls Meursault an "AntiChrist" (*S* 71), and means by this that he is a monster without moral values. Camus also sees Meursault as an AntiChrist, not in the judge's sense, but in the Nietzschean sense of someone whose values are profound and deep, but antithetical to those embodied in Christ. Nowhere is this antithesis more evident than in Meursault's climactic confrontation with the priest at the end of the novel.

It is in the concrete confrontation between these two – between Meursault and the priest who is trying to minister to him in prison – that Camus plays out Pascal's thought experiment. The ascetic life of the priest is a perfect example of someone who stakes his entire life in this world on an infinity of happiness in the next. The priest constantly tries to remind Meursault that he stands to lose this heavenly happiness if he does not repent and believe. Although the priest does not specifically utilize Pascal's arguments, his approach and tone are similar. He stresses, for example, that Meursault can't be sure of his unbelief and that, as long as there

---

8. Mark 3:31-35.

is any hope at all, belief offers the possibility of far more happiness than the nothingness of his present prison life.

In his passionate denunciation of the priest's logic, Meursault for the first time becomes conscious of his own convictions. It is also here that Camus offers a counterargument to Pascal. Yes, at first glance the priest and Meursault may seem to embody, in their respective lives, the Infinity/Nothing polarity of Pascal. But Meursault insists that we look more closely. "Whereas it looked as if [he] was the one who'd come up emptyhanded" (*S* 120), he at least had something definite – the joys of this life. True, they might seem like nothing when weighted against infinity, but infinity is only a hope, whereas Meursault's joys are as absolutely certain as any founding truth Descartes ever sought. The absolute certainty of these joys must be added to the scale before they can be accurately weighed against the priest's infinite – but radically uncertain – faith. Once this is done, it is actually Meursault's life that becomes the more reasonable bet; his life is the one "vindicated" (*S* 121).

But what exactly are the joys of Meursault's life? As he is listening to his lawyer's inept summary at the end of the trial, he hears in the distance the familiar sound of an ice cream vendor out on the street. "I was assailed by memories of a life that wasn't anymore, but one in which I had found the simplest and most lasting joys: the smells of summer, the part of town I loved, a certain evening sky, Marie's dresses and the way she laughed" (*S* 104). These "joys" are not the stuff of crass hedonism. They are more akin to the aesthetic, to the kind of nuanced joys that are the aim of high art. Meursault's senses are attuned to savoring joys in ways that would embarrass most people. In fact, he reflects that one day intensely lived is enough to provide one with a hundred years of memories (*S* 79). This is why, when the priest pressures him to imagine heaven, he wants only a place where he can remember this life (*S* 120).

The priest cannot fathom this kind of devotion to joys he considers minor and ephemeral. He runs his hand slowly over the prison wall. He is steeped in a tradition that envisions the body – the world itself – as a prison from which death will finally free him. " 'Do you really love this earth as much as all that?' he murmured" (*S* 119). The priest is following the call of Christ, the call to another world; Meursault is instinctively following the call of another prophet, Nietzsche's Zarathustra: "I beseech you, my brothers, remain *faithful to the earth,* and do not believe those who speak to you of otherworldly hopes! Poison-mixers are they, whether they know it or not."[9]

But, Pascal might argue, betting on God does not eliminate the joys that Meursault describes. Sunsets, dresses, and laughter are as accessible to the believer as to Meursault. Camus disagrees. Like Christ, he is convinced that "where one's treasure is, there also one's heart will be." Any time spent hoping and praying, any time fastened onto a treasured future, is an inherent distraction which inevitably dilutes the multiple, nuanced joys of the present. It is only after his anger at the priest has "rid [him] of hope" that Meursault can, "for the first time," be thoroughly open "to the gentle indifference of the world" (*S* 122). He realizes that even the time he has spent worrying about a reprieve is time wasted. Ultimately, there is no reprieve! One must choose: either the present or the future. One cannot have them both.

In *The Stranger* Camus, like Pascal, sees our basic metaphysical choices resting on something like a wager. Meursault cannot be sure there is no future, no god, no afterlife. But such considerations only distract from the very real joys that he can be sure of. To Meursault, the wager is not between Infinity and Nothing; it is between infinities hoped for and simple but absolutely certain joys. Meursault's choice is clear: "none of his [the priest's] certainties was worth one hair of a woman's head" (*S* 120). Camus agrees: the reasonable choice is the single hair – or even the salty smell it leaves behind on the pillow!

The strategy Camus uses in *The Stranger* to determine whether immanence or transcendence should be chosen focuses primarily on weighing the joys that each option offers and assessing their respective chances. However, there is something incomplete, even simplistic, about this focus. Most of life's joys are imperiled and finally overpowered by pain. Does the option of immanence offer better chances for escaping pain than does transcendence? *The*

---

9. Friedrich Nietzsche, *Thus Spoke Zarathustra* in *The Portable Nietzsche*, trans. Walter Kaufmann (New York: Viking Press, 1968), 125.

Plague struggles to deal with this aspect of Pascal's problem.

Although death is a pervasive presence in *The Stranger*, its deaths (Mamam's, the Arab's, Meursault's execution) are essentially quick and painless. In the early novel, death's presence is felt mainly as a mark of finality and termination, as "a dark wind . . . rising toward me from somewhere deep in my future" (*S* 121). Death also pervades *The Plague*. It begins with Dr. Rieux stepping on a dead rat, and ends with a telegram about the death of his wife. In the later novel, however, death is not merely "a dark wind," but "a never ending wail,"[10] an excruciating and individual agony.

The different characters in the novel represent various possible reactions to this "never ending wail." Rambert, for example, is a sophisticated Meursault, seeking to savor life's richest joys – especially love – while he can. Grand is a humanist; Cottard an opportunist; Tarrou a revolutionary. But here, as in *The Stranger*, the issue of belief, the wager on transcendence, is best explored by contrasting the life of the novel's narrator, Bernard Rieux, with that of its priest, Father Paneloux.

Paneloux is, by far, the most benevolently drawn believer in Camus' fiction. His faith is intelligent, expansive and capable of productive action. In his character, belief becomes a forceful option. To understand the logic of his belief, it is necessary to trace its growth from the sermon that he delivers at the onset of the plague to the one he delivers after witnessing the death of Othon's young son.

The belief articulated in Paneloux's first sermon is the traditional one: suffering and death are deserved punishments, the "wages of sin" (*P* 89). Although God desires only our joy, his justice must address our perverse tendency to undermine our own happiness and drive ourselves out of paradise. Pain and death restore our chance for any lasting joy. "For the plague is the flail of God and the world His threshing-floor, and implacably He will thresh out His harvest until the wheat is separated from the chaff" (*P* 90). Yet, even amidst this image, Paneloux's intent is not to instill a Jonathan Edward's fear in his audience. He closes the sermon with

---

10. Albert Camus, *The Plague,* trans. Stuart Gilbert (New York: Vintage, 1972), 196-202; hereafter cited parenthetically in the text as *P*.

a call to hope, a call to realize that God is at work on our happiness, if only we do our minimal part.

But Paneloux himself comes to see that this type of faith, his "flailing God," is not an intelligent option. This realization is due primarily to his vigil at the deathbed of Othon's son. It isn't just Rieux's angry protestation that "that child, anyhow, was innocent, and you know it as well as I do!" (*P* 202), which gives the lie to his "wages of sin" view of God; it is Paneloux's deepening realization, as he watches the plague expand and invade people's lives, that there is simply no rational proportionality between sin and human suffering. The sheer extent of the agony overpowers the possibility that any human action, however heinous, could ever be equal to it, be the cause of it. In fact, if the world were governed by this sort of perverse calculation, it would elicit from any moral individual not reverence but revulsion. If such a flailing God exists, as Camus insists repeatedly in *The Rebel*, he must be met with revolt rather than reverence. "The metaphysical rebel is therefore not definitely an atheist, as one might think him, but he is inevitably a blasphemer."[11]

The faith that Paneloux articulates in the second sermon is a very different one, one that offers a more meaningful option to the wagerer. In this faith, God is not interested in retribution, but cares only for human happiness and identifies with it even to the point of self-crucifixion. However, this God's love is so totally beyond human understanding, so mysterious, that mere rationality is useless in understanding it. Given this incomprehensibility, a complete "All or Nothing" trust in God's plan for human happiness becomes necessary.

> The love of God is a hard love. It demands total self-surrender, disdain of our human personality. And yet it alone can reconcile us to the suffering and deaths of children, it alone can justify them, since we cannot understand them, and we can only make God's will ours. That is the hard lesson I would share with you today. That is the faith,

---

11. Albert Camus, *The Rebel*, trans. Anthony Bower (New York: Vintage Press, 1955), 24.

cruel in men's eyes, and crucial in God's, which we must
ever strive to compose. (*P* 211ff.)

In other words, the God of belief is not a flailing God, but a
loving God. Every event in the universe has one and only one root
explanation: divine love. However, human reason is not in a
position, does not have the intellectual wherewithal, to understand
the relationship between specific events – the suffering of innocent
children, for example – and this love. Attempts at explanation (that
suffering is a punishment or some sort of test) inevitably self-de-
struct. Humans must disdain such ineffectual efforts, sacrifice the
need to control by comprehension, and trust that what is ultimately
happening in the world is benevolent and generous. Only within
such a trust is there any possibility that the child's suffering will
be redeemed; only through this smallest crack of hope can such
pain become anything more than the cruelest waste. Either there
is a God, and human misery has some redemption beyond our
possibility to understand, or human misery is the empty grinding
of the universe. Belief alone offers the possibility of redemption
from suffering; unbelief offers only an eternity of human screaming.
Isn't belief, then, the reasonable choice?

As in *The Stranger,* Camus' response to this argument for
belief is contained in the personality and values of his narrator.
Rieux's profession places him, especially in this time of plague, in
daily contact with human suffering and death. Priesthood is
Paneloux's response to human misery; medicine is Rieux's. Camus
uses these two vocations to analyze the alternate sides of Pascal's
wager: Is it more reasonable to work for salvation or to work for
health?

The respective merits of each choice are evaluated in a
conversation between Rieux and his friend, Tarrou, about the
difference between his "devotion" and Paneloux's. Rieux says,

I've never managed to get used to seeing people die. . . .
but, since the order of the world is shaped by death,
mightn't it be better for God if we refuse to believe in Him
and struggle with all our might against death, without
raising our eyes toward the heavens where He sits in
silence? (*P* 121)

It is certainly a possibility that the world, in all its painful and negative particulars, is the result of God's incomprehensibly generous love. But if we believe that, if we choose to live that option, the urgency to provide relief loses some of its edge. As Rieux argues, "if he believed in an all-powerful God he would cease curing the sick and leave that to Him" (*P* 120).

There is a sense in which Paneloux agrees with Rieux's logic. It isn't that, in a simplistic way, his otherworldly faith leaves him indifferent to human misery. Quite the contrary, he becomes one of Rieux's most avid volunteers in the menial daily work of trying to contain the plague and comfort its victims. But when Paneloux himself falls ill, due more to sympathy with its victims than to the disease itself, he staunchly rejects any medical treatment. His passivity is an acknowledgment that since his faith implies a metaphysical acceptance of suffering, it should also, in its extreme, imply a practical acceptance as well. And even if believers don't go to Paneloux's extreme, Camus argues that their metaphysical acceptance of suffering, their conviction that it is part of God's allowing will, cannot help but influence the extent of their efforts to alleviate it.

Camus seems to agree with Paneloux's claim that the only thing that could possibly justify innocent suffering is a God whose love transcends any human ability to comprehend it. There may be such a God. But it is equally possible that there is no such God and that suffering happens absurdly, without any divine plan or purpose to justify it. If this is the case, then suffering has no redeeming value whatever and deserves only extinction – or whatever degree of it human efforts can bring about. As Rieux explains to Paneloux: "Salvation's much too big a word for me. I don't aim so high. I'm concerned with man's health; and for me his health comes first" (*P* 203). God may redeem all suffering, but the reasonable person can't risk believing that because that would make one less devoted to the surety of eliminating some degree of suffering.

If the believer is correct, all suffering will be redeemed, whether one believes it will or not. Thus, if the choice for nonbelief proves incorrect, it will not alter the final value gained, since all suffering will be redeemed. But if the believer is incorrect, that choice would negatively affect the final value gained, because the amount of pain alleviated would be less in the case of belief. It is by this reasoning that Camus reaches his (Rieux's) paradoxical conclusion that, if there is a loving God who desires only our happiness, it really would be "better for God," that is, serve God's purposes more effectively, if our energies for alleviating human misery achieved the intensified earthly focus that only nonbelief can give.

It should be noted, however, that if the nonbeliever is correct, the victory is very much a Pyrrhic one, for it leaves human beings with, as Rieux concedes to Tarrou, "a never ending defeat" (*P* 121). The ethical nonbeliever[12] will alleviate more suffering than the believer, but suffering itself will never be overcome. Thus, nonbelief calls for Sisyphean courage, for impassioned struggle, even though final victory is hopeless. Such struggle is, as Camus' famous meditation on Sisyphus makes quite clear, precariously close to foolishness, but it is our best bet, for it alone guarantees that at least some battles will be won, even though the war never can be.

Although *The Plague* evaluates the options of belief and nonbelief primarily by analyzing how each would affect the level of suffering in human life, it also offers an insight into the joys associated with each choice that goes beyond that presented in *The Stranger*. As we have seen, Camus argued in the earlier work that the quantity and vividness of joys could not be as great in the believer as in the nonbeliever. In *The Plague* he demonstrates that it is not just a question of quantity; there is a unique and profound joy accessible only to nonbelievers.

---

12. Camus' argument here assumes an existing level of altruistic concern for the suffering of others. He argues that the goals of such a concern are better served by nonbelief than by belief. He seems very aware, however, that, unlike the Christian, he has no reasons to justify his concern for others. When the stranded journalist, Rambert, has the opportunity to illicitly escape the suffering city of Oran and join his lover in Paris, Rieux is insistent that pursuit of personal happiness is just as logical an option as ministering to human suffering (*P* 204). Rieux claims his own concern for suffering is just "common decency" (*P* 163), but in terms of quantity it is surely not common at all and probably found more often among believers than nonbelievers.

This joy is exemplified by the unusual and powerful bond formed between Rieux and Tarrou. These men meet when Tarrou volunteers to help combat the plague. His commitment seems as total as Rieux's, but the urgency of the work gives them little chance to talk. Together they witness both the screaming death of Othon's son and the "blank serenity" of Paneloux's. After weeks of exhausting and seemingly fruitless struggle, they decide it is time to "take an hour off for friendship" (*P* 228).

Camus' account of this hour draws heavily on Matthew's Gospel account of Christ's Transfiguration (Matt. 17:1-8). The two men climb up to a rooftop terrace and watch as the night sky transforms the suffering town below into a thing of shimmering beauty. Tarrou, echoing Peter, says "It's good to be here" (*P* 244). In friendship they share the stories of their lives, not so much in their concrete details as in their motivating sources. Both men are unflinching in their acknowledgment of the world's brutality, yet both have chosen "a path of sympathy" (*P* 237), a path identifying as much as possible with the victims of that brutality. Because they have chosen nonbelief, they are acutely aware that all responsibility for the world, for "reducing the damage done," is on their shoulders. The world is in no greater hands than their own. This realization, both frightening and ennobling, unites them and gives them "a strange happiness" (*P* 239). They decide to go for a midnight swim. As they move through the water in unison, in the same perfect rhythm, they are given a type of baptismal grace that believers cannot know.

Pascal was convinced that in choosing God, one chose all. He argued that, since God is infinite, there can be no real value outside of God, no joy that the nonbeliever could possibly experience that the believer could not experience as well. Camus disagrees. The kind of happiness that Rieux and Tarrou experience in their communing swim flows from their shared realization that the good of the world is ultimately their responsibility. This happiness cannot possibly be experienced in the communion of saints, for it is a happiness born in the shared wielding of power, not the worshipping of it.

Camus' argument is a limited one here. He is not claiming that unbelief offers more joys than belief, nor that there are no joys possible to believers that are impossible to nonbelievers. He is simply demonstrating that the "all" of belief is mistaken. Some real and genuine values are eternally lost to the believer, excluded by the very nature of belief itself. These losses must be acknowledged in any honest calculation of the two options. Unbelief is not nothing; nor is belief everything.

Camus' entire work can be seen as an effort to demonstrate that being human is morally superior to being holy. I have argued that one of the ways he does this, particularly in *The Stranger* and *The Plague,* is to accept the general strategy of Pascal's wager, but show how it leads to the opposite conclusion: nonbelief is the more reasonable choice. In *The Stranger* he argues that the believer risks the sure joys of this life, hoping for an infinite but uncertain joy in the next. In *The Plague* he argues that the believer risks the sure elimination of some misery in this life, hoping for an uncertain redemption from all misery in the next. Also, in *The Plague,* he undercuts Pascal's contention that, should the believer win, nothing would be lost in that victory; there are real and positive values that can be had only in nonbelief.

One final point should be made. Pascal had argued that, although reason could not help us determine whether God exists, it could help us decide whether belief or nonbelief is in our best interest. His analysis of the gains and losses of each is an attempt to prove that belief is the rational choice. Implicit in his calculations, however, is his Jansenist sense that the nonbeliever must "fall forever either into annihilation or into the hands of an angry God."[13] Camus argued angrily for the rejection of such a "flailing" God. Interestingly, many contemporary believers share in his rejection. Their God is characterized far more by love and concern for human happiness than by any judicial rectitude. In the face of this God, Camus' arguments become especially poignant. If a God of love really does exist, perhaps, as Rieux paradoxically argues, it might be better – *for God* – if we choose not to believe in him.

---

13. Pascal, *Pensées,* 68 (194).

Author's Note:

Unlike his predecessor, Nietzsche, and his contemporary, Sartre, Camus was never confident in his nonbelief, never able to dismiss transcendence as a mere opiate or illusion. For him, there were undeniable aspects of human experience – beauty, for one – which raised doubts about a naturalistic explanation of the human condition.

He was an odd atheist in another way. Unlike Sartre, who saw God as desirable, but impossible, Camus did not feel "condemned" to a world without God, but drawn to it. His struggle was not so much whether to have faith, but what kind of faith to have. Like Nietzsche, he saw that, all too often, the move to transcend this world was motivated by resentment against it, by a reluctance to embrace its challenges and an inability to inhabit the present moment with enough focus to savor its pleasures. Camus' own faith fought mightily against this sort of motivation.

Is faith itself more important for the human than its object, whatever it might be? Does not belief in an other-worldly, transcendent reality necessarily condition the quality of earthly pleasures?

J.C.

Works Cited

Camus, Albert. *Lyrical and Critical Essays*. Edited by Philip Tody. Translated by Ellen Conroy Kennedy. New York: Alfred A. Knopf, 1986.

_____. *The Myth of Sisyphus*. Translated by Justin O'Brien. New York: Vintage, 1955.

_____. *The Plague*. Translated by Stuart Gilbert. New York: Vintage, 1972.

_____. *The Rebel*. Translated by Anthony Bower. New York: Vintage, 1955.

_____. *The Stranger*. Translated by Matthew Ward. New York: Vintage, 1988.

Garvey, John. "The Gnostics Among Us," *Commonweal* 58 (22 May 1981): 300.

Küng, Hans. *Does God Exist?* Translated by Edward Quinn. Garden City, N.Y.: Doubleday, 1980.

Nietzsche, Friedrich. *Thus Spoke Zarathustra*. *The Portable Nietzsche*. Translated by Walter Kaufmann. New York: Viking, 1968.

Pascal, Blaise. *Pensées* and *The Provincial Letters*. Translated by W. F. Trotter and Thomas M'Crie. New York: The Modern Library, 1941.

Steiner, George. *Real Presences*. Chicago: University of Chicago Press, 1989.

Chapter Fifteen

Face to Face: Samuel Beckett and Václav Havel

Phyllis Carey

In his provocative and witty novel *Immortality,* the Czech writer Milan Kundera describes Agnes, his protagonist, perusing a magazine on politics and culture and counting the pictures of faces. Struck by the gratuitous and redundant photographs, Agnes muses that "nowadays God's eye has been replaced by a camera. The eye of one has been replaced by the eyes of all. Life has changed into one vast orgy in which everyone takes part. . . . [It] has nothing to do with delight but merely serves solemn notice to all that they have nowhere to hide and that everyone is at the mercy of everyone else."[1] The plethora of faces leads Agnes to the conclusion that "if you have two hundred and twenty-three faces side by side, you suddenly realize that it's all just one face in many variations and that no such thing as an individual ever existed."[2]

Some fifty years earlier, in her 1938 essay titled *Three Guineas,* the English writer Virginia Woolf contended that photographs of mangled, mutilated bodies comprised the most forceful argument against war. The mute pictures, according to Woolf, spoke a universal language, communicating at a primordial level before or beyond rhetoric and politics.

This essay was originally published in the Autumn 1994 issue of *Christianity and Literature* (Volume 44, Number 1). It is reprinted here by permission.

1. Milan Kundera, *Immortality,* trans. Peter Kussi (New York: Grove Weidenfeld, 1991), 31.

2. Ibid., 33.

Woolf was writing before the mass media so inundated humans with images that violence itself has become part of what Kundera facetiously terms the "imagological system."[3] Implicated in the voyeurism of the camera's eye and deadened by continual exposure to images of the human body and violence, viewers, rather than identifying with victims, seem increasingly drawn into a stance of detached observation of the "one face in many variations."

The question of even minimal transcendence in a world increasingly dominated by the image and numbed by violence necessarily becomes enmeshed with the question of human identity, both individually and socially. For Woolf, "the human figure even in a photograph . . . suggests that we cannot dissociate ourselves from that figure but are ourselves that figure. It suggests that we are not passive spectators doomed to unresisting obedience but by our thoughts and actions can ourselves change that figure."[4] From Woolf's point of view, the recognition of identity between the observer and the observed can lead to individual and social transcendence, a changing of individual and social perspectives, leading to action that would render war unthinkable.

Although Woolf's identification of the observer with the observed produces a form of idealistic humanism,[5] Kundera's Agnes sees in the shared humanity of the redundant faces precisely the opposite: the loss of individual identity in a banal collectivity, a seemingly neuter state, where the notion of individual or social transcendence succumbs to the primacy and relativity of the image. While Woolf and Kundera typify, respectively, modernist and postmodernist approaches to the human, their views complement one another to some extent in their appeal to identification between

---

3. Ibid., 116ff.

4. Virginia Woolf, *Three Guineas* (New York: Harcourt Brace Jovanovich, 1938), 142.

5. From a postmodern perspective, idealism betrays a certain egoism, "for in idealism, although the self is at odds with the world, the self does not question itself. The self is unwilling to accept its limitations; the ego is perceived as self-sufficient. There is behind this concern for autonomy and independence traces of ontologism." See Lucien Richard, "The Possibility of the Incarnation according to Emmanuel Lévinas," *Studies in Religion / Sciences Religieuses* 17.4 (1988): 392.

subject and object, observer and observed. Woolf prioritizes the subject and appeals to the *sameness* in the object as a motivating factor for humane action. Kundera, on the other hand, prioritizes the *relationship of sameness* between the subject and the object in a world-weary, albeit entertaining, cynicism. Paradoxically, the postmodern distrust of the dominating subject – a central Enlightenment concept that has inspired various forms of humanism as well as tyranny in Western culture – and the subsequent attempt to elude the subject-object dichotomy have led to a tendency to prioritize that which mediates the relationship, e.g., image and language systems. Both subject and object, subsumed in the play of signs, have no identity apart from the signifiers and yet no unique identity within them. Subject and object disappear in an endless play of signifiers. Like the faces in Agnes' magazine, which lose individual meaning in their functioning as image, humans in language become part of a seemingly endless text, where meaning is relative, and transcendence – as meaning beyond the system – is self-deluding nostalgia.

The postmodern attempt to escape the dominating subject, however, does not of necessity lead to the fragmentation of the human nor the denial of transcendent meaning. On the contrary, in the works of such writers as Samuel Beckett and Václav Havel, the rethinking of the human vis-à-vis the subject-object impasse provides profound insights into the questions of human identity and transcendence in the late twentieth century.

For Beckett early on, the subject-object relationship was a source of great concern. As he indicated in his 1931 essay on Proust, the modern "subject" has excluded from reality anything that cannot be represented in intelligible terms. The "object," in turn, has become "a mere intellectual pretext or motive,"[6] reduced to what can be represented or to "the illusion that the object lets itself be represented."[7] Beckett's excavation of the rational subject and his deconstruction of the Cartesian *cogito*, particularly in his trilogy,

---

6. Samuel Beckett, *Proust* (1931) (New York: Grove Press, 1970), 11-12, 56.

7. Samuel Beckett, "Peintres de l'Empêchement" (1948), in *Disjecta*, ed. Ruby Cohn (New York: Grove Press, 1984), 136.

led to the apparent absence of a definable "I" as ego and the impossibility of isolating and defining the "self."

In the early 1980s, Beckett, who up until recently had been widely regarded as apolitical, was one of the first writers to respond to an invitation from the Association Internationale de Défense des Artistes (A.I.D.A.) for contributions of works to show support for Václav Havel, a Czech playwright, who was serving a prison sentence at the time for his *dissident* activities. Beckett wrote *Catastrophe* (1982) and dedicated it to Havel. After his release from prison, Havel, whose own work as a dramatist was influenced by Beckett, wrote and dedicated *Mistake* (1983) to Beckett. Although Beckett and Havel never met, *Catastrophe* and *Mistake* provide a literary face-to-face encounter between these prominent twentieth-century dramatists of Western and Eastern Europe. Through the lens of the philosophical insights of Emmanuel Lévinas, a contemporary Jewish-Lithuanian philosopher whose ideas show intriguing affinities with many of Beckett's works and who was a major influence on Havel, one can discern the recasting of the human in the drama of Beckett and Havel. Both shape their respective plays to *evoke* a human response that cannot be reduced to rational assertions.

Catastrophe, like many of Beckett's plays, foregrounds its own medium. It is a play about a play, supposedly a dress rehearsal for the final scene of a drama. A Director (D) and his female Assistant (A), whose age and physique are respectively "unimportant," put the "final touches" on the Protagonist, (P), also of "unimportant" age and physique, until the Director is satisfied that the representation of (P) as a "catastrophe" is "in the bag." The audience within the play, itself "canned" and staged, applauds noisily in the "dress rehearsal" until (P), apparently departing from the script, raises his head and "fixes" the audience, both imaginary and live. The canned applause dies, followed by a "long pause." The light on the face fades out in silence.

Beckett's (D), who wears a fur coat and matching toque, is director, designer, and dictator. He barks orders to (A), snapping impatiently at some of (A)'s suggestions. Like Pozzo in *Godot,* he is filled with self-importance, frequently checking his *chronometer;* presumably he is in a hurry because he has a caucus to attend. As he gradually shapes (P) into the "catastrophe" that he envisions, he focuses on the "clawlike" hands and the amount of flesh he wants displayed.[8] His final direction to (L), or Luke, in charge of lighting,[9] sounds like an order to a firing squad: "Now . . . let 'em have it" (12). Pleased with the "image" he has created, (D) anticipates success: "Terrific! He'll have them on their feet. I can hear it from here" (12).

Like Havel's protagonist in *Mistake,* Beckett's (P) never utters a word. He is a human prop, fashioned like a sculpture, designed by (D) to produce a predetermined effect. When (A) timidly suggests a "little . . . gag?" (D) treats the notion as an exercise in redundancy: "For God's sake! This craze for explicitation! Every i dotted to death! Little gag! For God's sake!" (11). (D) assumes that "not a squeak" will come from (P). When (A) suggests raising (P)'s head, (D) provides a parallel response: "For God's sake! What next? Raise his head? Where do you think we are? In Patagonia? Raise his head? For God's sake!" (12).[10] Not "a trace of face" must show. (P) is to be an inert, faceless object.

(P) ostensibly becomes a more and more dehumanized victim, presumably designed by (D) to feed vicariously the sadistic appetite of onlookers. The references to his "clawlike" hands and the "moulting" of his hair equate him with an animal. (D) is concerned

---

8. Samuel Beckett, *Catastrophe. Index on Censorship* 13.1 (February 1984): 11; hereafter cited parenthetically in the text.

9. The name *Luke* would seem to be significant as he is the only character given a name. The names of other Beckett characters – e.g., *Hamm, Clov, Krapp, Godot* – are certainly suggestive. *Luke* as the writer of a Gospel and the association with the Latin *lux,* light, seem to be obvious ironic referents. In *Catastrophe* Luke is the light technician who has trouble hearing directives from backstage, but who executes commands when they are transmitted "in technical terms." "Light" is a constant motif in the play as the director repeatedly demands a light for his cigar from (A) and directs that the general light fade out, followed by the fade-out of the light on (P)'s body, leaving only his bowed head: "*Light on head alone*" (12).

10. The chiasmic shaping of the Director's words echo the shaping of some of the dialogue in *Waiting for Godot* – e.g., the famous passage on "the dead voices" that make a noise "E: Like leaves. V: Like sand. E: Like leaves." "E: They rustle. V: They murmur. E: They rustle." "E: Like leaves. V: Like ashes. E: Like leaves." See Samuel Beckett, *Waiting for Godot* (New York: Grove Press, 1954), 40b. The shaping draws attention to what is enframed: "For God's sake!"

primarily with the parts of the body, particularly with exposing and whitening more and more flesh, an activity that draws attention primarily to (P)'s materiality. The fists must be unclenched, but when (A) joins the hands and raises them to the chest, (P) with bowed head resembles a silently praying victim.[11]

While he dramatizes (D)'s and (A)'s objectifying of (P) as though he were an inert mannequin, Beckett shapes the barest of gestures to express the possibility of transcendence. (P)'s mere raising of his head defies the role in which he has been cast. His "fixing" the audience breaks the totality of the intended image and disrupts the subject-object relationship suggested by (D)'s and (A)'s manipulative control of him. The fabricated response of the anonymous mass fades away into (P)'s face-to-face encounter with the live audience. (P)'s gesture is wordless but extremely powerful "dissent," essentially negating the drama that has shaped him.

As Howard Pearce has noted, the Assistant's conception of (P) as "catastrophe" differs from that of the Director: "The Protagonist is not merely an actor with whom the Assistant sympathizes but a character with whom she has an identity. . . . His apparent powerlessness is an expression of her subservience, her obedience, and her timidity."[12] Pearce suggests that (P)'s raising of his head can be read as the Assistant's "realization of character,"[13] a subversion of the Director's text with "the text within the text of the playwright's tribute [to Havel]."[14] In Pearce's reading, it is as though "the powerless," – that is, the Assistant and the Protagonist – together overcome the totalizing image of the Director.

---

11. In his *New York Times* review of several of Beckett's late dramatic works, Gussow noted that in discussing *Catastrophe* Beckett indicated that he did not intend that (P) face the audience at the end of the play in what Gussow called "abject supplication." Rather, "[P] is meant to cow onlookers into submission through the intensity of his gaze and of his stoicism." However, (D)'s "script," which is followed until (P) raises his head, seems to include in its aim the stance of "abject supplication." Mel Gussow, "Beckett Distills His Vision," *The New York Times*, 31 July 1983, sec. H:3.

12. Howard Pearce, "Text and Testimony: Samuel Beckett's *Catastrophe,*" *Journal of Beckett Studies* 2:1 (1992): 89.

13. Ibid., 90.

14. Ibid., 95.

While such a reading offers an intriguing political interpretation, it not only limits (P)'s transcendence to the political but also reduces (A) and (P) to *sameness*. But it is (A) – not (P) – who, despite her own "text," submits entirely to (D)'s directions; she is totally subservient to the end. Moreover, there is no evidence in the play to suggest that (P) has even heard (A)'s suggestions. Rather, (P) seems totally passive throughout until he raises his head after the canned applause begins. The "night attire" he wears under his cloak, while resembling a prison uniform, also suggests a state of unconsciousness. Like an animal in sleep, (P) seems unaware of the manipulation done to him until he "awakens" and lifts his head. It is only when he raises his head and "fixes" the audience that his consciousness becomes evident. Paradoxically, his action seems dramatically designed to suggest his escape from – his "transcending" – the formal boundaries of the predetermined dramatic role as a passive object. The "illusion" of his objectness is dispelled, but he does not take on the role of a defining or dominating subject. Rather, in his difference from both (D) and (A), in his rupture of the dramatic scenario, (P) becomes a living question confronting the audience. In transcending the subject-object dialectic, which (D) and (A) seem to reenact, (P) brings into question the meaning of the human. He confronts the audience with that which escapes the image.[15]

The mute face emerging from the darkness transforms the semblance of a prepackaged, manipulated object into a living, mysterious *Other*. For Emmanuel Lévinas, that *otherness* is essential to both human identity and transcendence. The *face* of the *Other* "exceeds all idea of the other in me";[16] the *face* bespeaks an infinite otherness beyond manipulation. In the response to that *face*, according to Lévinas, lies human identity, itself the revelation of

---

15. Pearce argues that (A) envisions (P) "representing old-fashioned ideas about human dignity and freedom, possibly even courage" (90). This interpretation may be valid as far as it goes, but it seems to me that Beckett's portrayal is more radical. (P) does not simply go from being (D)'s object to (A)'s. Nor is it at all clear that (P) represents "old-fashioned" ideas of dignity, freedom, and courage. While transcendence seems to be part of the thrust of (P)'s wordless gesture, ambiguity would seem to be a vital part of that transcendence.

16. Emmanuel Lévinas, *The Lévinas Reader*, ed. Seán Hand (Oxford: Basil Blackwell, 1989), 5.

the Infinite. As George Steiner notes in discussing Lévinas' theory of meaning, "the 'open impenetrability' of that visage, its alien yet confirmatory mirroring of our own, enact the intellectual and ethical challenge of the relations of man to man and of man to that which Lévinas terms 'infinity.'"[17] Lévinas notes that "the relation with the face is not an object-cognition. The transcendence of the face is at the same time its absence from this world into which it enters, the exiling . . . of a being, his condition of being stranger, destitute. . . . This gaze that supplicates and demands, that can supplicate only because it demands, deprived of everything because entitled to everything . . . this gaze is precisely the epiphany of the face as face."[18]

Beckett's dramatic shaping of the "epiphany of the face" seems to be an attempt to cut through not only the subject-object dialectic but the face as image as well. (P)'s face, staring at the audience, becomes a primordial, silent summoning to awareness of the human. The gaze of the face negates the totalizing system that would contain it to reveal that which cannot be controlled, manipulated, or rationalized. The internally determined "catastrophe" has been overturned by a catastrophe apparently designed, in turn, to awaken the audience. When (P) gazes at the audience, his "face" challenges the audience's role as *voyeurs,* as well as its complicity in the preceding manipulation. Implied in the overturning of the "catastrophe" is the disclosure of not only the empty "subjectivity" of the audience but also through its "canned" representation, its predictable *sameness.* The live audience, its mindless collectivity and conventional response parodied, is cast back into its individual members, unsure how to respond and yet compelled to respond to the face-to-face encounter. (P)'s face, "fixing" the audience, seems designed to awaken the individual viewer from the herd mentality of the consumer spectator – the role of passive objectness – to what Beckett terms in *Proust,* "the suffering of being."[19]

---

17. George Steiner, *Real Presences* (Chicago: The University of Chicago Press, 1989), 146-47.

18. Emmanuel Lévinas, *Totality and Infinity: An Essay on Exteriority*, trans. Alphonso Lingis (Pittsburgh: Duquesne University Press, 1969), 75; hereafter cited parenthetically in the text as *T&I.*

Havel's response to Beckett's dedication of *Catastrophe* ironically seems to make even greater demands on the audience.[20]
Mistake foregrounds the human tendency – regardless of political
system – toward totalitarianism. The plot seems simple and straightforward: four inmates in a prison, who have formed their own
subsystem with their own kingpin, indoctrinate a new prisoner,
who has inadvertently smoked a cigarette before breakfast, on his
"rights" and "responsibilities" within the subsystem. The new
inmate, XIBOY, says nothing throughout the play, merely shrug-
ging and looking embarrassed, to the increasing anger and frustra-
tion of the "King" and his cohorts. When the four inmates finally
realize that XIBOY is a "bloody foreigner," his fate is sealed. The
play ends with the prisoners approaching XIBOY "menacingly" and
King's final words: "Well, that's his bloody funeral. . . ."[21]

The prison setting as a totalitarian system, although probably
inspired by Havel's own experience, underscores the human propensity not only to adapt to repressive systems but also to duplicate
them and to subjugate others, attempting to force them into
conformity, into *sameness*. King's references to "rights" and "cus-
toms" make the civilized trappings of repression transparent.
XIBOY's death sentence flows logically from the primacy of the
system: speaking another language literally and perhaps metaphysically, he cannot be indoctrinated and subsumed into King's system
within the prison system. Violence is the logical consequence when
humans are objects to be manipulated, when difference is not to
be tolerated, when the system takes preeminence over the human.

Ironically, Havel's play appears much bleaker than Beckett's.
(P)'s raising his head in *Catastrophe*, an extremely significant
gesture in the context of Beckett's *oeuvre,* where gestures of hope
are rare, contrasts the bleak ending of *Mistake*, where the forces
of repression seem to be in complete control. But Havel's drama
consistently works through negation. The play is designed to

---

19. Samuel Beckett, *Proust,* 8.

20. *Mistake* was reportedly the first literary work Havel wrote after being released
    after almost four years in prison. The play premiered in Stockholm in
    November 1983.

21. Václav Havel, *Mistake,* trans. George Theiner, *Index on Censorship* 13.1
    (February 1984): 14; hereafter cited parenthetically in the text.

awaken a response through the careful shaping of absence. In XIBOY's silence and embarrassed gestures, his failure to understand what is being asked of him, and his innocence of the system, the play evokes questions in its viewers even though those questions are not articulated. Havel himself has said of his drama: "I at most can only help the spectator to formulate problems, which he must solve himself."[22]

One of the most basic questions *Mistake* raises is the relationship of power with human identity. It is clear that for King, power consists in reducing XIBOY to *sameness.* He is to be "Fourth Prisoner" in a potentially expandable number of conforming cellmates. King's identity, however, comes solely from his function of enforcing power; he is as anonymous as the other prisoners in his subservience to the arbitrary system: "That's how it's always been in this pad, and it's going to stay that way" (13). The fragility of King's "power" becomes manifest when the prisoners are confronted by XIBOY's *otherness.* XIBOY poses a threat primarily by being an individual, not yet reduced to *sameness.* XIBOY unwittingly threatens the entire system; the "power" of his *otherness* induces anger and fear in the prisoners. Unless they force him into the system, he poses a constant danger simply by being. The "power" of the system, in contrast, operates as a ruthless and dehumanizing force that can endure only through further brutality. Ludvik Vaculik, a noted Czech writer, defines "the first law of power" as the attempt "to maintain itself by reproducing itself more and more precisely. Secondly, it becomes more and more homogenous, purging everything foreign to it until each part is a replica of the whole and all parts are mutually interchangeable."[23]

Although XIBOY becomes the innocent victim sacrificed for the sake of the system, there is nothing redemptive about his suffering and implied death. *Mistake,* as the title of the play, includes in its ambiguity not only the mistaken identity of XIBOY and his "error" in smoking a cigarette before breakfast – in short, his being in the wrong place at the wrong time – but the "mistake"

---

22. Václav Havel, quoted in Jarka M. Burian, "Post-War Drama in Czechoslovakia," *Educational Theatre Journal,* 25.3 (October 1973): 313.

23. Ludvik Vaculik, quoted in Burian, 313.

of his death as well. XIBOY cannot be seen as a hero standing up to oppression because he apparently does not even realize why he is to be eliminated, nor will his death "protect" the system from future threats. Rather, XIBOY's death seems to be simply the logical, but meaningless, result of the inmates' becoming the instruments of systems.[24]

XIBOY's "trial" and "execution," though senseless and absurd, do not, however, suggest the absurdity of a universe where humans are caught in the meaningless of it all or can find meaning only in rebelling against the absurdity.[25] Rather, in drawing attention both to the absurdity of the system and the human complicity in perpetuating such systems, the play pushes its audience to confront the crisis of the human being in the late twentieth century. While the prison within the prison emphasizes the far-reaching effects of the totalizing structure,[26] the anonymity of King and his followers, the banality of their language, and their brutal adherence to the mechanics of the system manifest their collusion in the loss of their own humanity. Both the context and its slavish adherents manifest absurdity and meaninglessness, but Havel wagers on the dramatiz-

---

24. Karen Olsen, a colleague, suggests that X-Boy can be viewed as a "hero – by mistake." In being "outside" the totalizing system and acting simply as a human being, X-boy unintentionally represents the natural, not yet artificially controlled human.

25. In contrast, compare Sisyphus, whom Camus terms "the absurd hero" who is "superior to his fate." For Camus, the lucidity of the individual, conscious of the meaninglessness of the universe, constitutes as well one's victory over the absurdity: "There is no fate that cannot be surmounted by scorn." See Albert Camus, *The Myth of Sisyphus and Other Essays*, trans. Justin O'Brien (New York: Vintage), 89-90.

26. Havel sees prisons – and the fact that Czechoslovakia in the 1980s had a disproportionate number of people in prison – as an extension of the totalitarian regime: "The repressive apparatus that sends people to jail is an organic part, and, indeed, the culmination of the general pressure totalitarianism exerts against life: without this extreme threat, many other threats would lose their credibility." See Václav Havel, "Stories and Totalitarianism," trans. Paul Wilson, in *Open Letters: Selected Writings 1965-1990*, ed. Paul Wilson (New York: Alfred Knopf, 1991), 339. At the same time, Havel saw in the totalitarianism of Eastern Europe, "a kind of warning to the West, revealing to it its own latent tendencies." See "The Power of the Powerless," in *Living in Truth*, ed. Jan Vladislav (London: Faber, 1989), 54.

ing of that absurdity to awaken the audience to a sense of its own degradation.

Havel has described his own sense of the absurd as "the basic modalities of humanity in a state of collapse. . . . throw[ing] us into the question of meaning by manifesting its absence. . . . Modern man must descend the spiral of his own absurdity to the lowest point; only then can he look beyond it. It is obviously impossible to get around it, jump over it, or simply avoid it.[27] The absence of the human, which reduces the meaning of *Mistake* to the absurd, derives partially at least from the subject-object relationship of King and the prisoners vis-à-vis XIBOY. The prisoners see themselves as dominating subjects within the context, manipulating the new-comer as object into the system. The operative "modality of humanity" is one of exploitation for the sake of conformity. It is depicted as inherently totalitarian. Moreover, the "subjectivity" of the prisoners is itself revealed as illusory in their total lack of individuality.[28]

It is clear that the absurdity of XIBOY's death does not remove the threat to the neutral *sameness* of the other characters. The next inmate will have to be indoctrinated, coerced, perhaps murdered. Moreover, murder, according to Lévinas, attempts to "exercise a power over what escapes power." In murdering the other, one arrives only at the sensible. Because of this, murder always misses its target. XIBOY presumably will die, but the prisoners will not have eliminated the challenge to their power. Indeed, that "power," precisely because of its inhumanity, is ultimately impotent. Though it continues to kill again and again, it cannot touch that which exceeds the sensible in the resistance of *otherness*.[29] In the *Other* lies that which "exceeds my power infinitely" (*T&I* 198), the infinity of the human that makes murder so reprehensible. If humans were only their mere substances, murder would be merely power plays of egoisms exercising control over other substances. Havel wagers

---

27. Václav Havel, *Disturbing the Peace: A Conversation with Karel Hvízdala*, trans. Paul Wilson (New York: Alfred A. Knopf, 1990), 53-54, 57.

28. The prisoners are even similar in that they all have "*a variety of tatoos on their arms and torsos*" (13).

29. Lévinas' point here surely brings to mind the Holocaust, with the widening attempt at mass slaughter to produce *sameness*.

on the audience's horror of the utter dehumanization that *Mistake* dramatizes; in the explicit absence of transcendence, paradoxically, lies a witness to that which exceeds the mere measurable substance of the human.

XIBOY's identity as a foreigner, as an *Other,* not immediately subsumed into *sameness* – like (P)'s departure from his role in *Catastrophe*–opens the question of other potential modalities. That Beckett and Havel both use silent, seemingly powerless, almost passive protagonists, manipulated by other humans, suggests their attempts to represent naked human vulnerability. The condition of vulnerability would seem to be for Beckett and Havel, as well as for Emmanuel Lévinas, the primordial expression of humans in existence – separated, alien, exposed. In his letters from prison, Havel in another context addresses this very issue:

> This dramatic exposure of another, void of all obfuscating detail and all "appearances," reveals and presents to man his own primordial and half-forgotten vulnerability, throws him back into it, and abruptly reminds him that he, too, stands alone and isolated, helpless and unprotected, and that it is an image of his own basic situation, that is, a situation we all share, a common isolation, the isolation of humanity thrown into the world, and that this isolation injures us all the same way, regardless of who, concretely, happens to be injured in a given instant.[30]

But while Havel stresses that the exposure of the *Other* replicates our own individual defenselessness, that vulnerability does not thereby reduce all to *sameness*; rather, the helplessness of an *Other* seems to reveal both "its alien yet confirmatory mirroring of our own."[31] Moreover, for both Beckett and Havel, it would seem, the vulnerability of (P) and XIBOY opens the question of the primordially human, in the face of totalizing systems, in relation to other humans and in reference to transcendence.[32] The muteness of the

---

30. Václav Havel, *Letters to Olga*, trans. Paul Wilson (New York: Henry Holt, 1989), 323.

31. Steiner, 146.

32. Jan Patočka, eminent Czech philosopher, contributor to and signer of Charter 77, and a philosophical mentor of Havel, saw vulnerability as a defining characteristic of twentieth-century humanity. Using the term "the limping

protagonists does not invite the audience's identification with them as individual characters; rather, it evokes a recognition of naked human vulnerability and the *otherness* of the human that escapes the totalizing systems of modernity.[33] In responding to that vulnerability, viewers may awaken to what is ineradicably human, that which precedes individuality and the impersonal structures of knowledge and reason.

Throughout Beckett's works, the vulnerability of the human and the meaning of human existence between birth and death are a perennial concern. In one of the paradoxes underlying *Waiting for Godot,* Beckett poses the question of ultimate meaning: "Two thieves. One is supposed to have been saved and the other . . . damned."[34] The Augustine source, supposedly at the root of the play, puts the options more explicitly: "Do not despair; one of the thieves was saved. Do not hope; one of the thieves was damned."[35] Unlike Pascal, Beckett seems to have consistently refused to wager on either side of the issue, while nevertheless foregrounding the human agony that results from the dilemma. In Beckett's fictional

pilgrim" in one of his writings, Patocka depicted modern man as one who "no longer glories in the death of God: if anything, he wishes for God, but in His absence turns to his limitation, his finitude, to open the way to transcendence." See Erazim Kohák, *Jan Patocka: Philosophy and Selected Writings* (Chicago: The University of Chicago Press, 1989), 79.

33. Lévinas argues that war "is fixed in the concept of totality, which dominates Western philosophy. Individuals are reduced to being bearers of forces that command them unbeknown to themselves. The meaning of individuals (invisible outside of this totality) is derived from the totality" (*T&I* 21-22). Elsewhere Lévinas differentiates himself from Derrida in his "postmodernist" approach: "Whereas [Derrida] tends to see the deconstruction of the Western metaphysics of presence as an irredeemable crisis, I see it as a golden opportunity for Western philosophy to open itself to the dimension of otherness and transcendence beyond Being." See Emmanuel Lévinas, quoted in "Emmanuel Lévinas" in *Dialogues with Contemporary Continental Thinkers* by Richard Kearney (Manchester: Manchester University Press, 1984), 64. For a response by Derrida to Patocka, Lévinas, and Kierkegaard on such topics as responsibility and the *Other,* see Jacques Derrida, *The Gift of Death,* trans. David Wills (Chicago: University of Chicago Press, 1995).

34. Beckett, *Waiting for Godot,* 9a.

35. The exact source of this quote in Augustine has thus far eluded Beckett scholars. A recent note by David Green suggests some passages in Augustine that Beckett may have combined. See David Green, "A Note on Augustine's Thieves," *Journal of Beckett Studies* 3.2 (1994): 77-78.

and dramatic cosmos, humans cannot know with absolute certainty whether God does or does not exist, even though the latter possibility may seem very compelling. As a result, humans cannot know with any certainty if human existence has ultimate meaning or if it is ultimately meaningless. Stuck, immobilized, impotent, like one crucified,[36] human beings, awakened from the deadening weight of habit and convention, suffer the agony of not knowing why they exist: "Astride of a grave and a difficult birth. Down in the hole, lingeringly, the grave-digger puts on the forceps. We have time to grow old. The air is full of our cries."[37] The contemporary, conscious, "reason-ridden" human, fully aware of the rational uncertainty about ultimate meaning, certain only about his or her own death, experiences existence itself as hell. But such a stance is not simply an agnostic skepticism. It presupposes that all human meaning is dependent on the fundamental question of God's existence.[38] The persistent return to the question in Beckett's works and the stress on agonizing human desire and need suggest that confronting the question of transcendence is, for Beckett at least, the defining attribute of being human.

In a state of waiting and watching,[39] a prayer-like stance, the fully aware human is conscious only of need, impotence, and

---

36. A recurring motif in Beckett's texts is the use of cruciform shapes, e.g., the narrator in *How It Is* lies in the mud, "the arms spread yes like a cross no answer LIKE A CROSS no answer YES OR NO yes." See Samuel Beckett, *How It Is* (New York: Grove Press, 1964), 146; the lobster in "Dante and the Lobster" lies in a cruciform shape; Beckett in directing the German version of *Waiting for Godot* drew attention to all of the cross-shapes in the play in movements, action and speech.

37. Samuel Beckett, *Waiting for Godot*, 58b.

38. Beckett, of course, is not alone in recognizing the crucial link between the existence of God and human meaning. One can argue, for example, that many forms of "postmodernism" are dependent upon Nietzsche's articulation of "the death of God." Derrida's attack on "logocentrism," to cite but one instance, implicitly and negatively acknowledges the relationship between meaning and God. Asserting the relativity of all meaning, however, would seem to constitute not only an evasion of the crucial issue but also an implicit surrender to nihilism, by its presupposition that one can be rationally certain that there is no ultimate meaning.

39. Etymologically, both words come from the same root and provide recurring motifs in Beckett's works.

vulnerability vis-à-vis the central dilemma of human existence: Why are we here? In the light of utter impotence to determine with certainty the meaning of existence, the drive to control and manipulate becomes transparent as reprehensible stupidity. (P), staring at the audience, "fixes" them in the question of meaning. For Beckett, transcendence seems to consist in rising out of unconscious adaptations to forces molding our definitions of the human and, consequently, facing the agonizing question of meaning. In what the image cannot capture, in what escapes human control lies the naked human hunger for meaning, the question of the originary silence and gaze: "The supreme master submits to what cannot be mastered and trembles."[40]

Havel's works intersect with Beckett's in depicting the pettiness, mutual exploitation, and violence of perverted transcendence that leave the human frustrated, miserable, and essentially bestial. For Havel, in consonance with Lévinas, the response to the *Other* actually precedes human individuality: It is only in response to the *Other* that the self becomes a self, that subjectivity becomes possible. For Lévinas, "responsibility [is] the essential, primary and fundamental structure of subjectivity."[41] Havel echoes this idea frequently in his writings: "The crisis of today's world, obviously, is a crisis of human responsibility (both responsibility for oneself and responsibility 'toward' something else) and thus it is a crisis of human identity as well."[42] For Havel, in that which is betrayed one can still feel a vestigial, primordial responsibility, and his dramatic appeal is to the individual viewer: "But who should begin? Who should break this vicious circle? I agree with Lévinas when he says that responsibility cannot be preached, but only borne, and that

---

40. Samuel Beckett, "Hommage à Jack B. Yeats," *Les Lettres Nouvelles* 14 (1954): 620.

41. Emmanuel Lévinas, "Ethics and Infinity," *Cross Currents* (summer 1984): 194.

42. Havel, *Letters to Olga*, 365. For Havel, responding to the *Other* is the beginning of being human. He notes that "face-to-face with the existence of his neighbor, [the human] first experiences that primordial 'responsibility for everything' and thus becomes a special creature capable of fellow feeling with a complete stranger. . . . Another person, in short, is the only entity capable of opening the human heart" (370-71).

the only possible place to begin is with oneself. . . . Whether all is really lost or not depends entirely on whether or not I am lost."[43]

In neither *Catastrophe* nor in *Mistake* does a *deus ex machina* aid the human. Rather, for both Beckett and Havel, only in experiencing our humanness can transcendence become a possibility. As Lévinas puts it,

> God . . . reveals himself as a trace, not as an ontological presence. . . . The God of the Bible cannot be defined or proved by means of logical predictions and attributions. Even the superlatives of wisdom, power and causality advanced by medieval ontology are inadequate to the absolute otherness of God. It is not by superlatives that we can think of God, but by trying to identify the particular interhuman events which open towards transcendence and reveal the traces where God has passed.[44]

The watchful, waiting openness suggested by Beckett's (P) and the naked vulnerability of XIBOY seem to be attempts to evoke "otherness" in the audience, to awaken viewers to what precedes and goes beyond what can be represented. At the same time, the burden of the openness to the *Other* rests entirely on the human. Lévinas speaks of it as the need "to feel all the responsibilities of God on his shoulders."[45] Indeed, for Lévinas, one "can say 'I' only to the extent that he has already taken on [the whole suffering of everyone],"[46] meaning that "all persons are the Messiah."[47] The response to the *Other* not only constitutes the identity of the self but also opens the human to transcendence.

---

43. Ibid., 369.

44. Lévinas, quoted in Kearney, 67. This is a recurring motif in Lévinas' writing. For example, in *Difficult Freedom* he notes, "Through my relation to the other I am in touch with God." Emmanuel Lévinas, quoted in Robbins, 1058.

45. Emmanuel Lévinas, quoted in "An Inscribed Responsibility: Lévinas's *Difficult Freedom*," by Jill Robbins, *Modern Language Notes* 106 (1991): 1059.

46. Ibid., 1062.

47. Ibid., 1059. Lévinas points out that the notion of a God who distributes rewards, imposes penalties or pardons faults constitutes a God who treats humans as eternal children and rewards them with "the emptiness of a child's heaven." On the contrary, the apparent "absence" of God and the suffering of the human can "reveal a God who, in renouncing all beneficial manifestations, thus appeals to the full maturity of an entirely responsible man" (Ibid.).

The gratuitous violence of *Mistake* and (D)'s and (A)'s exploitation of (P) underscore the perversion and betrayal of the fundamentally human. In the works of Beckett and Havel, "man's inhumanity to man," which has assumed monstrous proportions in this century, is directly related not only to distorted conceptions of human identity but also, correspondingly, to denials and perversions of transcendence. Beckett dismantles illusions of power and control to reveal the shapes of naked need and desire for ultimate meaning that define existence as human; Havel shapes betrayal and cruelty to evoke a primordial response to the *Other* as the basis of human individuality and society. In their dramatic dialogue Beckett and Havel implicitly challenge audiences to emerge from their habitual passivity, from their self-comforting systems – from what Agnes in *Immortality* calls "the vast orgy." For only in entering into the agony and responsibility of being human, it would seem, can one begin to glimpse "the traces where God has passed."

Author's Note:

The minimum of transcendence in Beckett's plays is so powerful for so many, including prisoners at San Quentin and the war-savaged people of Sarajevo. Do Beckett's downtrodden protagonists embody the bleakness and helplessness so many humans feel at the end of the twentieth century?

Have humans from the beginning been destined like Didi and Gogo in Waiting for Godot *to wait endlessly for some assurance that their lives have meaning? Does yearning for meaning enable us to rise above being mere victims of one system or another, manipulated and predictable consumers, or extensions of the computer? And if desire enables us to at least persevere, is that kind of transcendence enough?*

Does being truly human depend on whether or not God exists? And what does wagering on transcendence mean? Can it mean simply to be responsible and responsive humans, attentive to the mystery of why we are here and, in Robert Coles' words, "what, if anything, who, if anyone, might be waiting around the great corner that is death"?

P.C.

Works Cited

Beckett, Samuel. *Catastrophe. Index on Censorship* 13.1 (February 1984): 11-12.

_____. "Hommage à Jack B. Yeats." *Les Lettres Nouvelles* 14 (1954): 619-20.

_____. *How It Is.* New York: Grove Press, 1964.

_____. "Peintres de l'Empêchement." In *Disjecta,* edited by Ruby Cohn, 133-37. New York: Grove Press, 1984.

_____. *Proust.* New York: Grove Press, 1970.

_____. *Waiting for Godot.* New York: Grove Press, 1954.

Burian, Jarka M. "Post-War Drama in Czechoslovakia." *Educational Theatre Journal* 25.3 (October 1973): 299-317.

Camus, Albert. *The Myth of Sisyphus and Other Essays.* Translated by Justin O'Brien. New York: Vintage, 1955.

Derrida, Jacques. *The Gift of Death.* Translated by David Wills. Chicago: University of Chicago Press, 1995.

Green, David. "A Note on Augustine's Thieves." *Journal of Beckett Studies* 3.2 (1994): 77-78.

Gussow, Mel. "Beckett Distills His Vision." *The New York Times* 31 July 1983, sec. H: 3.

Havel, Václav. *Disturbing the Peace: A Conversation with Karel Hvízdala.* Translated by Paul Wilson. New York: Alfred A. Knopf, 1990.

_____. *Letters to Olga.* Translated by Paul Wilson. New York: Henry Holt, 1989.

_____. *Mistake.* Translated by George Theiner. *Index on Censorship* 13.1 (February 1984): 13-14.

_____. "The Power of the Powerless." In *Living in Truth,* edited by Jan Vladislav, 36-122. London: Faber, 1989.

_____. "Stories and Totalitarianism." In *Open Letters: Selected Writings 1965-1990,* translated and edited by Paul Wilson. 328-50. New York: Alfred Knopf, 1991.

Kearney, Richard. "Emmanuel Lévinas." In *Dialogues with Contemporary Continental Thinkers,* 47-70. Manchester: Manchester University Press, 1984.

Kohák, Erazim. *Jan Patocka: Philosophy and Selected Writings.* Chicago: The University of Chicago Press, 1989.

Kundera, Milan. *Immortality.* Translated by Peter Kussi. New York: Grove Weidenfeld, 1991.

Lévinas, Emmanuel. "Ethics and Infinity." *Cross Currents* 34 (summer 1984): 191-203.

_____. *The Lévinas Reader.* Edited by Seán Hand. Oxford: Basil Blackwell, 1989.

_____. *Totality and Infinity: An Essay on Exteriority.* Translated by Alphonso Lingis. Pittsburgh: Duquesne University Press, 1969.

Pearce, Howard. "Text and Testimony: Samuel Beckett's *Catastrophe.*" *Journal of Beckett Studies* 2:1 (1992): 83-98.

Richard, Lucien. "The Possibility of the Incarnation according to Emmanuel Lévinas." *Studies in Religion / Sciences Religieuses* *17.4* (1988): 391-405.

Robbins, Jill. "An Inscribed Responsibility: Lévinas's *Difficult Freedom.*" *Modern Language Notes* 106 (1991): 1052-1062.

Steiner, George. *Real Presences.* Chicago: The University of Chicago Press, 1989.

Woolf, Virginia. *Three Guineas.* New York: Harcourt Brace Jovanovich, 1938.

Contributors

With the exceptions of Ann Angel, Paul J. McGuire, S.C.J., Caroline Sur, S.S.N.D., and Mary Hester Valentine, S.S.N.D., who have moved on to other endeavors, all of the contributors are currently members of the Mount Mary faculty (1992-98).

ANN ANGEL taught journalism courses and advised the student newspaper from 1987-96. Among her writing credits are *John Glenn: Pioneer in Space* (Fawcett, 1989), which received the Arthur Tofte Book Award, presented in 1989 by the Council for Wisconsin Writers; biographies of Louis Pasteur and Lech Walesa for a "People Who Made a Difference" school library series (Gareth Stevens, 1991); and two volumes, entitled *1900-1909* and *1910-1919* in a series entitled "The Twentieth Century" (Marshall Cavendish, 1995). Angel has written numerous articles for regional newspapers and magazines. She is currently working on a novel and is writing curricula for parenting teleconferencing classes for the Special Needs Adoption Network.

PHYLLIS CAREY is Associate Professor of English. She is the coeditor (with Catharine Malloy) of *Seamus Heaney: The Shaping Spirit* (University of Delaware Press, 1996) and (with Ed Jewinski) of *Re:Joyce 'n Beckett* (Fordham University Press, 1992). In addition, she has published essays on Samuel Beckett, James Joyce, Václav Havel, and interviews with Czeslaw Milosz and (with Catharine Malloy) Seamus Deane. She is currently coediting (with Marketa Goetz-Stankiewicz) a collection of essays on Havel, which will be part of Twayne's critical series on World Literature. Her essay in this volume, "Face to Face: Samuel Beckett and Václav Havel," was originally published in *Christianity and Literature*.

JAMES CONLON is Professor of Philosophy. He is especially interested in exploring philosophical themes in literature and film.

He has published in such journals as *The Modern Schoolman, Journal of Popular Film and Television, Journal of Aesthetic Education,* and *Post Script.* His essay in this volume, "Camus: Wagering on Immanence," was originally published in *The Modern Schoolman.*

MARY BETH DUFFEY is Lecturer of English. She has taught as an adjunct faculty member at Notre Dame University and at St. Mary's College, South Bend, Indiana, and at Marquette University, Milwaukee, Wisconsin. She joined the Mount Mary staff in 1984. Duffey has published articles on family and spirituality and on psychology and literature in *Scholastic Magazine, Rural Catholic Life,* and *Seasons, The Interfaith Family Journal.* In August 1995, she presented a lecture and led a discussion on the archetypal images of family in Eugene O'Neill's *Long Day's Journey into Night* at the Stratford Festival, Stratford, Ontario.

CHARLES JAMES KAISER is Professor or Art. He has taught courses in oil and acrylic painting, mixed media, basic drawing and life drawing since he joined the Mount Mary Art Department in 1973. Also a fine artist, he has exhibited watercolors, oil paintings, and drawings in numerous regional and national shows, including *Watercolor USA,* Springfield, Missouri, and *Chicago and Vincinity* at the Chicago Art Institute. Recent exhibitions include a duo show at the Gruen Gallery, Chicago, and the juried competitions *Watercolor Wisconsin 95,* Wustum Museum, Racine; *Self Portaits,* Charles Allis Art Museum, Milwaukee; and *Place/Wisconsin,* Cardinal Stritch College, Milwaukee.

MARY ELLEN KOHN is Assistant Professor of Spanish. She received her doctorate in Spanish from the University of Illinois (Urbana-Champaign). Kohn's doctoral dissertation was entitled "Violence against Women in the Novels of Maria de Zayas y Sotomayor." She has presented papers on Hispanic writers and on languages and international business. With Toni Wulff Martin she published an article entitled "Lending a new pair of eyes: A 'fresh and natural' approach to teaching 'small c' culture" in *Contact* (1993). Fluent in both Italian and Spanish, Kohn has traveled extensively in Europe and in Latin America.

CATHARINE MALLOY is Associate Professor of English. She is the coeditor (with Phyllis Carey) of *Seamus Heaney: The Shaping Spirit* (University of Delaware Press, 1996). In addition, she has read papers on Heaney at the International Association for the Study of Anglo/Irish Literature (University of Leiden, the Netherlands, 1991), the American Conference for Irish Studies (University of Wisconsin, 1991), the Modern Language Association (San Francisco, 1991), and the American Conference for Irish Studies (Belfast, 1995); she has published essays on Heaney, and (with Phyllis Carey) an interview with Seamus Deane.

PAUL J. MCGUIRE, S.C.J., was Assistant Professor of Theology at Mount Mary from 1989-1994. In 1994-95, he did research in Paris on the life of Father Leo Dehon, the founder of the Priests of the Sacred Heart. He is currently Director of the Dehon Study Center for the Priests of the Sacred Heart.

PATRICIA ANN OBREMSKI, S.S.N.D., is Associate Professor of Physics and Chair of the Physics Program. She is a published poet who describes herself as "appreciating the rich imagery imbedded in the physical world and the creativity of the questing mind that seeks to own the universe." Obremski's most recent papers include an editorial, "What is a Good Teacher?," an essay on critical thinking, "Critical Thinking; The Change Within," and a paper entitled ". . . everythingisconnectedtoeverything . . .," which links cosmology and nuclear physics.

JOAN PENZENSTADLER, S.S.N.D., is Associate Professor and Chair of the Theology and Religious Education Department. She has published five articles: "The Spiritual Dynamic in Education" (1989); "Contemplation and Education: Making Connections" (1994); "Teaching the Book of Job with a View to Human Wholeness" (1994). "Meeting Religious Diversity in a Catholic College" (1996); and "Attentive to Transcendence: The Life of Etty Hillesum" (1996).

PATRICIA ANN PRESTON, S.S.N.D., is Professor of Spanish. Recipient of a Fulbright Fellowship for study in Spain and two grants from the National Endowment for the Humanities Summer Seminars, she developed the essay in this volume, "The Search for

Transcendence as Manifested through Autobiography," as a result of a 1993 NEH seminar, "Spanish Autobiography in the European Context." Preston's publications include *A Study of Significant Variants in the Poetry of Gabriela Mistral* and "Gabriela Mistral" in *The New Catholic Encyclopedia.* Her other publications concern bilingual education. She received her B.A. *magna cum laude* with Honors in Spanish from Bryn Mawr College and the M.A. and Ph.D. in Spanish and French from Catholic University of America.

KATHLEEN SCULLIN is Associate Professor of English. Her dissertation, "Art and Strategy in Walker Percy's *Lancelot:* Visiting the Region of the Dead," gave rise to an abiding interest in religious writers and the novel of personal journey. She has given papers on Percy's philosophical kinship with Gabriel Marcel and on Percy's fundamental dispute with Jean Paul Sartre and has published essays on *Lancelot* and on *The Thanatos Syndrome.* Recently, she has become interested in women's novels and in reading fiction from an implicitly feminist perspective. Among the courses she teaches at Mount Mary are "The Literature of the Religious Imagination" and "The Seeker in the American Novel."

HEIDI N. SJOSTROM is Instructor in English and has taught writing at Mount Mary for nine years. Previously, she taught and studied at the University of Wisconsin-Milwaukee. An elder in the Presbyterian Church (U.S.A.) and Zen practioner, she has taught theology, journaling, and spiritual literature to adults and children. Her publications include many book reviews and articles on parenting and on historical figures. She also writes and teaches fiction and poetry.

CAROLYN SUR, S.S.N.D., is currently on the faculty of Greco Institute in Shreveport, Louisiana, where she teaches theology, church history, spirituality, and an interdisciplinary course in science and theology. She is also involved in spiritual direction and assists the bishop on theological issues. She taught at Mount Mary (1992, 1994-95) in the departments of Theology and Mathematics and also lectured for the Ewens Center. Sur has given retreat weekends in a variety of institutions, including the Benedictine Retreat Center, Madison, WI, Caroline Center, St. Louis, MO, and

Grailville, Loveland, OH. From 1992-94 she was assistant professor of Systematic Theology at Sacred Heart School of Theology. Sur received her Ph.D. from St. Louis University; the European research for her published dissertation, *Feminine Images of God in the Visions of Hildegard of Bingen's Scivias,* was funded by a grant from the Bogart Foundation for research in mysticism.

JANE THOMPSON is Instructor in English and a doctoral student at the University of Wisconsin-Milwaukee. Thompson presented the paper, "Take a Chance on Meaning: Teaching Alternate Worlds" – which discusses challenges in the teacher/student relationship and specifically in teaching *Riddley Walker* – at the Life, the Universe and Everything Conference XX; the paper was published in the volume *Deep Thoughts.* At the symposium "Rethinking Women's Reality" at Mount Mary (1994), Thompson presented a paper entitled "He Builds Houses She Can't Live In: Frances Hodgson Burnett Revises Henry James." At the 1996 Mid-Atlantic Popular Culture/American Culture Conference, Thompson and her collaborator, Kristi Siegel, presented the paper, "Whose Story: Class, Empire and Selfhood in Frances Hodgson Burnett's *A Little Princess.*" Thompson is currently engaged in further work with Burnett's novels.

MARY HESTER VALENTINE, S.S.N.D., is Professor Emerita of English. She taught for over forty years at Mount Mary College, with time out for a year on the faculty of Sogang University, Seoul, Korea, a lecture tour for the United States Information Agency, and editorial work for her congregation in Rome, resulting in the publication of the letters of the Foundress of the School Sisters of Notre Dame. Valentine has written poetry, short stories, historical, critical and education articles as well as book reviews. She has edited eight books and is the author of eight, the most recent being *Aging in the Lord* (Paulist Press, 1994).

Index